$6.95

HISTORIC MIDWEST HOUSES

John Drury

HISTORIC MIDWEST HOUSES

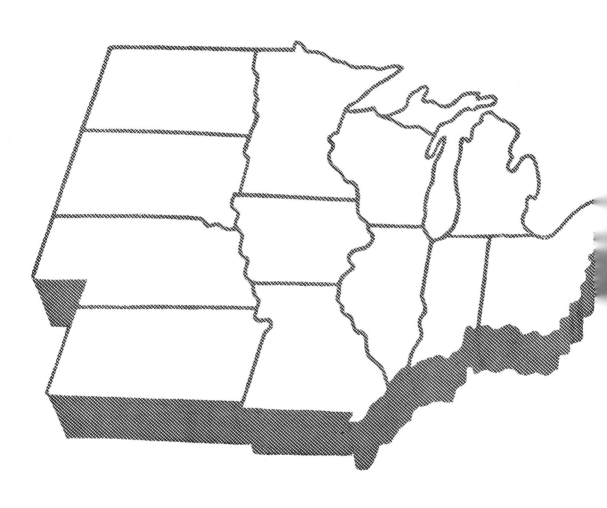

HISTORIC
MIDWEST HOUSES

by JOHN DRURY

THE UNIVERSITY OF CHICAGO PRESS
Chicago and London

F 351
D78
1977

THE UNIVERSITY OF CHICAGO PRESS, CHICAGO 60637
The University of Chicago Press, Ltd., London

Originally published by the University of Minnesota Press
© 1947 by the University of Minnesota, renewed in 1975. All rights reserved
Reprinted by arrangement with the University of Minnesota Press, Minneapolis
Published 1977
Printed in the United States of America

81 80 79 78 77   9 8 7 6 5 4 3 2 1

ISBN: 0-226-16551-5
Library of Congress Catalog Card Number: 77-78084

Preface

PERHAPS the most appealing relics of great men and women — and of those not so great — are the houses in which they lived. For just as a man is known by the company he keeps, so, too, is he known by the house he occupies. We may be awed by the lofty position to which history has elevated a man, but on visiting his home, on seeing his favorite rocker, his writing desk, his walking stick, or his slippers, we receive a comforting impression of kinship; we feel that underneath his greatness there was the simple humanity common to all of us. For this reason, in part, we preserve the homes of great statesmen, military heroes, writers, artists.

In studying the subject of old houses, I discovered that our people seem to believe, curiously, that the area of historic American houses ends with the Appalachian Mountains. It is in the seaboard region east of the Appalachians, especially in New England and the Old South, that we had thought were located America's only habitations worthy of our veneration, either from a historical or architectural point of view.

This attitude is shown in the list of what few books there are on the subject of old houses in America. In Laurence Vail Coleman's authoritative work, *Historic House Museums*, the bibliography of volumes by such leading house historians as Fiske Kimball, Montgomery Schuyler, Harold D. Eberlein, and William R. Ware, deals almost entirely with dwellings located east of the Appalachian range. So, too, are most of the country seats and residences which Elbert Hubbard described in his *Little Journeys to the Homes of Famous People*, which was so popular in the early years of the present century. Even in a later work than Hubbard's, a two-volume study by Chesla C. Sherlock entitled *Homes of Famous Americans*, we find few chapters devoted to historic houses west of the Atlantic seaboard, even though the author was a Midwesterner.

Other regions of the United States contain many historic houses as worthy of attention as those on the Eastern seaboard, and it is time they be recognized.

A significant step toward treating this matter on a broad, nationwide scale was taken fourteen years ago by the federal government when, during the administration of Franklin D. Roosevelt, there was established the Historic American Buildings Survey. During the eight years or so in which this project was operated jointly by the National Park Service, the American Institute of Architects, and the Library of Congress, architects composing the personnel of the project made scale drawings of 2639 historic buildings in all regions of the United States.

This was an architectural project, however, and no attempt was made to obtain the story of each house or public building drawn, to ascertain why these structures are historic. But this need was met, in part at least, by the Federal Writers' Project. In the useful and comprehensive guidebooks to each state prepared by the writers of this project, historic houses are included, along with all other landmarks in each state, but the information about the houses is necessarily brief. Nevertheless, great credit is due the writers of the project, as well as to the architects of the Historic American Buildings Survey, for locating these

v

dwellings in every city, town, village, and rural area in the United States.

I have taken as my own field of study my native Midwest, which is now generally accepted as embracing the twelve states of Ohio, Indiana, Illinois, Missouri, Michigan, Iowa, Wisconsin, Minnesota, Kansas, Nebraska, North Dakota, and South Dakota. Few of the houses in these states, of course, are as old as most of the notable historic dwellings in New England, Virginia, or the lower seaboard South. The interior regions were settled later. But to my mind the important factor is not so much age as historical association and importance.

A beginning has been made in telling the stories of Midwestern historic houses. Two volumes on the architecture of certain parts of this region have appeared — *Early Homes of Ohio* (1936), by I. T. Frary, and *Architecture in Old Chicago* (1941), by the late Thomas E. Tallmadge. There are also pamphlets on the architecture of Ste. Geneviève, Missouri, and on early Indiana by Charles E. Peterson and Lee Burns, respectively. And in preparation now is a comprehensive study of early Midwest architecture by Professor Rexford Newcomb of the University of Illinois.

An interesting and unusual treatment of this same field is the collection of colored drawings of Midwest buildings by the Illinois artist, Kenneth Becker. Another artist, Lane K. Newberry, has portrayed Midwestern historic buildings in a number of his oil paintings.

My own interest in the subject is more historical than architectural. What I have attempted to do is to tell the story of a house in terms of the person who made it historic, to describe that person within the framework of his or her house and its historical milieu. This was the method I employed in *Old Chicago Houses*, published in 1941 by the University of Chicago Press, and again in a series of articles on "Old Illinois Houses" in the *Chicago Daily News*. As in *Old Chicago Houses*, each dwelling in this book is described in "a blend of historical, biographical, architectural, and social facts." But the main emphasis is biographical. The architecture of a house is here considered as only one of the many aspects relating to it. This differs from most books on old houses in America, which treat of architecture entirely and are written from the point of view of the professional architect or the connoisseur of architectural details. Even the newest books in the field, *The Mansions of Virginia*, by Thomas T. Waterman, and *Old Vermont Houses*, by Herbert W. Congdon, both published in 1946, are architectural works, replete with technical information.

The biographical treatment of historic houses seems to have been applied for the first time in America in a volume published by G. P. Putnam in 1853. This was called *Homes of American Authors*, and each chapter was the work of some well-known writer of the day. It was followed in 1854 by another volume entitled *Homes of American Statesmen*. Then during the early 1920's, when Chesla C. Sherlock was editor of *Better Homes and Gardens*, he wrote for his magazine a series of articles on the homes of famous Americans, which were later published in book form. Sherlock, too, used the biographical approach. Although he considered mostly historic houses on the Atlantic seaboard, he did include in his series such outstanding Midwestern homes as those of Abraham Lincoln, General Grant, Mark Twain, John Brown, William Henry Harrison, and James Whitcomb Riley.

I make no claim to have included all historic Midwestern houses in this book. My aim was to choose representative houses — the most famous of the historic houses in the twelve states of the Midwest — limiting my survey to not more than ten houses in each of the states considered. This resulted in a total of eighty-seven dwellings, each of which I visited on a ten-thousand-mile tour of the Midwest. And more than half of these are museums open to visitors. My choices are admittedly somewhat arbitrary, and others would, and may, compile a different list.

In gathering material and pictures for this book I have become indebted to many persons, especially librarians and officials of historical associations, for their counsel and cooperation. Aside from these, however, I wish to thank in particular the staff of the University of Minnesota Press and the members of the University of Minnesota Committee on Regional Writing. The Regional Writing Fellowship awarded me brought *Historic Midwest Houses* into being much sooner than would otherwise have been possible.

Among librarians who have been especially helpful to me are Herbert H. Hewitt, head reference librarian of the Chicago Public Library, and his two assistants, Mrs. Barbara Sutton and Mrs. Mildred King, and Stanley Pargellis, head of the Newberry Library of Chicago. Assistance and advice were generously given by Laurence Schmeckebier, former chairman of the fine arts department of the University of Minnesota; August Der-

leth, the Wisconsin novelist; Erwin C. Zepp, curator of state memorials of the Ohio State Archaeological and Historical Society; Curtis W. Garrison, director of research of the Hayes Memorial at Fremont, Ohio; Edward P. Alexander, former director of the Wisconsin State Historical Society; Stanley D. Newton, of Sault Ste. Marie, Michigan; Marjory Douglas, curator of the Missouri Historical Society; James Lawrence, editor of the *Lincoln Star,* Lincoln, Nebraska; W. D. Newberry, secretary of the Chamber of Commerce, North Platte, Nebraska; Russell Reid, superintendent of the State Historical Society of North Dakota; Lawrence Fox, former superintendent of the State Historical Society of South Dakota; and Paul M. Angle, director of the Chicago Historical Society.

This list of persons who have aided me, however, would be incomplete without the inclusion of my wife, Marion Neville. Her knowledge of Midwestern manners and customs was especially helpful to me and her editorial skill was generously and untiringly afforded during the preparation of the entire manuscript.

JOHN DRURY

"Hawthornden"
Chesterton, Indiana, June 1947

Table of Contents

OHIO

Westward over the pine-covered mountains they came — men, women, and children from New England, from New York State, from the Piedmont and the Tidewater. On foot, on horseback, in ox carts and Conestoga wagons, carrying their axes and rifles and skillets, they climbed over the Alleghenies and down to the Ohio River. They drifted westward on the Ohio in flatboats, keelboats, barges. They moved into a new land — a vast, fertile, undeveloped region of dark forests and wide windy prairies. And here, in this new promised land, the men, women, and children from the East made clearings, built log cabins, and hewed out a new civilization. Their children and children's children came after them and grew corn, bred cattle, built roads, dug canals, erected towns and cities. And some of their children and children's children became men and women of destiny, leaders of the people.

Cradle of the Midwest

RUFUS PUTNAM HOUSE. MARIETTA. BUILT 1788. OPEN TO THE PUBLIC.

JUST beyond Front Street, the busy shopping thoroughfare of the Ohio River city of Marietta, stands a plain, old, unpainted dwelling. In appearance it is unimpressive, but without too much exaggeration it might be called the cradle of the Midwest. It survives as a reminder of the very earliest days of the Northwest Territory, from which were carved the states of Ohio, Indiana, Illinois, Michigan, Wisconsin, and part of Minnesota.

The man who built this house and made it historic was General Rufus Putnam, a patriot and a pioneer. As a boy in Massachusetts he polished boots and ran errands at his stepfather's inn to get money to buy books on mathematics and surveying. He joined the army in the last of the French and Indian Wars and later served with distinction as an engineer in the American Revolution.

When the independence of the colonies had been won, General Putnam took up the cause of the men of the Continental Army who wanted to exchange their military certificates for land in the vast new country west of the Alleghenies. With a companion-in-arms, Benjamin Tupper, he called a meeting at the Bunch of Grapes tavern in Boston on March 1, 1786, and organized the Ohio Company of Associates to acquire and settle land on the Ohio River.

Through the energy and the shrewdness of the Reverend Manasseh Cutler, the company's spokesman before the Continental Congress, the men of the Ohio Company succeeded in obtaining from that body a tract of one and a half million acres on the Ohio River at the mouth of the Muskingum. At the depreciated value of their military certificates, the land cost them about eight cents an acre.

This huge purchase was of little consequence without a civil government, and such government was promptly provided by the famous Ordinance of 1787, drawn up by the Continental Congress for the control of the "Territory of the United States North and West of the River Ohio."

When the ordinance had been enacted, General Putnam led forty-seven members of the Ohio Company — surveyors, mechanics, and carpenters — westward to the new claim. They traveled across the Alleghenies, floated down the Ohio on flatboats, and reached the mouth of the Muskingum on April 7, 1788. In gratitude to the country that had aided them in the War of Independence, they named the settlement they established here Marietta, after Queen Marie Antoinette of France.

Under the expert supervision of General Putnam the men of the Ohio Company built first a combination fortress and community dwelling place, which, because they were men of some classical learning, they called Campus Martius. The fortification, one hundred and eighty feet square, with blockhouses at each corner, was unusual in that the stockade on all four sides was composed of sturdy two-story, gabled houses.

And one of these houses, the one adjoining the blockhouse at the southeast corner, was General Putnam's.

Here the general lived with his large family: his wife, two sons, six daughters, and two grandchildren. Here was held the first town meeting in the West; here General Putnam

3

The Rufus Putnam house, one of the first frame houses in the Midwest

managed the affairs of the Northwest Territory until the arrival of the first territorial
governor, General Arthur St. Clair; and here
Putnam was notified of his appointment by
President Washington as a judge of the territory and later as surveyor-general of the
United States.

In this house, too, the Putnams entertained
a number of well-known persons who came to
visit the new settlement: among them the Reverend Manasseh Cutler, who drove all the
way from Massachusetts in a sulky; the exiled
Duke of Orleans, Louis Philippe, who afterward became king of France; and Harman
Blennerhassett, lord of Blennerhassett Island,
who later was a partner in the ill-fated Burr
conspiracy.

If the old General Putnam house seems un-
imposing to the layman, it is a building of
considerable interest to the student of archi-

Front parlor and living room, furnished as they were in Putnam's day

tecture. It was one of the first examples in the Midwest of the simple frame house built by the Puritans of Massachusetts in the late seventeenth century, and it was a great advance in comfort over the primitive log cabin that had to do for most frontiersmen. Interesting features of the house are its hand-hewn timbers and beams, the use of wooden pins instead of nails, the mortise and tenon joints, and the vertical planking in one of the exterior walls. It has also the small-paned windows and brick chimneys, as well as the fireplaces, of the typical early Puritan dwelling.

When "Mad Anthony" Wayne's victory at the Battle of Fallen Timbers in 1794 put an end to the Indian menace in the Ohio country, the men of the Ohio Company went out from Marietta and settled on distant claims, made clearings in the forest, started farms, and established new settlements. There was no further need for the fortification at Marietta and in 1795 it was razed — all, that is, but the Putnam house. Here the general continued to live. Using timbers and planks from the dismantled blockhouse, he enlarged his house, adding two more rooms and a wing kitchen. From this house, then, he served as a delegate to the constitutional convention that paved the way for the admission of Ohio into statehood in 1803, and he became one of the first trustees of Ohio University. On May 4, 1824, he died in his Marietta house at the age of eighty-seven.

OHIO STATE ARCHAEOLOGICAL AND HISTORICAL SOCIETY

The kitchen of the Putnam House

The subsequent story of this historic dwelling is recorded in a pamphlet by Norris F. Schneider. Some years after the death of General Putnam, the house was sold by his two sons, William R. and David Putnam, to Judge Arius Nye of Marietta, a descendant of one of the men of the Ohio Company. The purchase price was six hundred dollars. Judge Nye removed the wing kitchen. When he died, the old house came into the possession of his daughter, Minerva Tupper Nye. After serving as a residence until 1900, it was acquired by the Marietta chapter of the Daughters of the American Revolution and was used as a chapter house. Eventually the chapter persuaded the state of Ohio to purchase the house as a historic shrine.

Today the old, weather-beaten house, still standing on its original site (now the northwest corner of Washington and Second streets), is enclosed in a large brick building, a wing of the magnificent new Campus Martius State Memorial Museum built by the Ohio State Archaeological and Historical Society. The visitor to the old house finds its low-ceilinged rooms completely furnished as they were in General Putnam's day. Though few of the pieces belonged to the general himself, the rush-seated chairs, trundle beds, spinning wheels, mantel clocks, candle molds, hooked rugs, warming pans, harpsichord, long-barreled rifles, and powder horns are all authentically from the days when the Northwest Territory was young.

Queen City Showplace

THE TAFT MUSEUM. CINCINNATI. BUILT ABOUT 1820. OPEN TO THE PUBLIC.

AS THE westward movement grew, many settlements and towns sprang up along the routes of immigrant travel, principally on the Ohio River. And the first of these towns to become a city was Cincinnati. Because of its strategic location as a river port, serving both the newer Midwest to the north and the older Southland below, Cincinnati prospered; its commerce and manufacturing expanded quickly, many of its citizens grew rich, culture and the arts appeared, and it became known throughout the country as the "Queen City of the West."

One of the few surviving landmarks of Cincinnati's early days, when its riverfront streets and taverns were crowded with land specu-

lators, horse traders, steamboat men, cotton merchants, and roustabouts, is the fine old mansion at 316 Pike Street. This was perhaps the Midwest's first great house, a splendid example of formal domestic architecture as it first appeared in a rough land still used to log cabins.

From the very beginning, this historic house was a showplace of Cincinnati. It was built by Martin Baum, a German immigrant who made a fortune from his numerous enterprises: a flour mill, woolen mill, iron foundry, sugar refinery, and exporting company. Wanting men to work in his various mills, Martin Baum went to Philadelphia and Baltimore and persuaded many recently arrived German immi-

Greek Revival mansion. Front portico,
doorway to the Gray Room, music room

grants to come west to the booming young metropolis on the Ohio River. Their coming contributed greatly to the large German element in Cincinnati's population.

The year Baum's home was completed is not known but it was under construction in 1820. The house and the nine-acre estate surrounding it were valued at thirty thousand dollars. Legend has it that the house was designed by James Hoban, the architect for the White House, but this has never been proved. "Better grounds exist," says I. T. Frary in his *Early Homes of Ohio*, "for attributing it to Benjamin Henry Latrobe, who was Surveyor of Public Buildings under Presidents Jefferson and Madison." This could be, for Latrobe was the father of the Greek Revival style in America, and this Midwest mansion is a good example of that style.

Installed in his new home, Baum entertained many leading personages of the river town, among them the famous pioneer physician, Dr. Daniel Drake. Here, too, Baum helped organize a library, a school, a literary society, an agricultural club, various singing societies, and a museum. This last was called the Western Museum and one of its first employees was a young taxidermist named John James Audubon.

When financial reverses forced Martin Baum to give up his elegant house, it served for a time as quarters for a "respectable female seminary" known as Belmont House. Then in 1830 the mansion was acquired by Nicholas Longworth I, and soon became the acknowledged social and cultural capitol of the Ohio Valley.

Longworth was a native of New Jersey. Like many other young men of his time, he had caught the westward fever, and had come to Cincinnati when he was twenty-one, with "hardly a stitch to his back." He studied law and hung out his shingle. The story is often told that he undertook to defend a man for

horse-stealing, was given two old copper stills as a retainer's fee, and exchanged these stills for thirty-three acres of land which were then valued at only a few dollars but which later were appraised at two million dollars.

In any case, young Longworth soon came to devote more attention to buying land than to practicing law, and as Cincinnati grew, his fortune in real estate grew with it. So he was able to buy the Martin Baum home, retire from the practice of law, and devote himself to his favorite hobby, grape-growing.

He was a skilled horticulturist, and in time his vineyards occupied the entire Longworth estate and even climbed to the top of nearby Mount Adams. His Catawba and Isabella wines became nationally famous, even inspiring Longfellow to a tribute in verse, and the cultivation of grapes and strawberries spread throughout the Midwest largely as a result of his encouragement.

The Longworths were lavish entertainers. Among their noted guests were Robert Owen, founder of an unsuccessful utopia at New Harmony, Indiana; Frances Trollope, the English writer whose book, *Domestic Manners of the Americans*, caused a tempest by its unrestrained criticism of American ways; and General William Henry Harrison, afterward president of the United States. Harriet Martineau, another famous English writer, was also a guest at the Pike Street mansion, and in her book, *Retrospect of Western Travel*, published in 1838, she wrote:

"The party at this house was the largest and most elegant of any that I attended in Cincinnati. Among many other guests, we met one of the judges of the Supreme Court, a member of Congress and his lady, two Catholic priests, Judge Hall, the popular writer, with divines, physicians, lawyers, merchants, and their families. The spirit and superiority of the conversation were worthy of the people assembled."

When "Old Nick," as he was familiarly

Gray and Violet Room

known to the Cincinnatians of his day, died in 1863 at the age of eighty-one, his estate was valued at fifteen million dollars. It was his grandson, Nicholas Longworth III, who was for many years speaker of the House of Representatives, and who married Theodore Roosevelt's daughter Alice. Together they became the social arbiters of the national capital.

In 1871 the old Longworth mansion became the home of David Sinton, another prominent citizen of Cincinnati, and so the home of his daughter Anna's husband, a young man named Charles Phelps Taft, whose half-brother, William Howard Taft, was then preparing to enter Yale College. Nine years later Charles Phelps Taft, in partnership with his father-in-law, established the *Cincinnati Times-Star* and entered on a career in journalism that brought

him wealth and national political power. He had more than a little to do with the elevation of his half-brother to the presidency of the United States, and it was from the portico of the Pike Street mansion that William Howard Taft accepted the nomination to that office.

Charles Phelps Taft and his wife were discerning art collectors, and during the long years of their residence in the Pike Street house, they acquired one of the finest art collections in the Midwest. They also helped to establish the Art Academy of Cincinnati, promoted that city's famous "Zoo Opera," and presented to the metropolis its notable Lincoln statue by George Grey Barnard.

Appreciating the value of their residence as a historic and architectural landmark, and wishing to keep their large art collection intact within the walls of the dwelling they had occupied most of their lives, Mr. and Mrs. Taft decided to present their home to the city of Cincinnati. Accordingly in 1927 Charles Taft announced that he would give the house, the land on which it stood, the art collection it contained, and the sum of one million dollars for remodeling and maintenance to the people of Cincinnati if others would contribute a total of two and a half million dollars. His offer was accepted, the additional amount was subscribed, and the historic mansion and its art collection were turned over to the Cincinnati Institute of Fine Arts. The house was formally dedicated to its present use in 1932 and has since become known throughout the Ohio Valley as the Taft Museum.

As one approaches the house today, one notices first, through the sycamore trees that shade a well-kept lawn in front, the balanced proportions and graceful design of the Greek temple style. The white façade, the splendid classical portico, the finely wrought iron railings, and the dignified Colonial doorway with elliptical fanlight and slender side lights appear chastely beautiful in their Hellenic simplicity.

The interior, with its halls and thirteen rooms, is no less arresting. The downstairs rooms, in powder blue, lemon yellow, apple green, and other delicate shades, are elegantly fitted with brilliant crystal chandeliers, period rugs, and rare pieces of furniture — among them several pieces from the workshop of Duncan Phyfe. The many fireplaces in the house are exquisitely designed. Oil portraits of Mr. and Mrs. Taft hang in the music room.

In the main entrance hall, above the wainscot, the walls are covered with charming pastoral frescoes by the early Cincinnati painter,

The Blue Room in the Taft House

Robert S. Duncanson, and among the paintings on display in the salons are works by Goya, Gainsborough, Reynolds, Corot, and Rembrandt. On display, too, are collections of rare French enamels, Italian majolicas, historic jewelry and watches, and Chinese vases and porcelains. There are also several busts by the American sculptor, Hiram Powers, who was often in this house as a protegé of old Nicholas Longworth.

At Lawnfield

JAMES A. GARFIELD HOUSE. MENTOR. BUILT 1832. OPEN TO THE PUBLIC.

SOME houses are "born" and others, like Topsy, just "growed." Of the latter type is the residence of President James A. Garfield at Mentor, some twenty-three miles east of Cleveland.

Big and rambling, with a comfortable veranda, bay windows, many dormers, a carriage porch, and all the other appurtenances of a typical late Victorian mansion, this house had its origin more than a century ago in an unpretentious farmhouse built by James Dickey, an early settler in the old Western Reserve. In the years that followed, the house was added to, raised, and improved until it became a fairly representative example of the kind of house lived in by a moderately prosperous Midwestern family of the 1870's. A perfectionist in architecture would probably call it nondescript, of no particular style, but it belongs to the eclectic period in American architecture, when various styles were often combined in one house.

In the fall of 1876, when James A. Garfield bought the Dickey farm, paying one hundred and fifteen dollars an acre for the land, he was thinking of a suitable place to retire to a few years hence. Although he was only forty-nine, he had already served for seventeen years as a congressman from Ohio, and now he wanted a place, he said, "where my boys can learn to work and where I can get some exercise, where I can touch the earth and get some strength from it." So he bought the old farm on the shores of Lake Erie. He promptly named the place "Lawnfield," and set about enlarging and remodeling the house and improving the land. During the next four years, in the weeks when he was not on duty in Washington, Garfield spent long hours in his fields, digging drainage ditches, plowing, sowing, and cultivating.

He was elected to the Senate in 1880, and in that year, too, he was nominated for the presidency by the National Republican Convention in Chicago.

In the campaign that followed, Garfield made Lawnfield his headquarters. A small building was erected on the front lawn near the house to serve as the campaign office; it was equipped with telegraph wires; and it became the meeting place for Republican delegations from all over the country. This office on the candidate's estate led to the first of the "front porch" presidential campaigns.

*The rambling Garfield mansion — typically Victorian —
grew from an early settler's farmhouse*

From there on the story is a familiar one. Five months after his inauguration, President Garfield was shot in a Washington railroad station by a disappointed office seeker and he died from the wound on September 19, 1881. His family, including his aged mother, lived on at Lawnfield.

Today the rambling, white-painted house at Mentor, shaded by gnarled old maples and elms, is a museum open to the public. In its twenty-six rooms are displayed such objects as the hat President Garfield was wearing when he was shot, his familiar lunch basket, the Bible on which he took the presidential oath, the manuscript of his inaugural address, a set of monogrammed Haviland china used by the Garfields in the White House, Mrs. Garfield's gowns, numerous autographed photographs, portraits in oil, part of the president's library, and the bed used here by Garfield's mother. On the lawn outside still stands the campaign office of 1880.

Located on U.S. 20 in a setting reminiscent of New England — white picket fences, fine old shade trees, church spires, and trim, comfortable dwellings — the Garfield mansion has become one of the best known old houses of the Western Reserve.

A Nation's Schoolroom

Here is John.
And there are Ann and Jane.
Ann has got a new book.
It is the First Book.
Ann must keep it nice and clean.
John must not tear the book.
But he may see how fast he can learn.

THESE simple sentences, from which millions of backwoods Midwesterners first learned that books must be kept "nice and clean," that they must not be torn, and that you can learn things from them, are carved on the stone pedestal of a memorial to the man who wrote them, William Holmes McGuffey.

This memorial, a statue of McGuffey in bronze, stands on the campus of Miami University at Oxford, Ohio. It was erected by a grateful public to the man whose primers, spelling books, and readers shaped the character and social standards of millions of nineteenth-century Americans. Nearly unknown to the present generation, McGuffey's *Readers* were in their time almost as influential as the Bible in making the little Johnnies and Annies of a crude, expanding frontier region conscious of right and wrong, of good and bad.

Not far from the statue on the campus in Oxford stands the unpretentious house in which McGuffey was living when he conceived the idea of his common school readers and wrote the first four of them.

He was a young professor of ancient languages at Miami University at the time. He had come out from Pennsylvania in 1826, to take this position at an annual salary of six hundred dollars. He was then twenty-six years old. A year later he married Harriet Spinning, the sister of an Oxford merchant. The young couple immediately began saving their money to build a home of their own, and in 1833 the simple two-story brick house at the corner of Oak and Spring streets was completed. Into it the young professor moved with his wife, his three-year-old daughter Mary, a younger daughter, Henrietta, and the professor's seventeen-year-old brother, Alexander, whom he had brought with him from Pennsylvania. This brother was then a student at the university. Later he compiled, or helped to compile, some of the readers.

It was at about this time that the older brother began working on the idea of new and better common school readers — schoolbooks that would suit the needs of children in the fast-growing, multi-national civilization of the Ohio country. And he began using his house as a training school, experimenting with his first reader on his own and the neighbors' children.

By now McGuffey was not only a college professor but an ordained minister of the Presbyterian faith. From his new house he would cross the street daily to his classroom on the university campus — the Reverend Mr. McGuffey, always attired in a black bombazine suit and silk stovepipe hat, swinging his cane as he walked along. On Sundays, as he drove off in his buggy to preach in a church four miles from Oxford, he would wear a black frock coat and a white clerical cravat. Sometimes he preached in the university chapel and on these occasions there was always a crowd,

FRANK SNYDER, OXFORD

The birthplace of McGuffey's Readers

for, despite his youth, he was an orator of elo-quence.

At intervals he went to visit nearby Cin-cinnati. This river metropolis was at that time the intellectual center of the region and Pro-fessor McGuffey was a leading figure in its literary, educational, and bookselling circles. It was these associations, in part, which led to the creation of the McGuffey *Readers*. With the manuscript of his first reader already com-pleted, McGuffey was visiting in Cincinnati on one occasion in 1834 when a member of the publishing firm of Truman and Smith (now the American Book Company) suggested that he write a series of common school readers. He had been recommended for the job by his friends the Beechers: Lyman Beecher, then president of a Cincinnati seminary, and his son

and daughters, Henry Ward Beecher, Cathar-ine Beecher, and Harriet Beecher Stowe.

McGuffey accepted the offer, returned to his Oxford home, and, between teaching in his classroom, delivering sermons, and caring for his family, managed to prepare four of his new-style readers. The first and second of the series, originally called *Eclectic Readers*, were brought out in 1836, and the *Third Reader* and *Fourth Reader* were published the following year. The others appeared in suc-ceeding years. The *Fifth Reader* was heralded as a volume of "Elegant Extracts in Prose and Poetry" and it was from this book that many young Americans got their introduction to the world of literature.

The popularity of the readers was phe-nomenal. In all they sold one hundred and wenty-two million copies. They were something new — they were human and interesting and varied. Children were fascinated by their stories, fables, mottoes, proverbs, poems, and pictures — especially the pictures. Here were textbooks that dealt with things they knew in real life, familiar things like dogs, games, houses, toys, and grandparents. Here were verses they could read and remember, like

> Twinkle, twinkle little star
> How I wonder what you are;
> Up above the world so high,
> Like a diamond in the sky.

From the later readers the older "scholars" could learn orations, perhaps Burke's plea for understanding of the colonies, Patrick Henry's demand for revolution, or Webster's call for the union of the states. Or they could learn some famous nineteenth-century poem, such as "The Sands of Dee," "Rock Me to Sleep," "Break, Break, Break," or "Landing of the Pilgrim Fathers."

With the appearance of the readers, McGuffey's fame as an educator spread. In 1836 he accepted an appointment as president of Cincinnati College and moved his family to the Queen City of the West. Three years later

he became president of Ohio University at Athens, and in 1845 he was named professor of moral philosophy at the University of Virginia, a position he held until his death in 1873.

Now, seventy-five years after his death, William Holmes McGuffey is by no means forgotten. There are McGuffey societies in many parts of the United States, and at Oxford, in addition to the bronze statue on the campus and the McGuffey house, there is a McGuffey memorial room in the public library which contains several interesting mementos, among them the odd, eight-sided table that the educator used as a desk.

At Dearborn, Michigan, in Henry Ford's Greenfield Village, stands the log cabin in which McGuffey was born. At Athens, on the campus of Ohio University, may be seen the McGuffey Elms, trees he planted while he was in residence there. And in Columbus, the state capital, there is the McGuffey Memorial Alcove of the Ohio State Archaeological and Historical Society. But of greatest interest to devotees of the readers is the Ohio house in which these books were written. Now occupied by the business manager of Miami University, it reminds us of the years when it was, not too figuratively, the nation's schoolroom.

House by the River

BENJAMIN HARRISON HOUSE. NEAR CINCINNATI. BUILT 1835.

SOME thirteen miles west of Cincinnati, among the thickets on the north bank of the Ohio River, stand the modern brick buildings of a branch power station of the Cincinnati

Gas & Electric Company. The power station, on its cindery, fenced-in grounds, appears at first sight to be the only landmark in a barren, desolate countryside. Then one discovers,

Benjamin Harrison's house on the Ohio

about a mile away, an old two-story house of red brick clinging to the riverside slope. It is occupied by a tenant family, and adjoining it is a small truck garden.

Although isolated and unmarked, this old house was the childhood and boyhood home of Benjamin Harrison, twenty-third president of the United States and scion of a family that did as much to shape American history as any clan in the country. Benjamin Harrison's grandfather, William Henry Harrison, also was a president of the United States, and the boy's great-grandfather, the first Benjamin Harrison, was a signer of the Declaration of Independence, a close friend of George Washington, a member of the Continental Congress, and an early governor of Virginia.

The old house by the river represents a real family chronicle. Its site was once part of the vast tract — including also the site of Cincinnati — called the Symmes Purchase. John Cleves Symmes was a member of the Continental Congress from New Jersey. Full of enthusiasm about the future of the Northwest Territory, he persuaded the Congress to sell him a million of its fertile acres and set out to populate them with emigrants from the East. John Cleves Symmes was Benjamin Harrison's maternal grandfather.

Symmes' dreams for his purchase did not materialize; North Bend, the settlement he founded in 1789, did not become the metropolis of the Ohio Valley as he had thought it would. He could not complete the payments on his purchase, and the grant was reduced to three hundred thousand acres along the Ohio River. A considerable part of this still sizable piece came into the possession of William Henry Harrison after his marriage in 1795 to Symmes' daughter Anna.

The Harrisons lived in a big log and frame house at North Bend, a rambling, thirteen-room country seat. And it was in this house, on August 20, 1833, that Benjamin Harrison was born, the eldest son of William Henry's son, John Scott Harrison.

Two years later, General Harrison, after the manner of fathers who can afford it, decided to set the young folks up on their own. He chose a pleasant spot on the river not far from his own place, built a simple but sturdy brick house, and presented it, together with five hundred acres around it, to John and his wife. So the house by the river became Benjamin Harrison's boyhood home.

It was not isolated then. North Bend was only a few miles away, and the flatboats and steam packets of the booming westward traffic crowded the river below.

John Scott Harrison, a quiet, hard-working man who preferred farming to public life, cultivated his corn and wheat, and in time his young son Benjamin helped with the chores. The father was not a rich man; his only means of support was the farm. When not helping his father, Benjamin, a chubby, tow-headed youth, would fish in the river below or hunt rabbits or squirrels in the hilly countryside above. He and his brothers and sisters attended school in an old log cabin on their father's farm.

Then, in 1841, when he was eight years old, Benjamin saw his grandfather become, after the exciting "Log Cabin and Hard Cider" campaign, the ninth president of the United States. Just one month after his inauguration, President Harrison died in the White House. And then young Benjamin saw his famous grandfather, the "Hero of Tippecanoe," brought back home in a river-boat funeral cortege and laid to rest in a hilltop grave at North Bend.

Although averse to public life, John Scott Harrison, the father of Benjamin, was called upon to serve two terms in Congress. Later the Democratic party wanted him to run for lieutenant governor of Ohio but he declined the honor.

Though Harrison preferred farming, he was not good at it, and through a series of mortgage foreclosures the size of his farm dwindled with the years. But he was able to educate his children. After two years at an academy in Cincinnati, young Benjamin entered Miami University at Oxford and was graduated with the class of 1852. The following year he married Caroline Scott, daughter of the president of the university.

He took his bride back to his boyhood home by the river, but they did not stay there long. When Benjamin decided to become a lawyer, they moved to Cincinnati and a few years later went on westward to Indianapolis. Benjamin's father continued to live in the old house by the river and died there at an advanced age in 1878.

Plans have recently been made for restoring the house near North Bend. The Cincinnati Gas & Electric Company has donated to the city of Cincinnati a tract of more than a hundred acres for a riverside park, and the grant will include the Benjamin Harrison house. Architecturally, this house is an example of post-Colonial style and was copied from houses in Virginia contemporary with the first Benjamin Harrison. This old dwelling, then, will join the fourteen-acre William Henry Harrison Memorial State Park at North Bend, which contains a stone shaft over the grave of the "Hero of Tippecanoe," as a memorial of the flourishing Harrison regime in southwestern Ohio.

In the Firelands

WHEN Connecticut gave up its claims to its western lands after the establishment of the United States, it reserved a vast tract for settlement by its own people, "Connecticut Yankees," as they were often called. This was the Western Reserve, in which today are the cities of Cleveland, Akron, Youngstown, and Sandusky. At the west end of the Reserve, along the shore of Lake Erie, some five hundred thousand acres were awarded to Connecticut citizens whose homes had been destroyed by fire and pillage during the Revolution, and when they settled on their new grants in the west, their part of the Reserve became known as the Firelands.

A few trim, white, New England-style houses still survive from the early days of the Firelands, but none of these has as much historical interest as a modest red brick dwelling in the little tree-shaded town of Milan, some thirteen miles south of the city of Sandusky. For this was the birthplace of Thomas Alva Edison.

It was rather a long and twisting road by which the Edisons came to be living in Milan when Thomas was born. His great-grand-

The house in which Edison was born

19

father, also named Thomas, was a stanch American patriot during the Revolutionary War. He believed firmly in American independence. But his son John was just as stanch a believer in the continuance of British rule, and he fought actively on the side of the Crown. When the Americans won, young John, like many other royalists, fled to Canada.

His son Samuel was born and reared in Canada, and in the little town of Vienna, in Ontario, he married a schoolteacher, Nancy Elliott, whose grandfather had been a Connecticut officer in the American Revolution. Samuel and Nancy were earning their living as innkeepers in Vienna when the Canadian Rebellion of 1837 broke out. Inclined toward his grandfather's convictions rather than his father's, Samuel took up arms on the side of the insurgents, who wanted to set up a republic. So, when the rebellion collapsed in defeat, Samuel in his turn had to flee. He and his wife crossed the border into the United States and settled at Milan in 1840.

Father John, still on the side of the Crown, remained behind, and he was still living in Canada, at the age of ninety-seven, when his grandson was born in Milan in 1847.

Milan, though still pretty much a frontier town, was then an important center for wheat shipping, principally because a good-sized canal connected it with Lake Erie to the north. Every day hundreds of wagons unloaded grain at the long row of Milan's warehouses, from which it was shipped to distant points in lake schooners. And alongside the warehouses there were busy shipyards and many small craftsmen's shops.

One of these shops was Samuel Edison's. In it, with the aid of several helpers, he made hand-wrought shingles, or "shakes," as they were called in that day, and from this source he derived a modest income, enough to provide for his wife and three small children.

In this humble Milan home Thomas Alva Edison spent the first seven years of his life. He was named Thomas after his great-grandfather and Alva after a lakeboat captain, Alva Bradley, whom Samuel Edison knew and admired. But in his childhood the future inventor was always known to his family and playmates as "Al." He was a very inquisitive lad, curious about everything. The ox-drawn grain wagons and the boats in the canal filled him with wonder and he was often down by the warehouses and shipyards, asking questions and watching the men work. Once he fell into the canal and had to be rescued by a workman. Another time he fell into a grain elevator and was nearly smothered.

Little Al's curiosity and the scrapes it got him into soon were the talk of the town. Seeing a hen sitting on eggs in the barn behind the house, he decided to sit on some eggs too, eager to know if he could hatch out little chicks. And in that same barn Al tried to solve the mystery of fire. The barn was destroyed, and the spanking Al's father gave him was staged in the public square, as a lesson to other boys.

Meanwhile, the fortunes of Milan turned downward; the coming of the "Iron Horse" caused a decline in canal traffic. Feeling that the Firelands town had lived through its best days, Samuel Edison decided to move away. And so the wizard-to-be spent the next eight years at Port Huron, Michigan.

It was at Port Huron that young Al attended school, but only for three months. His mother took him out of school when the teacher reported that he was "addle-brained"! This was the only formal schooling he ever had. From then on his mother taught him herself.

The story of Thomas A. Edison's career from the Port Huron days onward is a familiar one: his rise from train butcher and journeyman telegraph operator to become the "Wizard of Menlo Park," one of the modern world's foremost inventors, the man who changed night into day. He died at West Orange, New Jersey, on October 18, 1931, at the age of eighty-four.

Menlo Park, the New Jersey home in which Edison achieved some of his most important inventions, has been transplanted to Dearborn, Michigan, to stand with other historic American houses in Henry Ford's Greenfield Village. But the red brick house in which he was born still stands on its original site in the quiet village of Milan in the old Firelands.

Spiegel Grove

RUTHERFORD B. HAYES HOUSE. FREMONT. BUILT 1859. THE ADJOINING HAYES MEMORIAL MUSEUM OPEN TO THE PUBLIC.

WHEN he completed his term of office, Rutherford B. Hayes, nineteenth president of the United States, retired to an Ohio home that was as beautiful in its appointments and surroundings as were the homes of Washington at Mount Vernon and Jefferson at Monticello. Carefully preserved since then, the Hayes mansion in its park-like estate is today an outstanding Midwestern landmark, a first-rate example of the spacious country house of the mid-nineteenth century.

The twenty-five acre estate, in the residential section of Fremont about a mile from the central business district, is now owned by the state of Ohio and is known as Spiegel Grove State Park. In the center of it stands the old Hayes mansion. Although the park, with its many old trees, its Hayes mausoleum, and its new museum and library building, is open to the public, the Hayes residence itself is still a private dwelling, the home of President Hayes' grandson, Captain Webb C. Hayes II.

As the sightseer now views it, this red brick residence appears to be a double house — that is, two big gable-roofed dwellings built together, with a spacious porch across the entire front to give unity to the whole. Originally there was only one gable-roofed house, the south half of the present mansion. It was built in 1859 by Sardis Birchard, a prosperous Fremont merchant who was Rutherford Hayes' uncle and guardian. The elder Hayes, whose wife Sophia was Birchard's sister, had died several months before the boy's birth.

In 1834 Birchard had bought a large tract of land on the outskirts of Fremont, and as he walked over his acres from time to time in the years that followed, he was captivated by the beauty of one particular grove of trees, especially by several reedy pools of water which, mirrorlike, reflected the elms, oaks, and walnuts that grew around them. Here he decided to lay out an estate and build a house. And when the house was completed, he named the place Spiegel Grove from the German word *spiegel,* which means "mirror."

As a boy, Rutherford Hayes was often at his uncle's house, watching the birds, studying the flowers, or reading in his uncle's library. And it was his uncle who gave him his education, first at Kenyon College in Gambier, Ohio, then at the law school of Harvard University.

When the Civil War began, Hayes was practicing law in Cincinnati. He volunteered for army service, was commissioned a major in the 23d Ohio Infantry, served through the whole conflict, and was wounded four times. At the end he was brevetted a major general.

Although Spiegel Grove was now his, General Hayes could live there only at brief intervals. After the Civil War he took up residence in Washington as a congressman from Ohio, and this service was followed by three terms as governor of Ohio, during which time he lived in Columbus, the state capital, but spent his summers at Spiegel Grove. From Colum-

bus, in 1877, he went back to Washington again – this time as president of the United States.

At the close of his term in 1881, Hayes returned to Spiegel Grove and lived there in retirement until his death in 1893 at the age of seventy-one.

Afterward his son, Colonel Webb C. Hayes, gave the estate to the Ohio State Archaeological and Historical Society, which built on the grounds a combination museum and library. The library wing of the building houses the former president's large collection of books, and in the museum section are displayed many relics and mementos of Hayes' career as lawyer, soldier, and president. The exhibits include the sedately elegant gowns

HAYES MEMORIAL

The Hayes house – a Victorian country mansion

Mrs. Hayes wore as mistress of the White House.

With its many spacious rooms, great open fireplaces, ornate chandeliers, marble-topped tables, and walnut and mahogany chests and chairs, the Hayes residence is itself a museum of the household comforts and luxuries of the late Victorian era. It has been left almost intact since the days when Mr. and Mrs. Hayes entertained there many of their distinguished contemporaries. A guest in the house today can see, through tall windows, the many historic trees of Spiegel Grove, among them the McKinley Oak, the General Sherman Elm, the Garfield Maple, the Cleveland Hickory, and the Taft Oak. Each of these trees, identified by a brass tablet, was personally planted or selected by the man after whom it is named. And among the roots of these fine old hardwoods one may pick out the traces of the old General Harrison Military Trail of the War of 1812, which winds through the estate on its way from Lake Erie to the Ohio River.

A Literary Shrine

PAUL LAURENCE DUNBAR HOUSE. DAYTON. BUILT ABOUT 1875. OPEN TO THE PUBLIC.

IN THE year 1896, when the city of Dayton was celebrating the one hundredth anniversary of its founding, one of the elevators in a downtown office building was operated by a slender Negro boy of twenty-four. Few of the distinguished guests of the city paid any attention to the elevator operator; he was merely one of the hundreds of Negroes who lived and labored in Dayton. And for his part, the young Negro was not greatly concerned with the white people he carried up and down in his rickety cage; he was working for the four dollars a week that meant bread and butter to him.

Today the city of Dayton and the state of Ohio are proud to claim as one of their historic buildings the Dayton house in which that Negro elevator operator afterward lived. This house is now maintained as a public museum by the Ohio State Archaeological and Historical Society and is visited annually by several thousand persons from all parts of the United States, and even from foreign countries.

For in this house lived Paul Laurence Dunbar, the first Negro poet to become widely popular in the United States. He was the author of *Lyrics of Lowly Life*, a volume of Negro dialect poems that was as widely read as any other book of poetry in the America of its time.

Much of Dunbar's work seems out of date today because he wrote about Negro slave life on Southern plantations in the days before the Emancipation Proclamation. Nonetheless there is little doubt that Dunbar and another Negro writer of his period, Charles W. Chestnutt, whose best book is a volume of stories called *The Conjure Woman*, prepared the way by their success for a large number of later Negro writers, among them James Weldon Johnson, Countee Cullen, Langston Hughes, and Richard Wright.

*Dunbar's house, now a state museum, is
furnished with many of its original pieces*

The son of parents who had been slaves,
Paul Laurence Dunbar was born at Dayton
in 1872. As a boy he played in the city streets
and along the banks of the Great Miami River.
His father died when Paul was twelve, so the
boy worked his own way through grammar
and high school, and although he was the only
Negro in his high school class, he became
president of the literary club and editor of the
school paper. He did a great deal of reading
and soon began to write verses. Eventually,
his poems were printed in the Dayton newspapers, and some of them appeared in the
Chicago Daily News as well.   •

When Dunbar was twenty-one, his first volume of poetry appeared. It was called *Oak
and Ivy* and was printed in a small edition by
the United Brethren Publishing House of Day-

ton. By selling copies of the book on his elevator at one dollar each, young Dunbar was
able to cover the modest cost of publishing it:
one hundred and twenty-five dollars.

A few years later his *Lyrics of Lowly Life*
was published and this brought him almost instantaneous fame as well as financial rewards.
Other books followed. In time he was acclaimed "the sweetest singer of his race," and
was invited to read his poems in recitals in
Eastern cities and even in England.

It was after his return to Dayton following
an eastern recital tour that Paul Laurence Dunbar purchased the house at 219 North Summit
Street. It stands in a middle-class neighborhood of plain, well-kept homes shaded by
oaks, elms, and maples. To this house the Negro poet, who was then twenty-eight years
old, took his mother, and here they lived a
quiet, comfortable existence, now and then entertaining some distinguished white or Negro
visitor.

Dunbar continued his writing, but only for
a few years. He died in his Dayton home on
February 10, 1906, at the age of thirty-four.
His mother, who was the inspiration of one of
his most popular poems, "When Malindy
Sings," continued to live in the Summit Street
house until her death in 1934. Four years later
the house was acquired by the state and converted into the Paul Laurence Dunbar Museum.

The Dunbar house is a typical example of
a middle-class dwelling built in the 1870's
or 1880's. It is two stories high and built of
red brick, with a gabled slate roof, a small
side porch, and green shutters adorning its
front. The small porch on the south side of
the house is of interest for its cast-iron supports, made of grill work shaped in an intricate
floral design.

There are nine rooms in the house. In the
entrance hall, over a black marble fireplace,
hangs a large oil painting of Dunbar. Here
also are displayed first editions of the poet's

OHIO STATE ARCHAEOLOGICAL AND HISTORICAL SOCIETY

*Dunbar's workroom and library, where "the sweetest singer
of his race" wrote some of his later poems*

books, his original manuscripts, songs inspired by his poems, and many autographed volumes presented to him by his writer friends, including Theodore Roosevelt. All the articles of furniture in the front parlor remain as they were when Dunbar lived there: the marble-topped table with the family Bible on it, a kerosene lamp, a folding bed, a settee, and the poet's favorite rocker.

The bedroom and library are on the second floor. In addition to the poet's large walnut bed, the bedroom contains his baby shoes, the bicycle he used in his later years, a folding rocker, and the formal clothes, including a silk top hat, that he wore when he visited the White House at the invitation of President Theodore Roosevelt. In Dunbar's library and workroom are his books and his work table with an old-fashioned typewriter on it. Here, too, are his pipes, a collection of walking sticks, a Morris chair, and a comfortable couch with a taboret and tea set in front of it.

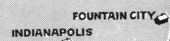

FOUNTAIN CITY

INDIANAPOLIS

TERRE HAUTE   VEVAY

MADISON

VINCENNES

NEW ALBANY

NEW HARMONY

INDIANA

They continued to move westward – the men, women, and children from New England, from New York State, from Virginia. But now their numbers were greater. With them now came Germans from Pennsylvania, and Southerners from Kentucky, Tennessee, and North and South Carolina to settle along the north bank of the Ohio. More and more and more were coming, along the old pikes, the rivers, the National Road. They organized the Territory of Indiana and when enough of them had settled there they made a new state in 1816. And still more people came into Indiana after it became a state. Some of them continued to come from the South and one of these was Tom Lincoln, bringing with him his young son, Abe. Others continued to come from the East, and these arrived in larger numbers after the opening of the Erie Canal. They made settlements, towns, county seats, cities. They reared sturdy children. And when some of these children grew up, they wrote about what they saw in the raw, new Midwest and so made Hoosier life, and Midwestern life, known throughout the land.

The White House of the West

WILLIAM HENRY HARRISON RESIDENCE. VINCENNES. BUILT 1804. OPEN TO THE PUBLIC.

AT THE north end of the historic Wabash River town of Vincennes, one of the centers of early French civilization in the Mississippi Valley, there stands what has often been called the White House of the West.

This was an apt designation in its time, for the house was the home of General William Henry Harrison while he was governor of the Territory of Indiana — an immense domain that included the present states of Illinois, Michigan, Wisconsin, eastern Minnesota, and of course Indiana itself. Indeed, for a short period the extent was much greater, because the Louisiana Purchase of 1803 brought into Indiana Territory for some nine months the huge region west of the Mississippi that became the states of Missouri, Arkansas, Iowa, western Minnesota, Kansas, Nebraska, Colorado, North Dakota, South Dakota, Montana, Wyoming, and Oklahoma.

General Harrison was no newcomer to the frontier when he took up residence in Vincennes. Entering the army as a young man in Virginia, he served for seven years in campaigns against the Indians throughout the Northwest Territory, was aide-de-camp to General "Mad Anthony" Wayne, and eventually resigned from the army to accept an appointment as secretary of the Northwest Territory in 1798. Three years before he had married Anna Symmes, daughter of John Cleves Symmes, a pioneer colonizer in southwestern Ohio.

In 1799 he was elected the Northwest Territory's first delegate to Congress and in this position he brought about, the following year, the creation of the Territory of Indiana, an act accomplished by cutting a large area off from Ohio. The seat of government for the new territory was fixed at Vincennes, and William Henry Harrison, at the age of thirty-four, was named its governor.

At Vincennes, then, he built the mansion that came to be known as the White House of the West. The house was completed early in 1804 and is said to have cost twenty thousand dollars, a sizable amount for those days. In keeping with Harrison's Southern background, the residence was designed after the plantation houses of Tidewater Virginia, which were usually spacious, two-story brick buildings in the Georgian style. It stood in a walnut grove and was surrounded by such outbuildings as a kitchen, Negro servants' quarters, barns, and stables. Nearby were orchards, gardens, and vineyards. The whole was set in the midst of a three-hundred-acre estate, which the governor called Grouseland.

During the twelve years he served as governor of Indiana Territory, General Harrison, with Mrs. Harrison, entertained many celebrated guests at Grouseland. The most dramatic of them came uninvited: the Indian chief, Tecumseh, who violently defied the governor and the American people in general at a meeting in the walnut grove in front of the mansion. The tree under which Tecumseh is supposed to have stood when he uttered this defiance is all that is left of the beautiful walnut grove at Grouseland.

After defeating the Indians in the famous Battle of Tippecanoe, and after serving as a general in the War of 1812, Harrison did not go back to Indiana but retired to a country

William Henry Harrison's house from territorial days; its entrance hall and basement fireplace

home he owned at North Bend, Ohio. It was from this house he went to become president of the United States in 1841.

For a time after General Harrison left Indiana, his mansion was used as a hotel, then it became a storage shed for grain, and finally it was left unoccupied entirely. Then in 1909 the Francis Vigo chapter of the Daughters of the American Revolution obtained custody of the house, restored it, installed Harrison relics and articles of furniture, and opened it to the public as a museum. Today it is one of the principal sights in a town of many memorials and historic landmarks, among which are the impressive George Rogers Clark Memorial Building, old St. Francis Xavier Cathedral, the Lincoln Memorial Bridge, and Indiana's territorial capitol.

Under the Golden Rain Trees

RAPP-MACLURE HOUSE. NEW HARMONY. BUILT 1821.

ONE of the most interesting American historic survivals is the Wabash River village of New Harmony. It has been the scene of two attempts to better the lot of man by a new social order. It was founded by the Rappites as an experiment in Christian communism and later was the setting for Robert Owen's famous experiment in utopian socialism.

Many of the original brick buildings are still standing in New Harmony, structures now heavy with age and covered with climbing vines. The oldest and best preserved of them is the one known as the Rapp-Maclure house. It stands on spacious, landscaped grounds at the northwest corner of Main and Church streets, almost in the center of the village. A square, white, one-story brick dwelling, with a low-pitched roof, it is spanned along its entire front by a wide veranda with Doric columns.

The best time to visit this house is in June, when it is bathed in yellow light from the "golden rain trees" that shade it. These trees, native to China, have bright yellow blossoms that in June fall like rain. They were first introduced to America at New Harmony, where the original seeds were planted alongside the gate of the Rapp-Maclure residence. For this reason, the trees, which now flourish throughout the village, are also called "gate trees" by the townspeople of New Harmony.

The Rapp-Maclure house takes its name from two men who lived in it. It was built as the home of Father George Rapp, the leader of a group of German pietists who came to America in the hope that here they could follow their principles without persecution. They settled first in Pennsylvania; then in 1815, wanting better land for their vineyards and orchards, Father Rapp led them westward to the banks of the Wabash.

The Rappites were patient, hard-working peasants, most of them, and they did a remarkable job of homemaking on the frontier. Within five years they had turned three thousand acres of wilderness land into flourishing farms and terraced vineyards; they had built sturdy, comfortable homes for themselves in

The "capitol" of two utopian experiments, in New Harmony

the village they named Harmony; and they had established a fairly wide range of industries: a tannery, flour and saw mills, a woolen factory, dyeworks, a distillery, and so on.

The Rappites' prosperity was the envy of their neighbors, but their beliefs were not. Their creed included common ownership of all property, strict celibacy, obedience to their leader, and toil on earth to prepare for the life hereafter. They were millennialists. Father Rapp lived only to present his followers to God, and the colony kept its affairs in order so as to be ready at any time for the Second Coming. One of the landmarks still to be seen at New Harmony is Gabriel's Rock, a boulder which, according to Rappite legend, contains the footprints made by the Angel Gabriel when he alighted there to bring a message to Father Rapp.

After ten years Father Rapp decided that

life had become too easy at Harmony; his followers did better when there was harder work to do. So he arranged the sale of the whole settlement—for a fraction of its value—and led his faithful band back into Pennsylvania, to start all over again at a place they named Economy.

The purchaser of the Indiana holdings was Robert Owen, a British industrialist who had been among the first to recognize the evils of the lag between industrial progress and social reorganization. He had introduced all kinds of reforms in his own factory in Scotland, but this was not enough. He wanted to establish a new settlement where a better social order might have a chance to grow, a utopia that would serve as a model for all mankind. The Rappite village on the American frontier seemed made to order for his purpose.

The sale was completed in the fall of 1824.

and Owen immediately announced his plan, inviting all who agreed with his purposes to come to New Harmony. Nine hundred answered his call, and the "community of equality" got under way in the spring and summer of 1825.

One striking thing about Owen's experiment was the number of scientists, artists, and educators who joined in it. Foremost among them was William Maclure, sometimes called the Father of American Geology — a man deeply interested in the new Pestalozzian education. When Maclure reached New Harmony he moved into the house that had been Father Rapp's, and it was Maclure who brought the seeds of the golden rain trees to be planted at its gate.

Others of the intelligentsia who came to work for the creation of the new social order were Thomas Say, eminent zoologist, who lived with Maclure; Charles Alexander Lesueur, painter and naturalist; Constantine Rafinesque, an ichthyologist; and Dr. Gerard Troost, a noted Dutch geologist. Joseph Neef, William Phiquepal D'Arusmont, and Madame Marie Fretageot were well-known Pestalozzians who came to assist Maclure in trying out the new kind of education at New Harmony. Added to these was a succession of interesting visitors: Frances Wright, an Englishwoman who was conducting a social experiment of her own in Tennessee; Sir Charles Lyell, distinguished British geologist; John James Audubon; Prince Maximilian von Neuwied, traveler and explorer; and Bernhard, Duke of Saxe-Weimar Eisenach, who included a long description of life at New Harmony in his account of his travels in America.

With people like these in the group, the intellectual and social life at New Harmony was varied and stimulating, and the Rapp-Maclure house was the center of much of it. But other aspects of the colony's life were less successful. Some of the settlers were extremists; a few

were unprincipled sharpers; and most of them were more given to talking than to doing. The group was sadly lacking in masons, carpenters, cooks, and laundresses. When Robert Owen himself was there, the settlers worked and things went well, but Owen had to keep a hand on his affairs in England and could be in New Harmony only briefly and infrequently. And when he was away, dissension rather than harmony prevailed.

After two years without noticeable progress toward the utopia he had dreamed of, Robert Owen was ready to write the experiment off as a failure, and the colony was officially dissolved. But this was not the end of New Harmony. Many of the settlers stayed on, and for many years, even beyond the Civil War, the village on the Wabash was a scientific and cultural center of great influence. It was the headquarters of the United States Geological Survey for seventeen years.

In 1828 William Maclure went to Mexico for his health, leaving his residence in the care of his brother Alexander, but Thomas Say continued to live in the house until his death in 1834. He was buried in the grounds and his tombstone can be seen there today. In 1844 the upper story was destroyed by fire and the house was restored to its present form by Alexander Maclure.

Some years later it came into the possession of David Dale Owen, one of Robert Owen's sons and an able geologist in his own right. He lived there until his death in 1860. From his heirs the house was bought by John Corbin, a New Harmony businessman, and in 1946 it was the home of his daughter, Mrs. Laura Corbin Monical.

Because of the interesting history and associations of New Harmony, the village as a whole has been taken over by the New Harmony Memorial Commission, an official state group charged with maintaining it permanently as a historic spot.

Grand Central Station

LEVI COFFIN HOUSE. FOUNTAIN CITY. BUILT 1820's.

ONE cold, rainy night, long after everyone in the village had gone to sleep, a man knocked softly at the door of a two-story stone house in the little Indiana settlement of Fountain City. Awakened by the sound, the owner of the house got up quickly, lighted a candle, put on his trousers and coat, and hurried to the door. Outside he guided a two-horse wagon to stables in the rear of the house, and there three Negro men emerged from the wagon and were conducted into the house. They were made warm before the fireplace and were given dry clothing, food, and beds for the night.

The next night the house owner had another wagon ready and in this the three Negroes were hidden and driven away to the next village north of Fountain City. Three more Negroes who had been slaves in the South were on their way to freedom in the North.

The two-story stone house at Fountain City was a station of that strange, secret system of transportation known in American history as the Underground Railroad. In fact, the stone house was the "grand central station" of the Underground Railroad, for it was the home of Levi Coffin, the "president" of that railroad — the man who directed its far-flung activities in the Midwest during the period before the Civil War.

The stone house in Fountain City, a village some fifty miles north of the Ohio River, still stands and is almost as sound today as when it was first built. Although privately owned and occupied, it is appropriately identified as a historic landmark by a bronze plaque at the entrance and a large marker at the curb. This marker can be easily seen by motorists on U.S. 27, which follows an old road that was used by fugitive slaves a hundred years ago.

The house itself is an example of early stone construction in the Ohio Valley — solidly built of rough-faced limestone, gable-roofed, and with chimneys at each end and small-paned windows across the front. Today it stands flush with the sidewalk and is shaded by two old maples at the curb.

From this house Levi Coffin is said to have helped more than two thousand Negroes escape from bondage. Here, secretly and under cover of darkness, he directed the movements of his illegal transportation system, for the fugitive slave laws were then in effect and it was a federal offense to help a slave escape from his master. But Coffin did not greatly fear discovery by his neighbors at Fountain City, for they, like himself, were Quakers and abhorred the enslavement of one human being by another.

When Levi Coffin moved to Indiana in 1826, he was thirty-seven years old and already a confirmed abolitionist, although he was a Southerner by birth. A native of New Garden, North Carolina, where he was born of Quaker parents on October 28, 1789, he grew up on his father's farm and became a teacher. In 1821 he and his cousin, Vestal Coffin, organized a Sunday school for the Negro slaves of the countryside, but this was closed not long afterward because the plantation owners were alarmed at what Levi Coffin was teaching their slaves. So the young Quaker migrated to Indiana, built his stone house at

34

HENLEY STUDIO, KNIGHTSTOWN

Levi Coffin's combined house and store in Fountain City was one
of the most important depots of the Underground Railway

Fountain City, and moved into it a year later. He made his living by conducting a general store in the house.

Levi Coffin and his wife, who was known as Aunt Katie, lived in Fountain City for twenty years. Their house was the focal point of fugitive slave routes from Cincinnati, Madison, Jeffersonville, and other towns on the Ohio River, and from it spread other routes northward to Canada and freedom.

In order to increase the scope of their activities, the Coffins moved to Cincinnati in 1847 and there opened what was ostensibly a general store. Actually it was the dispatcher's office of the Underground Railroad. Escaping slaves were secretly conducted to the basement of the store through a tunnel from the Ohio River.

When the Civil War started, Levi Coffin came out into the open to lead the cause of the enslaved. In 1864, a year after the Emancipation Proclamation, he went to England to establish the English Freedmen's Aid Society, an organization that sent more than a hundred thousand dollars in money and clothing to the newly freed Negroes of America.

The last ten years of his life Levi Coffin spent in retirement. He died in 1877 at the age of eighty-eight.

Harriet Beecher Stowe, whom Coffin had

known in Cincinnati, was greatly influenced by his antislavery zeal. There is a long-standing tradition that the prototype of Eliza Harris, heroine of *Uncle Tom's Cabin*, was cared for by Levi Coffin in his Fountain City home after she crossed the Ohio River on the ice with her child in her arms, a fugitive from the bloodhounds of her outraged master.

Hoosier Birthplace

EDWARD EGGLESTON'S BOYHOOD HOME. VEVAY. BUILT ABOUT 1835.

THE Hoosier state is famous for its writers: Edward Eggleston, James Whitcomb Riley, George Ade, Lew Wallace, Meredith Nicholson, George Barr McCutcheon, Gene Stratton Porter, Booth Tarkington, Theodore Dreiser, Kin Hubbard . . . The list is a long one. But the forerunner of them all was Edward Eggleston, best known for *The Hoosier Schoolmaster*, a novel of backwoods life on the Midwestern frontier.

It has generally been thought that Midwestern realistic writing began with Mark Twain's *The Adventures of Tom Sawyer*, which was first published in 1876. But *The Hoosier Schoolmaster* preceded *Tom Sawyer* by five years, appearing first as a serial in the pages of *Hearth and Home*, a Sunday school magazine published in Chicago in the early 1870's. It might be called the first American classic to come out of the Midwest.

The modest house in which Edward Eggleston was born at Vevay, Indiana, is still standing. Now a quiet county seat of about a thousand persons, at a bend on the Ohio River, Vevay was originally settled by a group of Swiss immigrants who grew grapes there and became widely known for their wines. But the Swiss influence was on the decline when Eggleston was born; Vevay had begun to attract settlers from the South.

One of these Southerners was Joseph Cary Eggleston, a member of an old Virginia family. After graduating from the College of William and Mary, he came west and took up the practice of law in Vevay. Here he married Mary Jane Craig, daughter of a Kentuckian who had moved north to Indiana and bought a large farm some six miles west of Vevay. Shortly after his marriage, Joseph Cary Eggleston acquired a two-story brick house with an acre of ground around it, and in this house Edward Eggleston was born on December 10, 1837. This was the birthplace, too, of Edward's younger brother, George Cary Eggleston, who also became a writer.

In this Vevay house Edward spent his boyhood and was introduced to the world of books by his cultured and well-read parents. Of equal importance in his life were his experiences on the backwoods farm of his maternal grandfather, Captain George Craig, on the Ohio River just below Vevay. Here the boy first heard, among the farm hands and backwoods settlers, the early Hoosier dialect that he was later to put into his novels. And on the Craig farm and in its vicinity he had his first

Indiana: A Guide to the Hoosier State

The house in which Edward Eggleston was born

contact with the varied types of individuals who were later to people his pages.

When Edward was six years old he attended his first school. This was held in a log cabin about a mile from the Eggleston home and was a "loud school"; that is, one in which the pupils studied their lessons out loud, so the schoolmaster could be sure they were applying themselves. Being a delicate and sensitive child, Edward made little progress under this vocal form of education, and his schooling was often interrupted by ill health. So he was frequently sent to the Craig farm or allowed to play with his brother on the acre of ground surrounding his Vevay home, a plot his father had planted with fruit trees, vineyards, and vegetable gardens, as well as honeysuckle bushes and climbing roses. Here, too, was a small brick house which the elder Eggleston had built as a law office but which later became a combination playroom and library for the two boys.

For several years after their father's death in 1846, Edward and his brother lived with various kinsmen on farms or in towns in southern Indiana. But when Edward was sixteen, they returned to Vevay and entered the high school there. And a couple of years later Edward's brother taught school at Ryker's Ridge, in the backwoods near Vevay. His experiences there, as told to Edward, formed the major part of *The Hoosier Schoolmaster*.

When Edward Eggleston reached maturity he went north to Minnesota, feeling that the climate there would be better for his health. He stayed in Minnesota for about ten years, serving as a Methodist minister in St. Paul, Stillwater, Winona, and other communities. The times were hard, though, and Eggleston had often to supplement his minister's income by other activities. On one occasion he peddled soap from door to door in the Minnesota Valley.

After the Civil War Eggleston gave up the ministry and turned to journalism in Chicago, and there the publication of *The Hoosier Schoolmaster* brought him fame. This was followed by other stories of frontier life: *The Circuit Rider, The End of the World, The Mystery of Metropolisville, Roxy, The Hoosier Schoolboy*, and *The Graysons*.

Although built more than a century ago, the Edward Eggleston birthplace is still in sound condition. It is located half a block west of the courthouse square and in 1946 was the private home of Mr. Carrol Dodd, assistant postmaster of Vevay. Originally it was of red brick but its exterior is now painted a creamy yellow, and the acre plot on which the house first stood, on which the boy Edward Eggleston played under the apple blossoms in spring, has long since been divided into lots for other houses. The Eggleston birthplace, however, still stands on its original site.

Greek Revival Masterpiece

JAMES F. D. LANIER HOUSE. MADISON. BUILT 1844. OPEN TO THE PUBLIC.

WITH the rise of towns and cities in the Midwest and the construction of canals and stagecoach roads to link them together, the primitive log cabins of the first settlers were replaced by houses of frame construction or, if the materials were available, of stone and brick. At first these homes were of no particular structural distinction. Then came the appearance of a definite, traditional architectural style. Since most of the people who settled the Midwest were from Eastern or Southern states, they transplanted to the new country the domestic architecture they had known in their old homes. And the style most popular at the time the Midwest was being built up is that known in American architectural history as Greek Revival. This classic temple mode flourished from about 1820 to the Civil War.

"Not in the East alone were there imposing mansions in the Greek style," wrote Thomas E. Tallmadge in his *The Story of Architecture in America.* "In Madison, Indiana, on the Ohio River, is the home of James F. D. Lanier, built in 1844 at a cost of forty thousand dollars—a noble building with a tetrastyle Doric Colonnade and the unusual dignity of a great round cupola."

Another writer, Talbot Hamlin, in his *Greek Revival Architecture in America*, says that the Lanier residence is "sophisticated and beautiful" and that it was designed by Francis Costigan, one of the "most skillful" architect-builders of Madison—which, Hamlin adds,

*Lanier's Greek Revival mansion is a splendid example of the architectural
style that swept America in the mid-nineteenth century. It was used for
every type of building from state capitols to modest farmhouses*

South portico of the Lanier house. Looking toward the Ohio

*The interior furnishings reflect the leisurely, opulent, ante-bellum
days — the days of crinolines, candlelight, and shining landaus*

"seems to have been at this time rather a center of architectural sophistication."

Not the least interesting fact about this Midwestern Greek Revival mansion is that it was designed by an architect-builder, a combination of carpenter and architect who copied his house designs from books of ready-made plans. One of the earliest of these useful craftsmen to appear in the Ohio Valley was Francis Costigan, who had received his training as a carpenter's apprentice in Baltimore. The Lanier house is considered his masterpiece, and his name plate is embedded in its newel post.

The house was begun in 1840 and took four years to complete. At that time James F. D. Lanier was one of the best known and most successful bankers in Indiana. A native of North Carolina Lanier was seventeen years old when he was brought to Madison by his parents. After graduating from Transylvania Law School at Lexington, Kentucky, he returned to Madison, practiced law, served as clerk in the Indiana house of representatives, and in 1834 helped to found the State Bank of Indiana. Until 1842 he served as president of the Madison branch of the bank and as a member of its state board of control.

Lanier lived in his stately mansion for only

A second-floor bedroom and the children's nursery on the third floor

The furnishings of the front parlor, like all the other rooms,
have been carefully kept just as they were in Lanier's day

a few years, but they were years of brilliant social gatherings that made the house famous as a center of hospitality in the Southern manner. In 1851 Lanier left Madison for the financial world of New York. He specialized in railroad securities and became a millionaire.

At the outbreak of the Civil War the state of Indiana was heavily in debt. Lanier offered to finance its participation in the conflict with loans from his personal fortune, and Governor Oliver P. Morton accepted the offer. During the course of the war the financier advanced more than a million dollars to the state. He continued to live in New York City after the Civil War and died there in 1881.

After Lanier left Madison the mansion on the Ohio came into the possession of his eldest son, Alexander C. Lanier, who occupied it

until his death in 1895. It then passed through the hands of a number of other members of the family and was finally presented to the Jefferson County Historical Society by Charles Lanier, another son of the original owner. In 1925 the state of Indiana acquired the property and has since maintained it not only as a period museum but as a memorial to the man who came to the aid of Indiana at a critical period in its history.

The house is open to the public and a curator is in charge. To visit this mansion, with its many magnificent rooms, all retaining their original nineteenth-century furnishings, is to be transported back to the leisurely, opulent days of the ante-bellum era, the days of crinolines, beaver hats, candlelight, and shining landaus.

Poet's Home

AMONG literary historians of the Midwest, the old two-story house at 411 West Market Street, in the southern Indiana city of New Albany, has long been an object of interest. For this was the boyhood home of William Vaughn Moody, poet, dramatist, and educator.

Although born and reared in the Hoosier state, and associated during his entire mature life with Chicago, William Vaughn Moody did not derive his poetic inspiration from the Midwestern scene; following a traditional pattern of poetic composition, he obtained his figures of speech and imagery from Greek mythology and other Old World sources.

It was just a few years after the Civil War

JORDAN STUDIO, NEW ALBANY

The house in which William Vaughn Moody lived as a boy

that the Moody family moved to New Albany from Spencer, the small town farther north where the poet was born July 8, 1869. The elder Moody was a river steamboat captain, and New Albany was a steamboat capital of the Ohio River. Here, then, as a boy, William Vaughn Moody could have absorbed the pageantry of river life, as young Mark Twain did on the Mississippi. But Moody preferred the world of books, and he remained a scholarly booklover the rest of his life.

Moody lived in the Ohio River town only until he was seventeen years old. Then, both his parents being dead, he went East to school. After graduating from Harvard in 1892, he made the first of his many pilgrimages to Europe, then returned to teach at Harvard. His work as a teacher and writer soon attracted the attention of the enterprising western educator, William Rainey Harper, founder and first president of the University of Chicago, and in 1895 the twenty-six-year-old William Vaughn Moody returned to the Midwest as a member of the Chicago faculty.

In Chicago Moody became one of a brilliant group of faculty associates who achieved as much distinction in writing as in teaching, a group that included Robert Herrick, novelist, and Robert Morss Lovett and Percy H. Boynton, both critics of American life and letters.

Moody's first book, published soon after his move to Chicago, was a poetic drama called *The Masque of Judgment*, the first part of a trilogy Moody planned to write. In 1901 his lyrical and narrative poems were collected in a volume called, simply, *Poems*, and in 1904 *The Fire-Bringer*, the second drama of his trilogy, appeared. As a dramatist, however, Moody attained his widest fame with two prose plays, *The Great Divide* and *The Faith Healer*.

By this time, William Vaughn Moody had resigned from the faculty of the University of Chicago and was devoting his full time to writing. He was at work on the third part of his trilogy, "The Death of Eve," when he died suddenly at Colorado Springs on October 17, 1910. He was forty-one years old.

Mrs. William Vaughn Moody, a brilliant and engaging personality, was widely known as Chicago's outstanding literary hostess, both before and after her husband's death. A few years before her own death in 1932, she paid tribute to the life and work of her husband by establishing at the University of Chicago the William Vaughn Moody Lecture Foundation, which regularly brings famous authors to the Chicago campus, and the William Vaughn Moody Library of American Literature, which contains a comprehensive collection of books by American writers.

The modest, two-story house at New Albany, Indiana, where the poet grew to maturity, is time-stained and unkempt now, but it is still of architectural interest. Its design was simple but structurally sound and functional. In the sagging, recessed porches on one side there is still to be seen the striving of its builder for classical adornment, privacy, and shelter from the glare of Indiana's midsummer days.

The House in Lockerbie Street

JAMES WHITCOMB RILEY HOUSE. INDIANAPOLIS. BUILT 1865. OPEN TO THE PUBLIC.

AFTER having lived a bohemian and no-madic existence in hotels, garrets, boarding-houses, and hall bedrooms — in which sup-posedly uninspiring places he wrote most of the dialect poems that brought him national fame as the "Hoosier Poet" — James Whit-comb Riley soon after his fortieth year de-cided he wanted a home. He wanted a place where he could live permanently for the rest of his days, write more poetry, and entertain his friends.

He found this place in an old-fashioned house at 526 Lockerbie Street in Indianapolis. It was a house in which Riley had often been a guest, for John R. Nickum, the man who built it in 1865, was one of his earliest friends and one of the first to recognize his poetic gifts.

James Whitcomb Riley was born on Octo-ber 7, 1849, in the little county-seat town of Greenfield, some twenty miles east of Indian-apolis on the old National Road, America's first highway west of the Alleghenies. This his-toric highway is now U.S. 40, and still standing alongside it, in Greenfield, is the house in which Riley was born. At Greenfield, too, there is a statue of the poet in front of the county courthouse, and the James Whitcomb Riley Memorial Park, laid out around the "old swimmin'-hole" that Riley made famous in one of his poems.

In Greenfield — called "Griggsby's Station" in Riley's verse and prose — the Hoosier Poet grew up among rural types that were later to appear in his books as the Raggedy Man, Little Orphant Annie, Doc Sifers, Tradin' Joe, Old Aunt Mary, and Uncle Sidney. Riley's father was a lawyer, and the boy James was often around the courthouse, where he came to know the town characters and their stories, as well as their peculiar Hoosier speech.

Young Riley was not a very successful stu-dent and he quit "schoolin'" at sixteen to roam the countryside painting advertisements on the sides of barns.

After returning to Greenfield, where he joined the staff of the local newspaper, Riley began writing verse. He had a hankering for the stage, though, and a few years later he joined a traveling troupe of actors. He also served for a time as an assistant with various patent medicine shows.

This brief career as an actor influenced his work as a poet, for it gave him a slant in writ-ing that makes his verse highly successful as platform poetry. So effective was it that he afterward won wide fame as a public reader of his own poems, often appearing at joint recitals with the humorist, Bill Nye.

Riley resumed his career as a journalist at Anderson, a town about twenty miles north of Greenfield. And it was here that he perpe-trated his famous hoax. He had one of his own poems printed as a newly discovered poem by Edgar Allan Poe. It was taken seriously by many literary critics, and Riley was severely criticized when the fraud was exposed. But the incident brought him to the attention of Eastern literary circles and his newspaper verse began to find a wider and wider audience. In 1877 he joined the staff of the *Indianapolis Journal*, and he was still with that newspaper when his first book, *The Old Swimmin'-Hole and 'Leven More Poems*, appeared in 1883 un-

510 Lockerbie Street

der the pseudonym of "Benj. F. Johnson, of Boone." That book brought him fame, and from then on a new volume of his verse appeared every few years.

With some affluence came Riley's desire for the peace, security, and comfort of a home. As a frequent guest of John Nickum in the comfortable residence on Lockerbie Street, the poet had become more and more fond of the street, only one block long but pleasantly shaded by maples and sycamores. He had expressed his affection in a poem called "Lockerbie Street."

When he went there to live, in 1893, the house was occupied by Major Charles L. Hol-

stein and his wife, the former Magdalene Nickum. This couple continued the regard for Riley which the elder Nickums had shown, and after the death of Major Holstein, the poet was given the entire residence for his own use. Here he continued to reside with two Negro servants, Katie Kindall and Old Dennis, with his secretary, Marcus Dickey, and his nephew and traveling companion, Edmund H. Eitel.

The Lockerbie Street house was a perfect setting for the genial man who sang of old-fashioned things in American life, for surrounding him here were the overstuffed sofas and chairs, arched marble fireplaces, gaslight

JAMES WHITCOMB RILEY MEMORIAL ASSOCIATION

Riley would shut himself in his bedroom for hours at a time while he wrote

chandeliers, and all the ornamental bric-a-brac of the Victorian era. Seated in his favorite chair in the library, always neatly dressed, his gates-ajar collar and frock coat giving him the appearance of a clergyman, Riley received many distinguished persons from near and far. Delegations of school children came to see him too, eager to meet the author of "Out to Old Aunt Mary's," "When the Frost Is on the Punkin'," and many other poems they knew and loved.

Riley had been living comfortably and contentedly in his Lockerbie Street house for twenty-three years when he died, at the age of sixty-six, on July 22, 1916.

Now owned and maintained by the James Whitcomb Riley Memorial Association, an organization of Indianapolis civic leaders, the Riley house in Lockerbie Street is open to the public, with a hostess in charge. Inside and out, from its modified mansard, Italianate eave brackets, keystone-arched doorways and windows, to its florid interior furnishings, heavily ornamented with fringes and overdraperies, the house is a museum of its period. Of special interest are the enormous gilt-framed pier glasses and the mantels of onyx and white marble.

These and certain details of the interior woodwork show a gracious simplicity that suggests the transition from Greek Revival to later styles.

Shrine for Labor

EUGENE V. DEBS HOUSE. TERRE HAUTE. BUILT 1880.

THERE is nothing very remarkable physically about the house on Eighth Street in Terre Haute; hundreds, perhaps thousands, much like it are still to be found in the towns and cities of the Midwest. But this house was for almost fifty years the home of Eugene V. Debs, the champion and hero of the working-man at a time when it was not safe to be that in the United States. Denounced and persecuted in his own day as a dangerous radical and anarchist, Debs is today recognized by many as one of America's great men. Many of the ideas he was sent to prison for advocating are today accepted as custom and sanctioned by law.

As a labor leader, Eugene Debs had come up from the ranks. Born in Terre Haute (also the birthplace of the novelist, Theodore Drei-

ser) in 1855, young Gene had to leave school when he was fourteen. He went to work in the local railroad shops and soon became a fireman on the road. He educated himself beyond his formal schooling by reading widely and attending lectures. Later he worked for a wholesale grocery house, served Terre Haute as city clerk for four years, and was elected to the Indiana state legislature for one term. From this he moved into full-time labor union activities, first with the Brotherhood of Locomotive Firemen.

By this time Debs had married Katherine Metzel, a woman who shared his economic and political beliefs, and had acquired the two-and-a-half-story frame house at 451 North Eighth Street. Although the Debses had no children, their house was always full. Debs'

Eugene Debs' house in Terre Haute

parents lived with them, and also, much of the time, his brother Theodore, who became his secretary and aide. And the neighbors and their children were always in and out. Often, too, one or more of Debs' friends were guests, among them James Whitcomb Riley, Eugene Field, Susan B. Anthony, and Robert G. Ingersoll.

In June 1893 Debs organized and became the president of the American Railway Union, one of the first industrial unions, as distinguished from trade or craft unions, in America. Its strength and efficiency were demonstrated a year later by its surprising victory in a strike against Jim Hill's Great Northern Railway.

But its next engagement was not so successful. In May 1894 began the historic Pullman strike — one of the better examples of how contemporary verdicts can be judged mistaken by history. The roles of hero and villain in this struggle have been almost exactly reversed in the decades since they were played.

When the Pullman employees finally struck

to force a change in their intolerable working and living conditions, they appealed to the American Railway Union for a sympathy strike. Debs refused this, but he led his trainmen in a boycott of Pullman coaches, refusing to move any such cars. The boycott was amazingly effective and railway traffic came almost to a standstill.

The federal court in Chicago issued an injunction against Debs and his union members; then, without consulting Governor John P. Altgeld, indeed over his protests, President Cleveland, acting on the advice of his attorney general, a former railroad counsel, sent troops of the United States Army to Chicago to enforce the injunction — in order, he said, to protect the mails. Violence followed — induced, as an official investigation later proved, by the strikebreakers hired by the Pullman Company. Debs and six others were arrested for violation of the injunction, convicted of contempt of court, and sentenced to six months' imprisonment.

When Debs was released from the Woodstock, Illinois, jail in the closing weeks of 1895, he was greeted with one of the most spectacular demonstrations in the history of Chicago. A crowd of a hundred thousand met his train at the station. They had a carriage waiting for him, but he said he preferred to walk as they had to, and he led their march across to Battery D Armory on Chicago's lake front, where he addressed them with the inspired eloquence for which he was famous.

The next day he took a train for home and his wife Kate. And again in Terre Haute he found a huge crowd of workingmen waiting to welcome him with torchlights, Roman candles, and an enthusiastic brass band. That night he made another speech and when it was over stayed up far into the night shaking hands with hundreds of his neighbors and friends.

The prison term had not lessened Debs' fervor for his cause. He went into Woodstock

jail a union leader; he came out of it an advocate of general social reform. And now, in the library of his Terre Haute home, Debs set to work on plans for organizing an American Socialist party. The Social Democratic Party of America was launched in 1897, and Debs became its first presidential candidate in 1900.

Three more times he was its nominee, the last time while he was again in prison for his principles.

Debs was the most conspicuous of those who suffered from the hysterical hatreds that were aroused during World War I. In a speech at Canton, Ohio, on June 16, 1918, he dared to be sarcastic about the lateness of many conversions to the battle against militarism and autocracy. The Socialists had long been fighting these dangers, he said, but some good Americans had been slow to see the light. Theodore Roosevelt, for instance, had been proud to visit the German kaiser. "And while Roosevelt was being entertained royally by the German kaiser, that same kaiser was putting the leaders of the Socialist party in jail for fighting the kaiser and the Junkers of Germany. Roosevelt was the guest of honor in the white house of the kaiser, while the Socialists were in the jails of the kaiser, for fighting the kaiser."

For this, Debs was tried under the Espionage Act in a federal court in Cleveland on charges of inciting mutiny in the army, stirring up disloyalty, and promoting the cause of the enemy. He was convicted and sentenced to ten years in the federal penitentiary at Atlanta.

So from his Terre Haute home, Eugene Debs, tall, lanky, and bald now, walked away to prison a second time. And during this second term, he was again nominated as the Socialist candidate for president and in the election that followed polled almost a million votes. The next year, 1921, he was pardoned by President Harding.

He returned again to his house on Eighth Street, to his devoted wife, his books, and his friends. But the prison term had weakened him. He failed gradually, and in 1926 he died in the Lindlahr Sanatorium at Elmhurst, Illinois. He was then seventy-one years old.

In the years since then, the Debs house at Terre Haute, though still a privately owned dwelling, has come to be revered by workingmen everywhere for its associations with one of their most effective and most dramatic leaders.

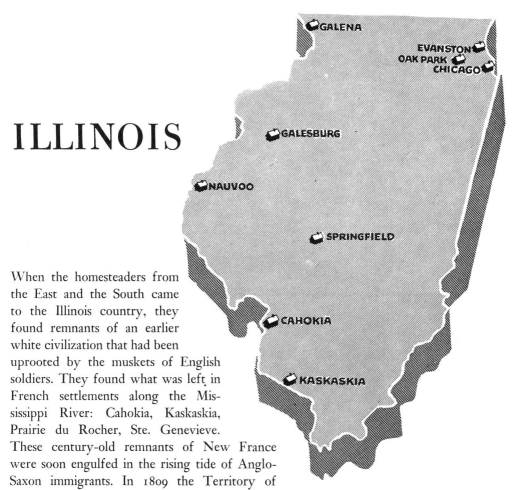

ILLINOIS

When the homesteaders from the East and the South came to the Illinois country, they found remnants of an earlier white civilization that had been uprooted by the muskets of English soldiers. They found what was left in French settlements along the Mississippi River: Cahokia, Kaskaskia, Prairie du Rocher, Ste. Genevieve. These century-old remnants of New France were soon engulfed in the rising tide of Anglo-Saxon immigrants. In 1809 the Territory of Illinois was formed, a great new land that included the present state of Wisconsin. Then in 1818 enough people had come to form a state, and Illinois, her territorial size reduced, came into the Union. In the years afterward her prairie sod was plowed, fields of corn and wheat appeared, fenced in by Osage orange hedges and rail fences, cattle and hogs were bred, and farmers began shipping their surplus products to the thriving new lake port of Chicago. As more people came from the East and later from Europe, as more corn, wheat, cattle, and hogs appeared, Chicago grew to become the commercial capital of the Midwest, the second largest metropolis in America.

Oldest Midwest House

JEAN BAPTISTE SAUCIER HOUSE. CAHOKIA. BUILT ABOUT 1737. OPEN TO THE PUBLIC.

THE ancient log house now generally known as the Cahokia Courthouse is Illinois' most historic building. And it seems to be the oldest private dwelling extant in the entire Midwest. It was used as a residence for almost half a century before it was converted into a courthouse, and then, after being abandoned as a courthouse, it once more became a private home.

A family was living in this historic house when it was acquired in 1904 for exhibition at the St. Louis Exposition. It was known then that various families had been occupying it successively since 1860, and before that time it had served for a period as a tavern and meeting hall. After the close of the St. Louis fair it was taken to Chicago and set up at the south end of Jackson Park, and there it remained until 1939. Today it stands on its original stone foundation at Cahokia and has been completely restored as a pioneer courthouse. It is now maintained by the state of Illinois and is open to the public as a museum.

The sturdy old house is believed to have been built about 1737, not so many years after the first white men settled in the wilderness of mid-America. These men were French missionaries and fur traders from Quebec who set up outposts of the French empire in the Mississippi Valley. Attracted by the luxuriant vegetation and rich bottom-land soil bordering the east bank of the Mississippi just above the Ohio, they established settlements here, the first at Cahokia in 1699 and the second a few years later at Kaskaskia some forty miles to the south. A little later still Ste. Genevieve was founded across the Mississippi in what is now Missouri. This entire region, full of reminders of the French period in American history, was long known as the American Bottom.

The identity of the man who built the Cahokia house has never been discovered. Records show, however, that in 1763, the year France lost the Illinois country to England, the house was acquired by Captain Jean Baptiste Saucier and his wife. Captain Saucier was a French military engineer who designed and built Fort de Chartres, located a few miles below the settlement of Cahokia. When France capitulated at the end of the French and Indian Wars, Saucier resigned from the colonial army and he and his wife went to live at Cahokia.

"Capt. Saucier and wife," writes John F. Snyder, one of the captain's descendants, "enamored with the country and the people, upon his resignation left New Chartres and purchased an elegant home in Cahokia, where they were accorded the highest respect and consideration by the entire community. . . . Capt. Saucier engaged actively in business pursuits and prospered." The house was still owned by the Saucier family when George Rogers Clark, in 1778, captured the Illinois country from the British and when, a few years later, the Northwest Territory was formed.

With the establishment of American civil government in the region, the Illinois country was divided into two counties and Cahokia became the seat of St. Clair County, which embraced most of northern Illinois, including the future site of Chicago. In 1793 François Saucier, son of Captain Saucier, sold the log house

*The oldest house in the Midwest, built about 1737, dates
from the French colonial period*

to the county for a courthouse and jail. Here were held the first American court sessions in the Illinois country, as well as part of the first election and the region's first public school sessions.

The construction of the Saucier house is evidence of its antiquity. It was built in the French style — that is, with the logs set perpendicularly, as in a palisade. The later American style of log house construction, introduced into this country by Swedish settlers on the Delaware River, is characterized by horizontal logs.

Writing of this two-century-old Illinois building in an issue of the *Bulletin* of the Illinois Society of Architects, a state architect, Joseph F. Booten, said: "It was a revelation to find that our structure originally had its interior walls plastered on split lath. Other refinements included casements with glass panes, shutters, beautiful wrought-iron hardware, beaded beams and ingenious roof trusses. . . . The interior had four rooms and an attic. A chimney was placed at each end and a gallery surrounded the whole. Many new wall logs were required (in the restoration) and the existing ones (of walnut) had to be lengthened."

French Colonial Residence

PIERRE MÉNARD HOUSE. KASKASKIA. BUILT 1802. OPEN TO THE PUBLIC.

ON A grassy slope above the Mississippi River, some fifty miles south of East St. Louis, stands a white-painted old house of French colonial architecture. Surviving from early territorial days, this house is one of Illinois' most famous dwellings. It occupies a plot in Fort Kaskaskia State Park, a fifty-seven-acre tract including what was once Fort Kaskaskia. This fort, which stood on a bluff above the house, was built by the French when they controlled the Mississippi Valley in the eighteenth century. One of its purposes was to protect the little French settlement at its feet, Kaskaskia. This settlement later became the first capital of the new American state of Illinois.

In the year 1791, when the Illinois country was still part of the Northwest Territory, there came to Kaskaskia a young Quebec-born fur trader named Pierre Ménard. He opened a store, prospered, and the next year married one of the village girls, Thérèse Godin. Soon afterward he was appointed a major, and later a lieutenant colonel, in the local militia.

When the Illinois country became part of Indiana Territory, the governor, William Henry Harrison, appointed Pierre Ménard a judge of the county court at Kaskaskia. After

ILLINOIS DEPARTMENT OF PUBLIC WORKS AND BUILDINGS

The Ménard house, famous throughout the early West for its hospitality

57

Ménard fireplace, with French mantel

house on the Mississippi, although small in outward appearance, was roomy enough to hold them all. They grew to maturity and lived in the house after their father's death in 1844, but one by one they moved away to other parts of the country.

Meanwhile, the old French settlement of Kaskaskia below the Ménard house fell into decay as East St. Louis and St. Louis grew; its houses crumbled into ruins, and finally most of what was left of the original settlement was submerged when the Mississippi formed a new channel at this point in 1880. All that is left today of Kaskaskia, once known as "the metropolis of the Northwest Territory," is the Ménard house, the foundations of the old French fort on the hill above, and a small cemetery nearby where lie the remains of the early Kaskaskians.

Illinois became a separate territory, Ménard served as presiding officer of the territorial legislature, and when the territory was admitted to statehood in 1818, he was elected the state's first lieutenant governor. All in all, he was a respected and substantial citizen of Kaskaskia.

It was in 1802, just after the Illinois country became part of Indiana Territory, that Pierre Ménard built the house which stands today on a grassy bluff above the broad expanse of the Mississippi. Before long, according to the *Dictionary of American Biography*, it was "a place famous throughout the West for its hospitality." Several years after it was built, Ménard's wife, who had borne him four children, died. He later married Angélique Saucier, sister-in-law of the famous fur trader and Indian agent, Jean Pierre Chouteau.

In the years following, six more children were added to the Ménard household. But the

The water basin in the kitchen is carved from solid rock

After the last of the Ménard descendants left the house, it was owned and occupied for some twenty-five years by Louis Younger and his family. Then in 1927 the state of Illinois acquired the house and the land around it. It was converted into a public museum, and gradually some of its original furnishings, as well as many of the personal belongings of Pierre Ménard, were restored to it. Today it stands as one of the noteworthy landmarks of early French civilization.

The design of the house is reminiscent of the minor French colonial plantation houses of Louisiana. It is long and low, just one story high. Two narrow dormers light the attic, and the roof sweeps out over a long columned porch.

In the entrance hall the visitor is shown numerous belongings of Ménard's, including his compass, Bible, spectacles, watch, flute, and flageolet. In the drawing room, where General Lafayette is said to have been entertained when he visited America in 1824–25, there is an elegant French mantel over the fireplace,

above which hangs an oil portrait of Ménard. Here, too, are Ménard's cowhide trunk and his mahogany chest.

Similar heirlooms and pieces of furniture, including Ménard's barber chair, what remain of his books, his embroidered velvet vest, a two-hundred-year-old clock, a walnut swivel chair, a cherry-wood desk, and a bear trap, are displayed in the parlor, dining room, and bedrooms. At the rear of the dwelling is the stone kitchen, with its Dutch oven, huge fireplace, and water basin carved out of solid rock. Beyond the kitchen stands the old slave house, also built of stone.

Most of the windows in the Ménard house still hold their original hand-pressed panes, imported from France. On the outside of one of these panes is an inscription, evidently scratched in with a diamond, that suggests romance in the Ménard family. It contains two names, "L. C. Menard" and "Augustin Louis Cyprian," the place name "Ste. Genevieve," and a date, "August 24, 1842."

Here Lived Lincoln

ABRAHAM LINCOLN HOUSE. SPRINGFIELD. BUILT 1839. OPEN TO THE PUBLIC.

WHEN Abraham Lincoln sought the services of a minister for his marriage to Mary Todd, he went to his friend, the Reverend Charles Dresser. This call was made at the minister's new Springfield home, and the story is that Lincoln was so impressed and pleased with the house, with its comfort and roominess, that he decided then and there he wanted to own one just like it. And two years later Abraham Lin-

coln became owner and occupant of the minister's dwelling.

To this green-shuttered, white frame house at the northeast corner of Eighth and Jackson streets in the Illinois capital city of Springfield more people come annually, from all parts of the world, than to any other historic shrine in the Midwest. Here they can get an impression of the plain, home-loving, chore-performing

*The home on Eighth Street in Springfield was the only
house Abraham Lincoln ever owned*

The parlor in the Lincoln house

Lincoln, as opposed to the public Lincoln of great deeds, immortal orations, and fateful decisions.

When the Reverend Mr. Dresser built the house in 1839, it was only a story-and-a-half dwelling and stood on the outskirts of the state capital in a new neighborhood of "nice" homes. Mr. Dresser lived in the house with his family until he sold it to Lincoln in 1844. For the two years since their marriage the Lincolns had been living in the Globe Hotel.

This house was the only one Lincoln ever owned. The price he paid for it and the lot on which it stands was fifteen hundred dollars in cash. Although it was not mentioned in the deed, there was a nine-hundred-dollar mort-

gage on the house which was cleared a few months after Lincoln bought it. In referring to this mortgage afterward, Lincoln is supposed to have said that he "reckoned he could trust the preacher that married him." In 1856 the house, at the suggestion of Mrs. Lincoln, was raised to the height of a full two-story residence.

When Lincoln was elected to Congress and moved his family to Washington in 1847, the Eighth Street house was rented to one Cornelius Ludlum. The Lincolns returned to their Springfield dwelling a year later and remained there until the tall, gaunt master of the house was elected president of the United States. Lincoln was formally notified of this event by a committee from the Wigwam in Chicago, where the Republican convention was held, and the notification was made in the south parlor of Lincoln's home.

After the Lincolns moved to Washington in 1861, the house on Eighth Street was rented first to L. Tilton, president of the Great Western Railroad, and next to George H. Harlow, who later became secretary of state for Illinois. Then, after several years' occupancy by a Dr. Gustav Wendlandt, the house was rented in 1884 to O. H. Oldroyd, a well-known collector of Lincolniana. It was Oldroyd who urged Robert Todd Lincoln, son of the martyred president, to deed the house to the state of Illinois. This was done in 1887, and Mr. Oldroyd became its first official custodian.

The house is very well preserved. Students of architecture note that its exterior is in the Greek Revival style, though with ornamental details that mark the beginning of the corruption of that chaste architectural pattern. The framework of the house is of oak while the siding, trim, and flooring are of black walnut. The few nails used in its construction — wooden pegs tie the main timbers together — are all hand-wrought. Standing on a slight elevation, the house is partly surrounded by a low brick retaining wall and a white picket fence of unusual design. The fence was built to Lincoln's order.

No changes have been made in the interior of the house since the Lincolns left it. Unfortunately, most of the original furniture was

ILLINOIS DEPARTMENT OF PUBLIC WORKS AND BUILDINGS

Lincoln's Springfield house has been restored with authentic furnishings from the Civil War period

destroyed in the Chicago fire of 1871, while it was in the possession of the widowed Mrs. Lincoln. As a result, only a few Lincoln pieces are on display in the house today. These include Lincoln's favorite rocking chair, a cupboard he used as a bookcase, and Mrs. Lincoln's sewing chair. But the house is not otherwise bare. Each of the twelve rooms has been restored with authentic mid-nineteenth-century furnishings and the total effect, inside and out, is of a comfortable Midwestern small-town residence of Lincoln's day.

The Mansion House

JOSEPH SMITH HOUSE. NAUVOO. BUILT 1841. OPEN TO THE PUBLIC.

ON January 19, 1841, according to the Mormon *Book of Doctrine and Covenants*, Joseph Smith, the Prophet of the Mormon church, received a divine revelation. Among other things, the revelation contained these words: "And again, verily, I say unto you, if my servant Robert Foster will obey my voice, let him build a house for my servant Joseph according to a contract which he has made with him."

This passage was in reference to the construction of a suitable residence for the Prophet, and soon after the revelation, the "Mansion House" was completed by its builder, Robert Foster. It survives today in Nauvoo as a shrine of the Mormon church, and also as a historic house of both Illinois and the Midwest.

Nauvoo was the third "Stake in Zion" the Mormons had attempted to establish in little more than a decade. The Church of Jesus Christ of Latter-day Saints was founded in Palmyra, New York, but Joseph Smith soon afterward moved his family and his little band of followers out to Kirtland, Ohio, in the Western Reserve. There the group grew and prospered and the organization and procedures of the church were crystallized.

Most of these gains were lost, however, in the failure of a bank the Prophet had promoted, and Smith moved once again, this time to a colony of the Saints his missionaries had established in Missouri. But there, too, within a very short time, his people and their neighbors found themselves in trouble. The authorities intervened, Smith was arrested, and his followers were driven across the river into Illinois. Smith managed to escape from custody and joined them, in the settlement he soon renamed Nauvoo. This event took place in April 1839.

The early years at Nauvoo were the most successful of Smith's career. He was in his mid-thirties then, tall, handsome, full of self-confidence and good spirits. But trouble was developing in Nauvoo.

There were rumors that the Prophet and a chosen few among the church elders, in accordance with a secret revelation of 1843, were beginning to sanction plural marriages. The rumors grew into open charges, some of the Mormons rebelled, and the non-Mormons in surrounding counties were roused to frenzy.

Soon a full-scale civilian mob, backed by no less hostile county militiamen, were storm-

CLYDE BROWN, *Chicago Daily News*

The Mansion House of the early Mormon church

ing the gates of Nauvoo. Governor Thomas Ford then stepped in with the state militia to prevent bloodshed. Under promise of a fair trial, Joseph Smith and his brother Hyrum, the Patriarch of the church, were persuaded to surrender. They were lodged in the jail at nearby Carthage, and there on June 27, 1844, they were murdered by an infuriated mob of two hundred men.

After some dissension among the Twelve Apostles, Brigham Young led a large body of the church westward across the mountains to establish a new Stake in Zion in what is now Utah. A minority of the members refused to ac-

cept Young's leadership, however, and stayed behind to follow the banner of Joseph Smith's family. This branch of the sect became the Reorganized Church of Jesus Christ of the Latter-day Saints. Its headquarters are still in Independence, Missouri.

After the murder of the Prophet, the Mansion House was occupied by his widow, Emma Hale Smith. She was the mother of his five children, one of whom, Joseph, became in 1860 the head of the Reorganized Church. When Mrs. Smith died in 1889, the house was inherited by two of her other sons, Alexander and David.

Research by the northern Illinois unit of the Historic American Buildings Survey, under the direction of Earl H. Reed, reveals that the house and property were deeded to the Reorganized Church (the Missouri group) in 1918 by Frederick A. Smith, grandson of the Prophet. "Intensive repairs," says Mr. Reed's report, "were undertaken immediately and the house stands today in excellent condition, with most of the original details still intact."

Of white pine construction, two stories high, and with a hip roof, the Mansion House bears evidence of the Greek Revival style in the pilasters and cornices of its façade. Now maintained as a public museum by the Reorganized Church, the house contains numerous exhibits, such as Joseph Smith's desk, foreign

editions of *The Book of Mormon*, early copies of the *Book of Doctrine and Covenants*, and bound volumes of a pioneer Mormon newspaper, *Times and Seasons*.

"Every year," says Harry M. Beardsley in *Joseph Smith and His Mormon Empire*, "scores of earnest young men visit Nauvoo to spend a night in meditation in Joseph Smith's room in The Mansion House before setting out on their missionary journeys in behalf of the Reorganized Church. A few miles away at Carthage, other equally earnest young men arrive every year from Utah to spend a night in solemn contemplation in the cell tower at Carthage jail in which Joseph Smith was murdered, so that they may set forth on their missions imbued with the spirit of the Prophet."

Gift to the General

ULYSSES S. GRANT HOUSE. GALENA. BUILT 1857. OPEN TO THE PUBLIC.

THE one-time home of General Ulysses S. Grant is the principal sight of Galena, an old and picturesque city in a hollow of the hills at the extreme northwest corner of Illinois, not far from the Mississippi River. Actually located on the Galena River, which winds through this section, Galena was once a boom town, owing to the discovery of lead mines in its vicinity. But with the coming of the railroads in the 1850's, Galena declined and soon lost its position as a lead-producing center. Still standing, however, are the fine old Greek Revival mansions of the men who made fortunes in the lead mines. These, as well as General Grant's home, attract sightseers to Galena in increasing numbers each year.

It was just after the close of the Civil War in 1865 that General Grant, acclaimed in the North as the military savior of the Union, was presented with the spacious, two-story brick residence in Galena that was in after years to become a memorial to him. Here the Grants lived until 1868, when the general was elected president of the United States.

Grant had gone to Galena some years before the outbreak of the Civil War at a time when he was low in funds. He was then an obscure civilian, and he went to work, at six hundred dollars a year, as a clerk in a leather goods store operated by his two younger brothers. This modest store is still standing at 120 Main Street. The unpretentious home which

General Grant's house was one of the showplaces of Galena

Grant and his family occupied at this time stands at 121 High Street, and from its hillside position commands a view of the lower town. Here Grant and his wife and four children were living when Lincoln was elected president and Fort Sumter was bombarded.

As a graduate of West Point who had fought in the Mexican War, the Galena store clerk offered his services to the War Department. Response to his offer was slow in coming, but he was eventually commissioned a colonel of the 21st Regiment of Illinois Infantry. Thus he began the Civil War career that brought him fame.

At the close of the war the people of Galena, wanting General Grant to return, offered him one of the city's most imposing mansions as an inducement. When Grant accepted the gift he found himself in possession of one of the showplaces of Galena. It had been built in 1857 by Alexander Jackson, a leading citizen of the town in its boom days. To obtain the house as a gift for General Grant, the citizens of Galena are said to have paid sixteen thousand dollars for it. This sum included the lot and the furnishings of the house.

Writes Florence Gratiot Bale in her booklet *Galena Yesterdays:* "The Grants established themselves in this sightly and comfortable house and renewed the friendships of early days, and General Grant showed his intention of making it his permanent home by bringing his war trophies with him."

Mrs. Bale tells us that "people in the town entertained the Grants at dinners and other social affairs; all the ladies made formal calls on Mrs. Grant and once more the old town felt Grant was a citizen of Galena. His official duties took him to Washington and he was away a great deal of the time, but he always considered Galena his legal home."

After the Grants left for the White House in Washington, the mansion in Galena was occupied by H. H. Houghton and his wife. Mr. Houghton was editor of the *Galena Gazette* and at one time had been postmaster of the town. When General Grant completed his second term as president, he and his family came back to live in the Galena residence in the intervals of their extensive travels. Here he was living when, in 1880, he was prevailed upon to become a candidate for president once more. Upon losing the election to Garfield, Grant moved to New York. His last days were spent in writing his *Personal Memoirs,* a two-volume work which became a best seller of the day. He died on July 23, 1885.

Following the departure of the Grants, the Galena house was rented to the Reverend Ambrose Smith, pastor of the South Presbyterian Church of Galena. Subsequently, the house was occupied by David Nash Corwith and his family and later by the C. C. Matheys. It was given to the city in 1904.

The house today, open free to the public, is an almost intact relic of Civil War days, both in architecture and in interior domestic equipment. It has been completely furnished with the household effects of the Grants. On the plate rail in the dining room are displayed dishes which were used in the White House during Grant's two administrations, and on the dining table stands a glass bell jar containing fruits that were preserved in wax by Mrs. Grant herself.

Rest Cottage

FRANCES E. WILLARD HOUSE. EVANSTON. BUILT 1865. OPEN TO THE PUBLIC.

IN THE year that saw the end of the Civil War and the assassination of President Lincoln there was built in Evanston, a university suburb just north of Chicago, a frame cottage with board-and-batten siding and lacy scroll-work trim depending from its gables and porches. The man who built it was employed in a Chicago bank. With him when he moved into it were his wife, his son, and his twenty-six-year-old daughter.

Today, that somewhat ornate cottage, with its quasi-Gothic roof structure, is one of the noteworthy houses of the Midwest, because the young lady who moved into it in 1865 with her father and mother was Frances E. Willard, one of America's best known temperance crusaders and champion of woman's rights.

At the time the Evanston house was built, Miss Willard was by no means famous, although only the year before she had attracted some attention with the publication of her first book, *Nineteen Beautiful Years*, the story of her younger sister Mary, who had died. The two sisters had gone to Evanston in 1858 to attend Northwestern Female College (later absorbed into Northwestern University), and liking the town, they had persuaded their father and mother, sturdy and devout Vermonters who had taken up life on a farm in Wisconsin, to join them.

After receiving her diploma from the college, Miss Willard became a teacher in a country school near Evanston. Later she went abroad, to attend the University of Paris and to travel on the Continent. At this time she also began writing for weekly newspapers and

magazines. Upon her return to the United States she joined the temperance crusade of 1874, and this was the beginning of her career as a temperance leader. She was not only a writer of high merit but an effective speaker too, and she became a leader also in the movements that resulted in woman suffrage and the eight-hour working day.

During most of Miss Willard's active life her home was the old Willard cottage at 1728 Chicago Avenue in Evanston. She called it "Rest Cottage" and so it is known today, but her father called it "Rose Cottage" because of the numerous rose bushes planted around it by the family. He said the house was built "on some new lots reclaimed from the swamp." Miss Willard herself, in those early years, planted two chestnut trees in the yard at the rear of the cottage, and these are now full grown and shade the cottage in the summertime.

After serving as president of the Evanston College for Ladies in the early 1870's, Miss Willard was named the first dean of women at Northwestern University when that institution became coeducational. Later she founded the World Woman's Christian Temperance Union, and work in this organization took her to all parts of the United States and Europe. As an energetic crusader against alcohol, she won the approval and friendship of many noted persons in England; her work even attracted the attention of Queen Victoria.

The international scope of Miss Willard's career, the brilliance and versatility of her mind, and the honors bestowed on her for her achievements—all these are vividly illustrated

Memorial to Frances E. Willard

by the mementos and heirlooms on display in Rest Cottage. The house and its furnishings remain as they were when Miss Willard died on February 18, 1898. Because of this, the cottage is as much a period museum as it is a memorial to Miss Willard. It is now owned and maintained by the Woman's Christian Temperance Union, whose national headquarters occupy a modern two-story building at the rear of Rest Cottage.

Of greatest interest to visitors at Rest Cottage is a room in the southwest corner of the second floor which Miss Willard called her den. A combined workshop, study, and library, this room was the place where she did her writing and planned the many activities that made her one of America's outstanding women. Her annotated books, favorite Bible,

writing materials, furniture, and pictures are all still in the den, and on its brick fireplace is inscribed Miss Willard's favorite motto: LET SOMETHING GOOD BE SAID.

This room also contains the flat-topped oak desk on which she wrote her famous *Polyglot Petition for Home Protection*. This was a temperance petition addressed to the governments of the world and signed by more than seven and a half million persons of many different nationalities. The sheets of the petition were mounted on rolls by Mrs. Rebecca C. Shuman of Evanston, and these rolls are now one of the prized exhibits of Rest Cottage.

Other interesting exhibits in the den are Miss Willard's favorite rocker, in which she sat while writing her autobiography, *Glimpses of Fifty Years;* her "Old Faithful" traveling

The study and the dining room in the Willard house

bag; a tall grandfather's clock made by one of her ancestors, Simon Willard, a famous colonial clockmaker; and a large handsomely bound volume containing the letters sent to her by many famous persons on the occasion of a visit to England in 1893.

In rooms on the main floor of the house visitors are shown Miss Willard's parlor organ, an embroidered sampler she made at the age of fourteen, a bicycle she learned to ride when she was fifty-three, a music box which plays "Home, Sweet Home," her old-fashioned English tea basket, and her collections of china and glassware.

In the parlor on the north side of the cottage Miss Willard's long-time secretary and friend, Anna Gordon, maintained an office. This is now known as the Anna Gordon Memorial Room. Miss Gordon, who in 1898 wrote *The Beautiful Life of Frances E. Willard*, continued to live in Rest Cottage until her own death in 1931.

Home of the Merchant Prince

MARSHALL FIELD HOUSE. CHICAGO. BUILT 1873.

ONE of the few surviving landmarks of old Prairie Avenue, that once aristocratic street in Chicago where lived some of America's wealthiest families during the 1880's, is the three-story, red brick mansion of Marshall Field, the "merchant prince." The big old house stands almost alone now among weedy vacant lots where elegant Victorian residences and town houses once flourished.

At the time Marshall Field built his residence at 1905 Prairie Avenue, he was one of the wealthiest men in America. When he died in 1905 the Field estate was estimated "at about $100,000,000." Much of this fortune was derived from Chicago real estate, both in the Loop and in outlying neighborhoods, but the bulk of it came from the mercantile firm founded by the merchant prince, Marshall Field and Company of Chicago, the largest firm of its kind in the world.

A native of Massachusetts, where he was reared on a farm, Marshall Field moved to Chicago in 1856, at a time when the city was booming because of the first appearance of railroads. Without funds when he arrived, the young man soon was earning a living as a clerk in the wholesale dry goods house of Cooley, Wadsworth and Company. His abilities as a merchandiser were quickly recognized and in 1860 he was made a member of the firm. Then began a long and complicated series of changes in ownership and control, out of which emerged, in 1881, the present retail and wholesale house of Marshall Field and Company.

Some of the huge fortune Marshall Field acquired in the city of his adoption, he returned to the city in the form of cultural institutions that are now enjoyed not only by Chicagoans but by Midwesterners in general. He founded the great lake-front museum which originally bore his name and is now known as the Chicago Museum of Natural History, and he was in large measure respon-

Marshall Field house on old Prairie Avenue

sible for the creation of the Art Institute of Chicago. Field was also one of those who helped lay the groundwork for the University of Chicago and the now defunct Chicago Manual Training School.

It was shortly after the great Chicago fire of 1871 that Marshall Field built his Prairie Avenue residence, at a cost, it is said, of two million dollars. The house was designed by the noted American architect, Richard Morris Hunt, but it was far less elaborate than that other and more famous Hunt creation, the William K. Vanderbilt mansion in New York City. Typical features of the Field house are the French mansard so popular during the 1870's, the red brick construction, almost for-

midable in its solidity, and the heavy white stone lintels. The spacious grounds are enclosed in a grill-work iron fence, and there is a commodious coach house at the rear. This was the first house in Chicago in which electric lighting was installed.

Marshall Field lived in this Chicago mansion for almost thirty years, and here his first wife, the former Nannie Scott of Ironton, Ohio, ruled quietly but indisputably as social queen of Chicago during the 1870's and 1880's. In the years before and during the World's Columbian Exposition of 1893, the Fields entertained numerous American and European persons of note, but their social functions were always marked by decorous restraint.

They made at least one exception to this rule, however — when their son, Marshall Field II, reached the age of seventeen in January 1886. In honor of the event, the Fields invited more than five hundred guests to a ball in their mansion. Since Gilbert and Sullivan's operetta *The Mikado* was then the rage in the fashionable world, the Fields made this a "Mikado Ball," and the guests — youngsters and parents and grandparents — all came in colorful oriental costumes. Prairie Avenue was lighted that night with special calcium lamps, and the evening marked a high point in the festal history of the grand old avenue.

After the death of his wife in 1896, the austere and white-haired merchant prince remained a widower in his Prairie Avenue mansion for some years, but in 1905 he married Delia Spencer Caton, the widow of a well-known Chicago attorney who had been a friend and neighbor of the Fields in the Prairie Avenue section. The marriage was of short duration, however, for five months afterward Marshall Field died of pneumonia. He was seventy years old at the time of his death.

Mrs. Field lived on in the Prairie Avenue house for many years, much of that time with her niece, Mrs. Albert J. Beveridge, widow of the Indiana senator and Lincoln biographer. But just before World War I started, Mrs. Field took up permanent residence in Washington, D.C., and thereafter the old Field residence lapsed into obscurity. It was later inherited by Marshall Field III, who in turn deeded it to the Association of Arts and Industries for use by the New Bauhaus School of Design. Now no longer used for this purpose, the old mansion survives as a reminder of the vanished splendor of the old Prairie Avenue.

Cottage by the Railroad Shops

CARL SANDBURG COTTAGE. GALESBURG. BUILT 1875. OPEN TO THE PUBLIC.

ABOUT a hundred and fifty miles southwest of Chicago, in the smoky railroad town of Galesburg, stands the birthplace of Carl Sandburg, poet, ballad singer, columnist, lecturer, and biographer of Lincoln. He is known as the poetic voice of the Midwest, for his poems reflect as much of rural and prairie life as they do of metropolitan and industrial life in the great central states region.

The house in which Carl Sandburg was born and where he spent his earliest childhood is of the simplest construction — an ordinary workman's cottage, like millions of other workmen's cottages that huddle in the shadows of smoky industrial plants throughout the nation. Standing at 311 East Third Street, only a stone's throw from the Galesburg railroad shops, this small house is just a one-story frame dwelling with a gable roof, clapboard siding, front and rear doors, and a few windows. Nothing more. There is not even a porch or a stoop at the front entrance. One steps into the house from a rectangular flagstone.

In this plain and humble home Carl Sandburg was born on January 6, 1878. He was one of the sons of August Johnson, a Swedish

*One-story workman's cottage in Galesburg, where
Carl Sandburg was born*

immigrant who, upon arriving in Galesburg, discovered there were too many Johnsons among the numerous Swedish Americans there and changed his name to Sandburg. It is said that a mix-up in pay checks at the railroad shops, where August Johnson worked, caused him to make the change in name. The poet's mother was also a Swedish immigrant and, like her husband, had had no formal schooling.

In the smoky, sooty railroad shop, before a blazing forge, August Sandburg was sweating for ten hours a day six days a week when his son Carl was a baby. It is said he earned only fourteen cents an hour, or eight dollars and forty cents a week. At the end of each week

he had to indorse his pay check with an x because he could not write his name. He eventually learned to read a little English, however, and after supper each evening he would pick his way through a newspaper or try to read the Bible.

In the little Third Street cottage Carl Sandburg spent the first five or six years of his life. Here as his mind deepened and broadened, he heard the puffing of locomotives and the rumble of forge shops, but he saw, too, that there were blue morning-glories on the porches of workmen's cottages and yellow sunflowers along the railroad tracks. Or maybe at night his young mind wondered about the moon and the pale light it threw on the roofs of the railroad sheds and on the polished steel rails.

The elder Sandburg rented the cottage in which the poet spent his babyhood, but in spite of his meager wages, he managed to save a little money each year and when his savings mounted to eight hundred dollars he bought a house of his own in Galesburg. It was only a three-room house but the Sandburgs were happy to move into it. Unfortunately Carl's father lost the deed to the house through some mix-up with the courts and was forced to save the eight hundred dollars all over again and repurchase the house. Some years later the family was able to move from their three rooms into a larger and more comfortable home. When Carl was thirteen, he had to leave school and go to work, but he managed later to continue his studies at Lombard and Knox colleges.

The poet's subsequent career and his early struggles to become a writer are vividly told in *Carl Sandburg: A Study in Personality and Background* by Karl Detzer, published in 1941. His first book of poetry, *In Reckless Ecstasy,* by "Charles A. Sandburg," was published in 1904 by the Asgard Press of Lombard, Illinois, a small press run by Quincy Wright's father. Sandburg achieved his fame as the "Chicago Poet" after he became a newspaperman on the *Chicago Daily News.*

Sandburg was fascinated by the life and character of Abraham Lincoln, and working patiently over a period of many years he finally completed his monumental six-volume biography of the great Civil War president. With the publication of this work, Sandburg was acclaimed as one of the foremost of American writers. Harry Hansen wrote of him in *Midwest Portraits:*

"Carl Sandburg has become a figure of national significance. Today he is invariably named as one of the four or five outstanding poets of America. . . . He has helped direct our thinking back to the primitive forces of the land; to the soil, human labor, the great industries, the masses of men. . . . The cumulative effect of his poems will survive and be of great influence in our land."

As national, and international, fame came to Sandburg, more and more attention was centered on the little workman's cottage in Galesburg where he was born. Thanks largely to the efforts of Mrs. Adda George of Galesburg, the cottage is now owned and maintained by the Carl Sandburg Association and is open to the public as a museum of Sandburg and Lincoln memorabilia.

An Old New House

FRANK LLOYD WRIGHT HOUSE. OAK PARK. BUILT 1891.

A LANDMARK in the evolution of modern architecture is the rambling brick and shingle dwelling at the southeast corner of Forest and Chicago avenues in the Chicago suburb of Oak Park. Built late in the nineteenth century, this house pointed the way to twentieth-century building design. And it is of special interest as the former home of Frank Lloyd Wright, the man who conceived it.

Erected more than fifty years ago, at a

time when American domestic architecture was imitative and factitious, copying Gothic castles, Renaissance palaces, and Romanesque strongholds, this Oak Park house was a daring break with the past. In designing it Frank Lloyd Wright created a house whose form was determined, not by any French château or Viennese palace, but by its own function and site — in this case, a place on level ground in which a twentieth-century man could live comfortably with his family. Through much use of glass and brick, Wright achieved in this house a close unity between its interior rooms and the outside world of garden paths, flowers, bushes, and trees. It was the architect's earliest attempt at merging a house into the landscape; it was one of his first houses "designed for living."

Several other houses designed by Wright still stand on Forest Avenue, near the original Wright home, and as a result this section of Oak Park has become a kind of mecca for architectural students interested in the development of modern architecture.

Frank Lloyd Wright is of Welsh descent. He was born on June 8, 1869, at Richland Center, Wisconsin. His father, William Wright, was a traveling musician who later became a preacher, and his mother, Anna Lloyd Jones, had been a schoolteacher. After attending the public schools and studying engineering at the University of Wisconsin, Wright left college without completing his studies and went to Chicago.

This was in 1888. By that time young Wright had decided he wanted to be an architect, and he entered the office of Adler and Sullivan, one of Chicago's leading architectural firms, as an apprentice draftsman. It was his employer, Louis Sullivan, who evolved the doctrine that "form follows function," the principle underlying modern architecture, but it remained for Frank Lloyd Wright to make the practical application of the theory.

He stayed with Adler and Sullivan five years before striking out on his own. He was still with them when he built the Oak Park house in 1891, and in his autobiography he says Sullivan made the building of the house possible by giving him a substantial increase in salary. This was just after his marriage to Catherine Tobin of Chicago. She was not quite eighteen at the time and he was twenty-one.

In their Oak Park house, which was part home and part architect's studio, the Wrights became the parents of six children. Some idea of what life was like in this household may be gained from Wright's autobiography, first published in 1932. Here the architect tells us about his children and how he gave them musical instruments to play; about his own interest in books, prints, rugs, and handicraft articles; how the family once owed a grocery bill of eight hundred and fifty dollars which Wright paid by selling some of his rare Japanese prints; about the old willow tree around which he built a corridor to connect the main part of the house with the studio.

The Wrights lived in this house for nineteen years. Then in 1911, after he was divorced from his wife, Frank Lloyd Wright returned to Wisconsin, and there, at Spring Green, near his boyhood home, established the country estate on which he has resided since. It is called "Taliesin," a Welsh word meaning "shining brow," and the name of one of the greatest of the ancient Welsh bards. Taliesin has become internationally famous not only for its modern architecture but for its architectural school. Students from all parts of the world go to Taliesin for instruction in the "architecture of the future," which Wright calls "Usonian" and which he has outlined in his book *When Democracy Builds*.

In designing his Oak Park house, Frank Lloyd Wright was still somewhat under the influence of traditional architecture. This is

Frank Lloyd Wright's home, built more than fifty years
ago, made a daring break with the past

evidenced by the gabled roof. He had not yet achieved the flat or very low-pitched roof which marks later Frank Lloyd Wright houses. Aside from the roof, however, this Oak Park house has nearly all the earmarks of Wright's style: horizontal lines, overhanging eaves, terraces, and rows of windows.

This horizontal design was at first called prairie architecture because it was intended to fit the flatness of the Midwestern landscape. But as Wright developed and improved his method, and as it gained wider popularity, it came to be known as the international style. Having no unbreakable connection with the past, adaptable to any nation, and making use of the methods and materials of the industrial

era in which we live, the international style of architecture is as representative of the twentieth century as Gothic was of the twelfth.

In this style the Midwest has given to the modern world a form of architecture which is distinctively its own and not imitative of any other. And in this connection, it should be remembered that Chicago was the birthplace of the skyscraper, that most characteristic of twentieth-century buildings. In Illinois, then, one may observe in effect the whole range of American architecture: from the Cahokia courthouse, an eighteenth-century log cabin, to the first of the modern houses, which blazed the trail for a fresh approach to house design all over the world.

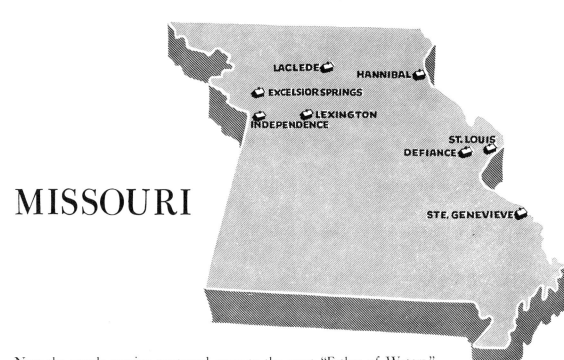

MISSOURI

Now the people moving westward came to the great "Father of Waters," and they crossed over it and pushed on into the old Spanish colony of Upper Louisiana, undeterred by the foreign flag that dominated its outposts. In flatboats they went up the Missouri River, or they journeyed overland on horseback or in wagons. As more and more of them settled on both sides of the Mississippi, they clamored for American control of the mighty midcontinent water highway, and the river and millions of acres beyond it became part of the United States in the Louisiana Purchase of 1803. By 1821 there were enough settlers beyond the Mississippi to form the state of Missouri. When steamboats appeared on the Ohio, the Mississippi, and the Missouri, St. Louis became the waterway capital of the midcontinent valley. Homeseekers came up to the new state from the South, joining there the migrants from the East and the German emigrants from the Old World. Some of the people remained in Missouri and established villages, towns, and cities, but others moved on toward the West, toward the Great Plains. And so Missouri, with its rugged and verdant hills, its rich pastures and stony knobs, became a pleasant settled land and at the same time became the starting point, the outfitting place, for the long wagon trains that carried men, women, and children over the alkaline wastes to the Far West.

Home of a Commandant

ALMOST in the center of the picturesque old Missouri town of Ste. Genevieve stands a story-and-a-half house of the kind the French Creoles built along the Mississippi. When this house, the oldest still standing in Missouri, was built by Jean Baptiste Vallé in 1785, all territory west of the Mississippi River was owned by Spain, to which it had been ceded by France in 1762.

Spanish rule did not materially affect the life of Ste. Genevieve. The town had been settled by habitants from the French villages of Kaskaskia and Cahokia across the river, and it remained a French settlement, preserving the customs, speech, and costumes of the days when France ruled the Mississippi Valley. Ste. Genevieve was then the principal settlement of what was called Upper Louisiana and New Orleans was the center of life in Lower Louisiana. St. Louis was still just a small fur trading post.

There was little change in the daily life of Ste. Genevieve residents when American control was established in 1804 and the "District of Louisiana" came temporarily under the jurisdiction of Governor William Henry Harrison of Indiana Territory. But now the old Creole dwelling built during the Spanish regime became in effect the "Statehouse" for that part of Upper Louisiana, for the man who had built it and was living in it, Jean Baptiste Vallé, was appointed civil commandant of the district of Ste. Genevieve by Governor Harrison.

Jean Baptiste Vallé was a member of the "ruling family" of Ste. Genevieve, one of the oldest, wealthiest, and most respected families of Upper Louisiana. His father, François Vallé, then his elder brother, François Jr., had been the commandants of the district of Ste. Genevieve under the Spaniards from 1762 to 1804.

It was while the younger François was commandant that Jean Baptiste built his French Creole house. The original site of Ste. Genevieve was on low ground near the Mississippi, and in 1785 a disastrous flood forced the residents to move their homes to higher ground. They chose a location some four miles to the northwest, and it was in this new village that Jean Baptiste Vallé built a home for his bride. He had recently married Jeanne Barbeau, daughter of the French army engineer who had built, on the Illinois side of the river, Fort de Chartres, France's Gibraltar in the Mississippi Valley.

In his home in the new village Jean Baptiste Vallé, then twenty-five years old, settled down to the comfortable existence of a colonial Frenchman of means. According to the Spanish census of 1787, the household of "Don Juan Baptista Vallé" included his wife, two children, and thirty-seven slaves. At this time Ste. Genevieve was a thriving center of the fur trade, its white, sunny streets crowded with colorful *voyageurs* and *coureurs de bois* from distant outposts in the Mississippi Valley. It was also a shipping center for salt and lead, as well as for farm products.

The prosperity of Ste. Genevieve continued for a time under the American regime, and the home of the commandant was its offi-

The "Statehouse" of Upper Louisiana

cial social center. It is very likely that when John James Audubon went to Ste. Genevieve in 1810, he was entertained in the Vallé home. Young Audubon and another man, Ferdinand Rozier, established a store in Ste. Genevieve, financing it with money they had received from the sale of three hundred barrels of whiskey they had brought up from Kentucky. Although Audubon soon withdrew from the partnership to continue his ornithological wanderings in the Mississippi Valley, Rozier maintained the business, prospered, became the first mayor of Ste. Genevieve in 1827, and established his mercantile firm so soundly that it is still in business today. Three of his sons were married to granddaughters of Jean Baptiste Vallé.

Vallé lived on in his French Creole house while Missouri became a territory and then a state, and while the importance of Ste. Genevieve waned as that of St. Louis grew. Vallé died in 1840 at the age of eighty years. "He was remembered," writes the Reverend Fran-

cis J. Yealy in *Sainte Genevieve: The Story of Missouri's Oldest Settlement* (1935), "as an old gentleman of culture and courteous manners who wore a cocked hat, knee breeches and an old-fashioned coat with broad cuffs,— altogether a striking memorial of the ancient regime."

After the death of this last of the Ste. Genevieve commandants, the house was occupied in turn by one of his sons and a grandson. Then in 1867 the house was sold to Leon Vion, a member of another old Ste. Genevieve family, and in 1946 it was still in the possession of Vion descendants.

Although built during the Spanish regime, the Vallé house, like most of the other old dwellings of Ste. Genevieve, is of French colonial design, which combined French-Canadian and West Indian features. It is located at the northwest corner of Main and Market streets, not far from Du Bourg Place, the center of the town.

The walls of the house, covered with white

plaster, are made of upright, rather than horizontal, logs, a mode of construction introduced into the Mississippi Valley by the French. Here, too, are the wide porches, or *galeries*, typical of the French Creole dwelling. Behind the house is an enclosed garden, in which stands an old ivy-covered hickory known as the Indian council tree. Much of the furniture and other household articles in the house are Vion family heirlooms.

Many Vallé family relics and heirlooms also survive in Ste. Genevieve. In 1946 they were in the possession of a great-great-grandson of Commandant Jean Baptiste, Jules F. Vallé, a retired St. Louis broker who was living in the old Jacques Guilbourd house at the northwest corner of Fourth and Merchant streets. Mr. Vallé's collection included rare pieces of furniture and china, old maps, documents in French, a pair of candlesticks made of Spanish coin silver and bearing the Vallé coat of arms, and some fine oil portraits of his ancestors, among them Jean Baptiste Vallé, last commandant of Ste. Genevieve.

Last Haven of a Frontiersman

DANIEL BOONE HOUSE. NEAR DEFIANCE. BUILT ABOUT 1817.

TRADITION has it that Daniel Boone, most famous of American frontiersmen, helped to build a substantial stone house that still stands some three miles northwest of Defiance, Missouri.

The story could well be true, because the builder and owner of the house was Daniel Boone's son, Nathan. After the house was completed sometime between 1810 and 1817, the white-haired old woodsman lived in it at intervals with his son, a room having been set aside for his use during these visits. And it was in this room, on September 26, 1820, that the almost legendary trail blazer of the early West died at the age of eighty-six.

An outstanding landmark in what has come to be known in Missouri as the Boone country, the stone house near Defiance is widely referred to in the state as the Daniel Boone house, although it was at no time his permanent home. Restless wanderer that Boone was, he rarely had a permanent home. Even in his last days, he almost always lived in temporary log shelters, and it is believed that none of the numerous Boone cabins have survived to the present time.

Although Daniel Boone might well be called the founder of the state of Kentucky, he lost most of his land there through faulty titles, and so he had to look westward to newer lands. When the authorities in the Spanish colony across the Mississippi promised him honors and large grants, he accepted their offers and marched his family off to the new wilderness west of the Mississippi. This was in the fall of 1799.

The Spaniards gave Boone one thousand arpents of land (845 acres) and later, when he promised to bring more settlers, an additional ten thousand arpents (8500 acres). They also appointed him syndic, or judge, of the Femme Osage district. This appointment made old Daniel Boone, then in his sixty-sixth year, the civil and military leader of the district.

When the Missouri country became part of the United States, Daniel Boone lost his position as syndic, and he also lost his ten-thousand-arpent tract, again because of a faulty title. Congress did, however, grant him a clear title to his thousand-arpent tract (though not until 1814), partly in recognition of his services to the country.

The general area in which these pieces of land were located is today, for that reason, called the Boone country. It lies some fifty miles west of St. Louis on the north bank of the Missouri River. A fertile region of rolling prairies, wooded creek valleys, and bottom lands, it was first settled by French colonists, then by Daniel Boone and his sons, and afterward by sturdy German families from the Old World who made it into a thriving agricultural area.

Daniel's son Nathan had come with him to the Missouri country in 1799, and the next year Nathan acquired in his own right a sizable tract of land in the Femme Osage district. It was on this land that Nathan began, about 1810, to build the stone house.

The house is said to have taken seven or eight years to complete, and when finished was regarded as the finest in that part of Mis-

ASHEN-BRENNER STUDIO, ST. LOUIS

The stone house in which Daniel Boone spent his last days

souri. It is constructed of blue limestone blocks, patiently quarried and shaped on the Nathan Boone farm. The two floors and gabled roof are supported by thick wooden beams, squared with an adz, and all interior woodwork is of walnut. It is said that Daniel Boone himself carved the sunburst decorations on the mantelpiece in each of the seven rooms. Similar in design to early Pennsylvania stone houses, the Boone house has a central hall and three rooms on the first floor. The first room on the right, at the northwest corner of the house, was the one set aside for Daniel Boone.

Although too old to join the army in the War of 1812, Daniel Boone helped guard the Missouri River settlements. Then when the war was over, he resumed his hunting, trapping, and exploring. His canoe, loaded with furs, was a familiar sight on the Missouri River.

After his wife Rebecca died in 1813, Boone began to spend more time in Nathan's home. He is said to have passed his last years polishing and ornamenting powder horns and dreaming of exploring trips to the Rocky Mountains. After his death in 1820 he was buried on a hill overlooking the Missouri River, but twenty-five years later his remains were removed to Frankfort, Kentucky, where a great stone shaft marks his grave.

Nathan Boone continued to live in the stone house on Femme Osage Creek until, after the Black Hawk War of 1832, he decided to enter the regular army. He did not return to the stone house near Defiance when he left the army, but instead built a new house for himself and his family at Ash Grove, near Springfield, Missouri. He lived there until his death in 1856.

Of remarkably sturdy construction, the stone house erected by Nathan Boone has been altered little since it was built more than a hundred and thirty years ago. In 1946 it was the summer residence of Colonel Francis M. Curlee, a St. Louis attorney. Aware of the historic significance of his country house, Colonel Curlee has furnished it as nearly as possible in the style of the period when Daniel Boone sometimes lived in it.

The Old Home Place

JESSE JAMES HOUSE. NEAR EXCELSIOR SPRINGS. BUILT 1822. OPEN TO THE PUBLIC.

SOME ten miles west of a popular Missouri spa, Excelsior Springs, there is a small farm with two old stone gateposts at its entrance. On one of the posts is carved the name "James" and on the other post "1845." Passing through this gate and along a hilltop road, the visitor shortly comes to a two-story frame house to which is joined a sagging old log cabin. This was "the old home place" of America's most famous outlaw and bandit, Jesse James.

It was in the sagging log cabin that Jesse James was born a hundred years ago, and it was from this cabin that he went out to become, as Carl Sandburg called him, the Robin Hood of America — the hero of a folk ballad whose opening lines are familiar to almost everyone:

> *Jesse James was a lad who killed many*
> *a man;*
> *He robbed the Glendale train.*
> *He stole from the rich and he gave to*
> *the poor,*
> *He'd a hand and a heart and a brain.*

To the old log house Jesse James, the hunted outlaw, alias "Mister Howard," often secretly returned to visit his mother, bringing with him at times his friend Robert Ford, the "dirty little coward" of the ballad's refrain:

> *Jesse had a wife to mourn for his life,*
> *Three children, they were brave,*
> *But that dirty little coward that shot*
> *Mister Howard,*
> *Has laid Jesse James in his grave.*

Now a folk hero of the American people, a "good bad man" as B. A. Botkin describes him in *A Treasury of American Folklore*, Jesse James, it would appear, was as much "sinned against as sinning." Once caught in the violence of his time and place, he could not extricate himself; and although he was certainly guilty of offenses against the law, many a train robbery and bank holdup were ascribed to him and his gang of which they were almost certainly not guilty. Jesse himself was never caught and brought to trial.

Jesse James was born in the old frontier cabin on September 5, 1847. His parents were Southerners. At the time of his birth his father, the Reverend Robert James, was pastor of the New Hope Baptist Church in the nearby town of Kearney. On week days the elder James farmed the fertile acres around his cabin, which he had bought from its builder, one Jacob Gromer, in 1845.

During the gold rush the Reverend Mr. James joined a wagon train to California, where he died not long after his arrival. Several years later the widowed Mrs. James married a respected physician of the region, Dr. Reuben Samuel, also a Southerner. Dr. Samuel and his wife, who had been educated in a Catholic convent, brought up young Jesse and his older brother Frank in a strict religious atmosphere. Both boys worked hard on the family farm, were taught the Bible, and attended Sunday school at Kearney.

Like many other Missourians, Dr. and Mrs. Samuel took the Southern side as the Civil War approached. Young Jesse was nine years old when he heard them talk about the John Brown attack at Osawatomie, Kansas, and he and his playmates made a game of shooting and hanging John Brown in effigy.

Then came the Civil War. One day when Jesse James was sixteen, a squad of Union militiamen, suspecting the Samuels of aiding Confederate guerrillas, hanged Dr. Samuel to a tree on the farm, leaving him for dead. They severely horsewhipped Jesse, who was at work in a cornfield. Dr. Samuel was revived, but young Jesse, swearing vengeance nonetheless, rode off on his horse to join a band of Confederate guerrillas. And that was the beginning of Jesse James' career as an outlaw.

Failing to surrender at the close of the Civil War, James became a hunted man. Then followed a series of bank robberies in western Missouri towns, and Jesse James was believed to be responsible for them. A little while later, in 1873, the first train robbery occurred, and again many said "Jesse James."

A year later, Jesse James, according to confessions by two of his companions, killed a Pinkerton detective who, posing as a farmer, had come to arrest him at the old home place. Then in 1875 occurred a tragic episode at the James farm home. Believing Jesse and Frank to be in the cabin, a group of men bent on capturing them tossed a bomb through the window. Little eight-year-old Archie Samuel was killed and Mrs. Samuel lost her right arm

PRESS ASSOCIATION, INC.

A nephew of Jesse James pumps water at the old home place

in the explosion. Neither of the outlaw brothers was there.

Next came the attempted robbery of the First National Bank at Northfield, Minnesota, in 1876. The James boys escaped, but three of their companions, the Younger brothers, were captured, and three others were killed. After this Jesse and Frank evaded public attention for several years.

It was about this time that the celebrated story of Jesse James' "perfect crime" arose: how he paid off a weeping widow's mortgage to save her home and then got the money back

again by holding up the mortgagee the same afternoon.

After a period of obscurity, Jesse James was definitely linked to the robbery of an express train at Glendale, not far from Kansas City, in 1879, and thereafter to several other train robberies in that part of Missouri.

When a reward of ten thousand dollars for the capture of the James brothers, dead or alive, was offered by Governor Crittenden of Missouri, the temptation was too much for Robert Ford, a member of the gang. On April 5, 1882, Ford shot Jesse James in the back in a house in St. Joseph, Missouri, in which Jesse had been living quietly with his wife and children under the name of Howard. The body was buried in the cemetery at Kearney.

A few months later Frank James made a dramatic surrender to the governor of Missouri, was tried on an old murder charge, found not guilty, and walked out of the courtroom a free man. He spent the rest of his life peacefully in various towns of Missouri, coming to the end of his days in 1915 at the old farm home near Excelsior Springs.

In 1893 Frank James built the two-story frame house that now adjoins the sagging cabin, and in 1946 the old home place was occupied by Robert James, Frank's son.

In both the frame house and the cabin are displayed many mementos of the James brothers: old photographs of the brothers and their relatives, pistols and rifles, holsters, cartridge belts, and saddles, old walnut furniture, a sampler made by Jesse's mother, a family Bible, and the minister's license granted to Jesse's father.

Where Tom Sawyer Lived

MARK TWAIN HOUSE. HANNIBAL. BUILT 1844. OPEN TO THE PUBLIC.

TO HUNDREDS of thousands the world over, the Mississippi River town of "St. Petersburg," in which Tom Sawyer and Huck Finn lived, is almost as real and familiar a place as their own childhood homes. The original of Mark Twain's St. Petersburg, of course, is Hannibal, Missouri.

Many landmarks associated with the boyhood days—the Tom Sawyer days—of Samuel Langhorne Clemens still survive in Hannibal and the surrounding countryside, and among them the most human and appealing is the modest little house in which young Sam lived. It is not so spectacular, perhaps, as Cardiff Hill, Lover's Leap, McDowell's Cave, or the great Mississippi itself, but its associations are more intimate.

This small frame house, built flush with the sidewalk, was the home of Mark Twain from the time he was nine years old until he was eighteen. This was the period that provided most of the boyhood experiences embodied in *Tom Sawyer* and *Huckleberry Finn*, and many of these experiences occurred in the Clemens home. In this little house the boy Sam Clemens did give painkiller to the cat, Peter, and here he stole out of his bedroom window at night to meet Tom Blankenship (Huck Finn) and the rest of his gang. Here, too, young Clemens supervised the whitewashing of the fence, gazed in admiration on Laura Hawkins (Becky Thatcher), and outwitted his mother (Aunt Polly). It is actually of record that he went from here one night on a pirate's expedition to an island in the Mississippi.

Samuel Langhorne Clemens was born at Florida, a small settlement some thirty miles west of Hannibal, on November 30, 1835. His birthplace still stands. When Samuel was four

*Mark Twain standing in front of the little house in Hannibal
where he lived as a boy*

years old, his father, John Marshall Clemens, feeling he might do better in his law practice in a larger town, moved the family to Hannibal. He was elected justice of the peace there, but he never really prospered; he lacked business acumen.

When Samuel was nine years old, the elder Clemens built the first floor of the Hill Street house; he could not afford to make it two stories at the time. But that mattered little to his children. In their new home Samuel and his two older brothers and a sister romped and played and squabbled happily, even though little Sam was not always in robust health.

In 1846 the Clemens family had to give up their house when John Clemens was forced to sell his furniture in order to pay a note he had indorsed for a friend. Taking pity on their plight, a Dr. and Mrs. Grant, who lived across the street, took the Clemenses under their roof, and there John Clemens became ill and died on March 24, 1847.

A few months later the Widow Clemens and her children moved back to their home across the street. Young Samuel was now twelve years old. Since the family was too poor to continue his education, Sam was apprenticed to a Hannibal printer, Joseph P. Ament, who also published the weekly *Missouri Courier*. Here the young man got his first smell of printer's ink. His older brother Orion had gone to St. Louis and obtained employment there as a book and job printer, and his sister Pamela began teaching music. Together the three of them supported the family in the small Hannibal house.

At about this time Sam's interest in history was awakened. He picked up a piece of paper from the sidewalk one day, and found that it was a page torn from a biography of Joan of Arc. What the young man read on that page aroused his curiosity and soon he was deeply absorbed in volumes of history.

In 1850 Orion returned from St. Louis and

became editor and owner of the *Western Union*, later the *Hannibal Journal*. Now a competent printer, fifteen-year-old Sam went to work for his brother. During Orion's absence on a trip, young Sam edited the paper himself and wrote a satirical piece about a rival Hannibal editor that nearly brought on a fight—and also, for a short time, increased the circulation of the *Journal*. Instead of fighting, as he had at first threatened, the rival editor left town. It was while working on his brother's newspaper, too, that prankish young Sam Clemens began his literary career with a short piece published in the *Carpet-Bag*, a small national magazine. The title of this sketch was "The Dandy Frightening the Squatter."

When fire destroyed his print shop, Orion transferred the editing and printing of his paper to the front room of the Clemens home. To do this, however, he added a second floor to the house, and it became the two-story structure it is today.

Young Sam continued to help Orion on the *Journal* for a time after this move, but he was restive under his brother's control and finally, at eighteen, broke away to wander the country as a journeyman printer. His subsequent career as river pilot, miner, newspaperman, author, and world celebrity is one of America's great stories.

Orion kept the *Journal* going for a short time after his brother left, even publishing some of the first letters Sam sent back from his travels. But the circulation was dropping and Orion decided to sell out. A long time afterward he remarked: "I could have distanced all competitors even then if I had recognized Sam's ability and let him go ahead, merely keeping him from offending worthy persons."

The Clemens family moved to Muscatine, Iowa, after the *Journal* was sold, and so Samuel Clemens did not return to Hannibal until his spectacular visit as the renowned Mark Twain in 1902. Viewing the house of his boyhood then, he said: "It all seems so small to me. A boy's home is a big place to him. I suppose if I should come back again ten years from now it would be the size of a bird house."

Two years after Mark Twain's death in 1910 his boyhood home was purchased by Mr. and Mrs. George A. Mahan and presented to the city of Hannibal. Located on its original site at 206 Hill Street, it is now a public museum containing Mark Twain relics and mementos, as well as furniture in the style of Clemens' boyhood days. As the source and setting of a great American classic, the house is perhaps the Midwest's outstanding literary shrine.

Nursery of the Children's Poet

EUGENE FIELD BIRTHPLACE. ST. LOUIS. BUILT ABOUT 1848. OPEN TO THE PUBLIC.

UNTIL a few years ago there stood on the south side of downtown St. Louis a group of old red brick dwellings known as Walsh's Row. Dating from the years when St. Louis was the steamboat capital of the Mississippi Valley, Walsh's Row had deteriorated into a run-down tenement block, and in 1934 it was announced that the houses would be torn down. Wreckers soon had demolished all the shabby old buildings — except one. This one was spared at the insistence of leading St. Louis citizens, because it was the birthplace and early childhood home of Eugene Field, "The Children's Poet."

It was on September 3, 1850, that Eugene Field was born in the three-story brick house on Walsh's Row (now 634 South Broadway). Here, from his educated Vermont mother, he heard his first lullabies and got his first glimpses into the world of fairies, hobgoblins, ghosts, and witches — a world he was later to make vivid in his poems for children. In this house, too, he first enjoyed the delights of those traditional holidays which fascinated him the rest of his life: Christmas Day, Thanksgiving Day, and the Fourth of July.

When Eugene was six years old, his mother died. His father, deep in the problems of the Dred Scott case, in which he was attorney for the defense, decided to entrust the care and education of his motherless boys to his sister, Mrs. Mary Field French, who lived in Amherst, Massachusetts. So Eugene Field was reared and educated in the cultured atmosphere of a New England college town.

When Field reached the age of twenty-one, he received a substantial legacy from his father's estate and spent a large part of it in a tour of Europe. He then returned to his native Missouri, married a sixteen-year-old girl, Julia Sutherland Comstock, at St. Joseph, Missouri, and in 1875 entered the newspaper field as city editor of the *St. Joseph Gazette*. After serving for brief periods on the *St. Louis Times-Journal*, the *Kansas City Times*, and the *Denver Tribune*, he went to Chicago in 1883. There, as the conductor of the "Sharps and Flats" column in the *Chicago Daily News*,

CHARLES TREFTS, ST. LOUIS

The hundred-year-old birthplace of Eugene Field

he attained national fame as a humorist, satirist, and prankster, and finally as the Children's Poet.

A tall, slender man, smooth-shaven and bald of head, with the animated, expressive features of an actor, Eugene Field was one of the most unusual characters in the Chicago of the nineties. Between madcap pranks and elaborate practical jokes, he wrote such poems as "Little Boy Blue" and "Wynken, Blynken and Nod," as well as many stories and pointed satirical pieces. His later satirical writings are more subtly conceived than his first book, *The Tribune Primer*, published while he was working on the *Denver Tribune*.

Eugene Field died in 1895 at the age of forty-five. Although Sabine Farm, his Chicago suburban home, has since been razed, Chicago has remembered Field with a statue in Lincoln Park.

The real memorial to the Children's Poet, though, is the St. Louis house in which he was born. Thanks to the efforts of St. Louis citizens and the cooperation of the poet's family, this house has become a museum of Eugene Field memorabilia.

Believed to be about a hundred years old, the house itself is well preserved and kept in excellent condition by the St. Louis Board of Education. On display inside is much of the furniture from Sabine Farm and many of the poet's personal belongings. There is also an interesting collection of innumerable curios and souvenirs that Field acquired during his life.

Period Piece

ROBERT CAMPBELL HOUSE. ST. LOUIS. BUILT 1851. OPEN TO THE PUBLIC.

FOR almost half a century the old brick mansion at 1508 Locust Street in St. Louis had been something of a house of mystery. Although its trim appearance indicated that it was occupied, no one seemed ever to leave it or to visit it. And as the business district crept up around it, the old mansion remained untouched, even though its neighboring residences disappeared one by one, replaced by modern commercial buildings.

The house was no mystery, though, to members of old St. Louis families. They knew it was occupied by two wealthy brothers, both bachelors and both recluses. They had inherited the mansion from their millionaire father, Robert Campbell, who in pioneer days had made history in St. Louis and the Far West.

When the two brothers died within a few years of each other in the 1930's, it was discovered that the interior of their home had been preserved intact, had been kept with exquisite care just as it was when first furnished and decorated a hundred years ago. Here, in this three-story mansion, were found many magnificent rooms furnished in the style of the mid-Victorian period. Though too heavy and elaborate for comfort, judged by modern standards, the tables, chairs, beds, dressers, and armoires are structurally superb.

As a result of this discovery, the house today is one of the outstanding period museums of the Midwest. It is now open to the public and is a St. Louis sight that few travelers fail to visit. Antiquarians, connoisseurs of furniture, interior decorators, and social historians are interested in it as possessing an authentic ante-bellum interior. It is also the lone survivor of old Lucas Place, the once fashionable and exclusive section of St. Louis, where, in elegant brick and stone mansions, lived most of the city's prominent families before the Civil War. The Campbell residence was then No. 20 Lucas Place.

The house was built in 1851, the same year Lucas Place was platted, for John H. Hall, and the architect appears to have been one William Fulton. But it was Robert Campbell who gave the house its name and distinction. He bought it from Hall in 1854 and lived in it the rest of his life. At the time he bought the house, Campbell was one of the wealthiest men in St. Louis, and behind him were years of exciting, dangerous adventure on the plains of the West.

A native of northern Ireland, where he was born in 1804, Robert Campbell came to America as a young man, headed west for St. Louis, and soon was engaged in the fur trade. Combining business with a search for health, he went on westward to the Rocky Mountains, where he joined forces with William Henry Ashley, a prominent fur trader. On the plains and in the mountains Campbell made friends with the Indians or fought them, rode with such noted frontiersmen as Jim Bridger and Kit Carson, and established numerous trading posts, notably the one at Fort Laramie.

When Ashley retired in 1830, Robert Campbell and another trader, William Sublette, continued the business of the Rocky Mountain Fur Company and in time made it the principal rival of the Chouteau-Astor fur company. This company had its headquarters in St. Louis, and there, too, Campbell set up his main office and established a permanent residence.

Campbell soon branched out into other business enterprises in St. Louis. He became president of the Bank of Missouri and the Merchant's Bank, owner of the Southern Hotel, and one of the city's leading real estate men. When the Mexican War started, he aided in recruiting and equipping troops for General Kearney's march to Santa Fé, serving as inspector general for Missouri. And in later years he put his early experiences to good use by acting as the government's representative in various negotiations with the western Indian tribes. He died in 1879 at the age of seventy-five.

As much a personality as Robert Campbell was his wife, whom he married in 1841, when she was nineteen and he was thirty-seven. She

CHARLES TREFTS, ST. LOUIS

The Robert Campbell house, an outstanding period museum of the Midwest

was Virginia Jane Kyle of Raleigh, North Carolina. Handsome and vivacious, she added the fine art of living of the Southern aristocracy to her husband's generous Irish hospitality, and together they made their home a social center of St. Louis. Among notable guests at some of the famous Campbell dinners were President and Mrs. Grant, General William T. Sherman, James B. Eads, builder of the renowned Eads Bridge in St. Louis, and Father Pierre De Smet, well-known missionary to the Indians.

The high spirits and social talents of Robert and Virginia Campbell were not transmitted to their two sons, Hazlett and Hugh, and after Virginia's death in 1882, the Campbell mansion was shuttered and locked against the world for half a century. The family fortune suffered little, though; the two recluse brothers left an estate valued at more than three million dollars.

It was owing to the active interest of Charles E. Peterson, Missouri historian, and the William Clark Society of St. Louis that the Robert Campbell house was saved from destruction and its furnishings preserved. It is now owned and maintained by the Campbell House Foundation, a nonprofit organization of St. Louis civic leaders.

On view now in the front entrance hall are oil portraits of Robert and Virginia Campbell, and on the landing of the stairway stands an eighteenth-century grandfather's clock, said to have been brought from Mrs. Campbell's girlhood home in North Carolina.

To the left is the parlor, the most stately room in the house and entirely representative of an ultrafashionable mid-Victorian interior.

On either side of a large, curtained bay window in the side wall are twin white marble fireplaces above which hang great French mirrors with ornate gilded frames. The design of the mirror frames is used in the gilded cornices of the bay window, as well as in the pier glasses at the far ends of the room. It is still possible to illuminate the parlor with gaslight by means of the handsome chandeliers of brass and bronze. Formally placed around the room are rosewood chairs upholstered in red damask, and in one corner stands a beautifully carved square piano.

Other rooms of the house have equally fine interior architecture and furniture. Not the least interesting of them is the kitchen, with its original copper utensils, ingeniously contrived call bells, cupboards, a copper-lined sink, and wooden chairs. Here, too, is Mrs. Campbell's cookbook, with recipes written in her own hand. A reproduction of it is on sale in the house. It is a "receipt book" that reflects the hospitable personality of Virginia Campbell almost as much as does the personal cookbook of that most renowned colonial hostess, Martha Washington.

Bullet-Scarred Memorial

WILLIAM O. ANDERSON HOUSE. LEXINGTON. BUILT 1853. OPEN TO THE PUBLIC.

AT LEXINGTON, a town some forty miles east of Kansas City on the Missouri River, stands a two-story red brick house marked inside and out with numerous scars and patched-up holes. Inside, in the attic, are vague discolorations said to be bloodstains. These bullet marks and old stains in the William Anderson house are reminders of the Battle of Lexington—not the famous one of the American Revolution but a minor though sharp encounter in the Civil War.

The story of this bullet-scarred mansion begins with the man who built it. William Oliver Anderson was born in Kentucky in 1794.

The William O. Anderson house, center of a Civil War battle

Early in life he engaged in flatboating on the Mississippi between his native state and New Orleans. Later he became a manufacturer of rope and bagging. He acquired the title of "colonel" when he served in the Kentucky militia during the War of 1812.

Attracted by the business opportunities in Lexington, which was then a thriving outfitting station for wagon trains about to set out for the Far West, Colonel Anderson moved north to the Missouri town in 1851 and established a new rope and bag manufacturing company there. Two years later he built his residence on the outskirts of Lexington. It was considered one of the handsomest mansions thereabouts, and in it the Andersons often entertained their neighbors, most of whom were slaveowning Southerners like themselves.

When guerrilla warfare broke out between antislavery Kansans and proslavery Missourians, Colonel Anderson was alarmed and did what he could to prevent. disorder and bloodshed. But then came the fateful firing on Fort Sumter. With the Civil War now under way, Federal troops quickly moved into Missouri, and Lexington was occupied by Colonel James A. Mulligan and his "Irish Brigade," composed of Chicagoans of Irish birth or parentage.

While throwing up earthworks for defense, Colonel Mulligan and his men were surprised by the arrival of Confederate troops under the command of General Sterling Price. Mulligan refused to surrender and firing began. This was the morning of September 18, 1861.

Not more than twenty yards west of the outer line of Colonel Mulligan's earthworks stood the Anderson mansion. It had been vacated by its occupants and was being used as a hospital by Mulligan's men. About noon on the opening day of the battle, the house was captured by a Confederate detachment. There is some question whether or not this taking of a hospital house was a violation of the rules of warfare. In any case, Colonel Mulligan thought it was and he gave orders for the house to be recaptured.

The fighting in and around the house was intense for several hours. About three o'clock in the afternoon the Union troops finally succeeded in retaking their hospital, but they lost it again an hour later and thereafter the house remained in Confederate hands.

At the end of the third day of the battle, Colonel Mulligan, finding his forces outnumbered almost three to one and with no reinforcements in sight, surrendered to General Price.

When the Civil War came to an end four years later and Colonel Anderson returned to his mansion at Lexington, he found it ruined beyond his means to restore it. He therefore returned to Kentucky and died there in 1873.

Mainly because of its association with a Civil War battle in the Midwest, the Anderson house was acquired in 1928 by the Lafayette County Historical Society and is now a public museum, part of the eighty-acre Lexington battlefield.

The house, almost a hundred years old now, is also interesting architecturally. Standing on a pine-shaded bluff above the Missouri River, it has the general appearance of an imposing, though faded, plantation mansion of the old South. A square porch at its front is supported by four Corinthian columns, and the ornate lintels over the windows are made of cast iron, an unusual feature in a dwelling of this kind.

The eighteen rooms of the interior have been almost completely restored by the Lafayette County Historical Society. A spacious entrance hall with a circular walnut stairway opens into high-ceilinged rooms furnished in ante-bellum style. Several of the rooms contain pieces of original Anderson furniture, among them a high-backed bed of Brazilian rosewood with inlaid miniatures of Colonel and Mrs. Anderson on the headboard. An 1834 coverlet is spread on top of the bed.

On display too are mementos of the Battle of Lexington: guns, maps, swords, flags, pistols, army equipment, and photographs — and, of course, the bullet holes and the bloodstains.

Prelude to West Point

JOHN J. PERSHING HOUSE. LACLEDE. BUILT ABOUT 1858.

THE birthplace of General John J. Pershing is still a matter of dispute. Some old-time Laclede residents claim the general was born in a railroad section house a little less than two miles west of the town; others insist he was born in a conventional house about four

miles to the west, near the hamlet of Mead-
ville. It matters little since neither of the
houses has survived, and both sites have been
included within the boundaries of Pershing
State Park, a wooded tract of two thousand
acres west of Laclede.

General John J. Pershing's boyhood home

There is no doubt whatever about General
Pershing's boyhood home. The two-story
frame house in Laclede to which the Pershings
moved when their first-born was a baby is
still standing. Though privately owned, it is
recognized as one of the Show-Me state's historic houses.

General Pershing was born September 13,
1860. His father, John F. Pershing, was then
a section foreman on the Hannibal and St.
Joseph Railroad. When the Civil War began,
he became regimental sutler of the 18th Missouri Regular Infantry, leaving his wife and
child in the care of friends.

It was on his return from war that the elder
Pershing established his family in the house
in Laclede. He opened a general store, became
the village postmaster, and helped to found
the local Methodist church. More children
arrived in the Pershing household, and they
were all given a strict, patriotic, and religious
upbringing. As a boy, General Pershing
watched his father conduct the first Memorial Day exercises in Laclede.

But the Pershing children were not denied
the normal pleasures of healthy young people.
In the big nine-room house there was plenty
of opportunity for fun and play, especially
during the cold winter months. But only after
their lessons were done. By the light of a kerosene lamp, young John studied his books and
did his homework, showing a particular aptitude for arithmetic. He was not so much brilliant as persistent, not giving up his lessons
until he had learned them thoroughly.

When summer and vacation time came, he
went adventuring afield with his companions,
swimming in a pool in Locust Creek, hunting
squirrels in the woods west of town, or tramp-
ing along the railroad right of way. One of
his companions described him in later years
as a boy with light, curly hair, large black
eyes, and a square jaw. Although there was
a dignified reserve about him, he was always
friendly and good-natured.

When he was seventeen years old, young
John became a teacher in the local Negro
school. The regular teacher had left suddenly
and no one else could be found to take his
place. Pershing later taught in white schools
of the district and earned money to be saved
for the college education he was determined
to have. He intended to become a lawyer.

Then one day, while he was at home on
vacation, he saw an item in the Laclede newspaper announcing that a competitive examination would be held for entrance to West
Point. Young Pershing, then twenty-one years
old, decided to take the examination. He
would gain what he wanted at West Point: a

thorough education. And, the story goes, he felt he need not worry about any future war; he didn't think there would be any for a hundred years to come.

Pershing was successful in the examination and went to West Point. His subsequent army career took him into the Spanish-American War of 1898 and made him commander in chief of the American Expeditionary Force in World War I. He emerged from the latter conflict as one of America's military heroes.

Today his name is engraved in bronze on a boulder at one corner of Laclede's little public park. Just one block north of the park, in the shade of some elms and pines, stands the now old-fashioned house in which General Pershing was reared. It has the bay window, roomy porch, and narrow clapboard siding of a conventional middle-class dwelling of the 1860's and 1870's. The gables are decorated with delicate scrollwork and rather pleasing wooden spires. The room occupied by General Pershing when he was a young man is on the second floor, in the northwest corner.

Summer White House

GATES-WALLACE-TRUMAN HOUSE. INDEPENDENCE. BUILT 1865.

ON A warm June day in 1919 a wedding reception was held in the rambling, manse-like residence at 219 North Delaware Street, in the Missouri town of Independence. The house was the home of the bride, a member of an old and respected Independence family. The groom, smooth-shaven, wearing glasses, and dressed in a dark blue double-breasted coat and white flannel trousers, had been a captain of artillery in the American Expeditionary Force in France. Before the war he had tilled the soil on his father's farm. Now he was planning to open a haberdashery in Kansas City.

The bride was Elizabeth Wallace, and the groom was Harry S. Truman, who became the thirty-second president of the United States in 1945. The Delaware Street house was their home until political office took Mr. Truman to Washington.

Few alterations have been made inside or outside the house since it was built in 1865. It is two stories high, though its fine mansard roof, with dormers, might be considered a third story. Its exterior is marked by big porches with intricate jigsaw trim. Inside are sixteen spacious, high-ceilinged rooms, some of which have fireplaces with tile facing. Most of the downstairs rooms can be shut off from the others by double sliding doors after the fashion of houses built before central heating appeared. The walnut and mahogany furniture is of the Civil War period.

The house is set well back on a wide lawn shaded by tall oaks and maples, with clumps of lilac bushes and other shrubs set close against the porches. At the rear of the lot is a barn, at one time a coach house, that has a framework of hand-hewn walnut timbers; the adz marks are still to be seen on its beams.

Kansas City Star, KANSAS CITY, MISSOURI

*The fine old Gates-Wallace-Truman house in Independence dates
from the Civil War period*

The builder of the house was George Porterfield Gates, Mrs. Truman's maternal grandfather. At the time he built his residence, George Gates was head of the Waggoner-Gates Milling Company, a firm that is still operating in Independence, with Mrs. Truman's brother Frank as its vice-president. In his comfortable Delaware Street house, George Gates raised his family, entertained his friends and neighbors, and later invited one of his daughters and her new husband to live with him. This newcomer into the family circle was David W. Wallace, a young Independence attorney. With the death of George Gates, his residence came into the possession of the Wallaces, and here was born and reared their daughter Elizabeth, called "Bess" by her friends.

Harry Truman was born in the small town of Lamar, Missouri, on May 8, 1884. His grandparents were Southerners who had settled in Missouri during the 1840's. When Harry was seven years old, his family moved to Independence, and there, three years later, he met Elizabeth Wallace at Sunday school.

Unable to attend college because of lack of funds, Harry Truman went to work after leaving high school. He became a timekeeper on the Santa Fé Railroad and later a clerk in several Kansas City banks. Meanwhile, he read books, many books, in several public libraries. And he continued his friendship with Elizabeth Wallace, visiting her in the big house on Delaware Street.

Then, when he was twenty-two years old, the Trumans moved to the ancestral farm at Grandview, just south of Kansas City, and there Harry Truman spent the next ten years of his life as a farmer, though he continued his part-time studies at the Kansas City Law School on the side. He soon owned a four-cylinder Stafford automobile and this was seen frequently in front of the Wallace home in Independence. Just before Harry Truman went to France in World War I, he and Bess Wallace became engaged, and they were married soon after the close of the war.

The young couple were invited to live with Mrs. Truman's parents and Grandmother Margaret Gates in the big old Gates-Wallace home, and this house is still their legal residence.

After a brief period as a Kansas City haberdasher, Harry S. Truman entered politics and became in 1923 county judge for the eastern district of Jackson County. He was elected to the United States Senate in 1935, and as vice-president of the United States in 1944. When he became president on the death of Franklin Roosevelt in 1945, he announced that his Independence home would be his "Summer White House."

MICHIGAN

They could journey now in canal boats and sailing vessels, the people moving westward from the upper East. After the opening of the Erie Canal in 1825, they could
travel on Lake Erie from Buffalo to points farther west, and many of them went
into the great woods of oak and pine between Lake Huron and Lake Michigan, and
there they made the commonwealth of Michigan, which was admitted into the Union
in 1837. The old French-Canadian trading post of Detroit became a gateway into the
new state and grew into a thriving city. And when the "iron horse" came, more people
from the East arrived, more villages and towns were established, and commerce and
industry multiplied. Now they were clearing the Michigan forests with great vigor,
hewing down oak and pine for the building of homes in the growing cities. When
the lumber barons had departed, their supply of timber exhausted, there was little left
of the Michigan forests but stumps. But the farmers came, cleared the fields of these
stubborn remnants, and planted corn and oats and fruit trees. Then copper and iron
ore were found in the Upper Peninsula, and in time the long lake ships passing through
the locks at Sault Ste. Marie, were carrying great loads of these ores to the smelters.
And in Detroit a young man named Henry Ford was perfecting the "horseless carriage," which was to develop into a revolutionary force in American life.

On the Island

SURVIVING from the busy fur trade days on Mackinac Island — the small green island in the straits which now is one of the Midwest's most popular summer resorts — stands the dwelling known as the Agent's House. Now restored and open to the public as a museum, this house is the main, and most interesting, unit of the American Fur Company buildings on Mackinac Island.

Immediately adjoining the Agent's House on either side are the employees' bunkhouse and a combination store and warehouse, and in the side of a hill to the rear are several stone vaults where money, whiskey, and ammunition were stored. The entire establishment is now owned by the Mackinac Island Community Association, a body formed to restore and preserve the buildings of the American Fur Company, the largest business enterprise in America during the first half of the nineteenth century.

When the Agent's House was built in 1817, Mackinac Island had already had a long history under the French and English flags. For the French it was a halfway station between Quebec and the wilderness settlements of New France: Vincennes, Detroit, Kaskaskia, Cahokia, and Ste. Genevieve. And for the British its importance was so great that they tried to keep control of it even after the American Revolution. Not until after the War of 1812 were the Americans able to attain a monopoly of the fur trade in the Mackinac country.

Properly speaking, it was one American who secured that monopoly: John Jacob Astor of New York. Astor's fur trading activities on the American frontier during the early decades of the nineteenth century brought him an immense fortune, one of the largest in the world.

In 1808 Astor organized the American Fur Company and two years later sent an expedition out to the Oregon country to establish a fur trading post on the Columbia River. A member of that expedition was young Robert Stuart, who had only recently come from his native Scotland. The new post was called Astoria. A year after its founding Robert Stuart was chosen as a courier to carry dispatches back to John Jacob Astor in New York. The dangers and hardships Stuart encountered in accomplishing his mission are vividly described by Washington Irving in his *Astoria*. Then, in 1817, young Stuart was sent to Mackinac Island, where he became assistant to Ramsay Crooks, general manager of the American Fur Company.

That was the same year in which the Agent's House was built, and in this house Robert Stuart became a guest upon his arrival at the island. He lived there for the next seventeen years, during the most flourishing period of the Mackinac fur trade. In 1820 he was appointed to succeed Ramsay Crooks as resident agent of the company at Mackinac, and he held this position for fourteen years.

Because of Stuart's prominence in the history of Mackinac Island, and because he lived so long in the Agent's House, his restored semi-official residence is often called the Robert Stuart house. During his years as agent, Robert Stuart ruled over a business enterprise that in 1822, its peak year, cleared more than three million dollars in pelts from all parts of

EMERSON DUFINA, MACKINAC ISLAND

The Robert Stuart House on Mackinac Island

the upper Midwest, and even from the distant Rockies. But by the middle 1830's the fur trade had begun to decline, and when John Jacob Astor withdrew from the American Fur Company, Robert Stuart decided to seek opportunities elsewhere. In 1835, at the age of fifty, he moved to Detroit, entering the real estate investment field there. Then in 1845 he went to Chicago, where he became active in promoting the construction of the Illinois and Michigan Canal, which was to link the Great Lakes with the Mississippi River. He died just a few months before the canal was opened to traffic in 1848.

With the decline of the fur trade and the departure of Robert Stuart, Mackinac Island began to emerge as a summer resort, and the Agent's House served as a boardinghouse in the years before and during the Civil War. In this period Edward Everett Hale came to Mackinac and, while a guest there, saw the newspaper obituary notice which inspired him to write *The Man Without a Country*. Constance Fenimore Woolson, a grandniece of James Fenimore Cooper, also visited Mackinac Island in these years, and her novel *Anne* (1882) is a romantic story of the island during the Civil War.

By this time the old Agent's House had acquired the status of a hotel and was called the John Jacob Astor House. But after a few years it was replaced by a new hostelry, the Grand Hotel, which still is the social center of Mackinac Island.

The Agent's House has become a historic building, and it attracts almost as many sight-seers as does the quaint, nineteenth-century town of Mackinac, where fringe-topped surreys and buckboards are still the only mode of transportation.

The house is of frame construction, two and a half stories high, with a gabled roof and projecting dormers. The framework is made of hand-hewn timbers. The small-paned windows and doorway pilasters, the simple entrance hall, the spacious rooms with fireplaces, and the graceful stairway are all reminiscent of the Colonial style in New England houses. Many relics of the great fur trade days, including ledgers and account books, maps and firearms, as well as period furniture, are on display in the several rooms.

The House at the Soo

HENRY ROWE SCHOOLCRAFT HOUSE. SAULT STE. MARIE. BUILT 1827.

AT THE intersection of Portage Avenue and Barbeau Street, in the old Great Lakes city of Sault Ste. Marie — "the third-oldest surviving community in the United States" and "the first permanent settlement in Michigan" — there rests a granite boulder to which is attached a historical tablet. This marker explains that a rambling old frame house nearby was the Sault Ste. Marie Indian Agency built in 1827 by Henry R. Schoolcraft.

As Van Wyck Brooks points out in *The World of Washington Irving*, it was Henry Rowe Schoolcraft who first brought to Americans the realization that the Indian has a soul as well as a body. It was Henry Rowe Schoolcraft, through his books on Indian lore and legend, who inspired Longfellow to write *The Song of Hiawatha*. And it was Schoolcraft, who, among other scientific explorers of the early Midwest, first traced the Mississippi to its source.

The house Schoolcraft built at the Soo is two and a half stories high, many gabled, clap-boarded, and now painted yellow. It stands alone on a wide tract of smooth grassy land not far from the long, steel-gray plant of the Union Carbide Company. Hardly more than half a mile to the northwest are the great St. Marys Locks, and beyond the locks rise the gentle hills of Ontario.

In this house, then on the Western frontier, Henry Schoolcraft carried on the studies of Indian life and customs which made him America's foremost authority in that field. It was in this house he wrote his scholarly, two-volume *Algic Researches* (1839), from which many Americans learned for the first time that the Indians had languages, customs, legends, and a religion of their own. And in this house at the Soo Schoolcraft laid the groundwork for his monumental *History and Statistical Information Respecting the History, Condition and Prospects of the Indian Tribes of the United States* (1851–57). This authoritative work, sponsored and financed by the United States government, consists of six folio vol-

umes and contains steel engravings of paintings by Seth Eastman.

But Schoolcraft was not altogether ignorant
of Indians before his arrival at Sault Ste. Marie.
He had met them firsthand on several occasions. Born in New York State on March 28,
1793, Schoolcraft, after graduating from
Union College at the age of fifteen, went west
on a geological and mineralogical tour of the
Ozark country in Missouri and Arkansas. His
book about this expedition, *A View of the
Lead Mines of Missouri* (1819), won him acceptance as a geologist and mineralogist of
consequence and led to his appointment as
scientist for the General Lewis Cass expedition, which in 1820 explored the Wisconsin

region, the Lake Superior country, and the
area at the headwaters of the Mississippi River.
General Cass was then civil governor of the
Territory of Michigan, to which the Wisconsin country had recently been added.

Certain that the Cass expedition had not
found the real source of the Mississippi River,
Schoolcraft returned to the Minnesota country in 1832 and traced the great river to its
beginnings in a lovely lake. With the aid of a
missionary companion who knew a bit of
Latin, Schoolcraft coined the name *Itasca* for
that lake — from the middle syllables of the
phrase *veritas caput*, meaning "true source."

It was the earlier Cass expedition, though,
that first took Schoolcraft to Sault Ste. Marie.

YOUNG'S STUDIO, SAULT STE. MARIE

*Henry Rowe Schoolcraft, Indian agent at Sault Ste. Marie, included
office space in his house when he built it in 1827*

Here, on a June day in 1820, the exploring party was entertained in the primitive home of John Johnston, a well-known and popular Irish fur trader. The Johnston house still stands in Sault Ste. Marie.

Mrs. Johnston was a fullblood Indian, the daughter of a Chippewa chief, Waub-ojeeg. Jane, the oldest daughter of the Johnstons, after a few years' schooling in England and Ireland, became the wife of Henry Schoolcraft in 1823. The year before, Schoolcraft had been appointed Indian agent at Sault Ste. Marie.

By now his second book had appeared. This was *Travels from Detroit to the Sources of the Mississippi*, a volume based on his experiences with the Cass expedition.

As Indian agent for the "Sault country," Schoolcraft at first lived in the home of his father-in-law, John Johnston. But as his family and his importance grew, he came to want a home of his own, and he applied to Washington for permission and the funds to build one. His request was granted and "the Agency" came into being.

In his *Memoirs* Schoolcraft describes the building of his house: "A site was selected on a handsomely elevated bank of the river, covered with elms, about half a mile east of the fort, where the foundation of a spacious building and office were laid in the autumn of 1826, and the frame raised as early in the ensuing spring as the snow left the ground. . . . I re-moved my family to this spot in October (1827)." He named his new residence Elm-wood.

Here for the next nine years Schoolcraft, according to his own account, lived happily with his family, acting both as agent and as student of Indian affairs. "It was Schoolcraft's custom," writes Stanley Newton in *The Story of Sault Ste. Marie and Chippewa County*, "to assemble the Saulteur (Sault) Chippewas at intervals on the green in front of his office near the bank of the river and distribute various articles of merchandise among them. Whiskey is not mentioned; indeed Schoolcraft had a horror of its effects on the Indians, and continually bewailed its influence on particular Indian acquaintances of his. The gifts were received with appreciation and satisfaction, and helped to cement his influence and his friendship with the Saulteurs."

When Michigan became a state in 1837, Schoolcraft was named state superintendent of Indian affairs and moved from Elmwood to nearby Mackinac Island. Four years later he returned to the East and began writing his six-volume history of North American Indian tribes. He died in Washington, D.C., on December 10, 1864, at the age of seventy-one.

Today the house in which Schoolcraft lived as Indian agent is pointed out with pride by residents of the Soo, many of whom are descendants of Indians and French-Canadians he befriended.

A Wayside Inn

BOTSFORD TAVERN. NEAR DETROIT. BUILT 1836. OPEN TO THE PUBLIC.

THE old and well-known Botsford Tavern on the outskirts of Detroit was originally built as a private home and served as such for some five years before it was converted into a public stopping place.

The original frame farmhouse was built by one Orrin Weston in 1836, one year before Michigan Territory was admitted to statehood. In constructing it, Weston's carpenters used the familiar method of that early day: a framework of hand-hewn timbers held together by wooden pegs. This outmoded basic construction can be seen today in the cellars of Botsford Tavern.

Here Weston lived with his family, tilled his acres, and saw horsemen and wagons pass his house, on their way to or from Detroit. The dusty road in front of the Weston house, an old Indian trail, was to become the Grand River Road, running northwestward out of Detroit to Lansing and Grand Rapids. Today the old Grand River Road is a modern, paved highway: U.S. 16.

When wheeled traffic increased on the Grand River Road, and stagecoaches and covered wagons appeared in greater numbers, the Weston farmhouse, sixteen miles from the central business district of Detroit, became a wayside inn called the "Sixteen Mile House." This conversion was brought about by Stephen Jennings, who had purchased the dwelling in 1841. As host at the Sixteen Mile House, Stephen Jennings became well known to travelers between Detroit and the state capital, Lansing.

In 1860 the roadside inn passed into the hands of Milton Botsford, and since that time it has been known as the Botsford Tavern. Under the management of the Botsford family, the inn grew steadily in favor with the public, reaching its peak of popularity during the horse-and-buggy days of the 1880's and 1890's.

Abandoned as an inn with the coming of the automobile age, the Botsford place was acquired by Henry Ford in 1924, together with forty acres of land surrounding it. Since then, under the Ford management, the house has been restored as nearly as possible to its original state, and it is again serving as a tavern.

The long, white, two-story building is set back from the highway on spacious grounds shaded by old elms and maples. A white fence separates the lawn from the highway. Across the entire front of the tavern stretches a two-story porch, which resembles the gallery of a Southern plantation house. On each side of the small-paned windows hang green shutters. An attractive doorway, with sidelights, invites the visitor inside.

The interior is truly of the mid-nineteenth century period in America. Although it is at once evident that the house was built as a dwelling place, the large rooms on either side of the narrow central hallway have been converted into dining rooms, and an atmosphere of quiet elegance pervades each room. Indicative of the general old-fashioned charm of the place is the parlor to the left of the entrance hall, which now is used as a waiting room. Here, against a background of white and gold wallpaper, are authentic pieces of mid-Victorian walnut and mahogany furniture, all meticulously arranged. On the marble-topped

The Botsford Tavern near Detroit

*The original kitchen of the Botsford Tavern has been restored with
authentic furnishings of the American pioneer period*

table in the center rests a velvet-covered family album and in one corner of the room stands a parlor organ, lavishly ornamented with scrollwork. Several horsehair chairs, a sofa, a whatnot, and a few oval-framed pictures complete the room's furnishings.

At the east end of the house, with a separate entrance from the porch, is the establishment's small taproom. Behind its service bar, whose walnut surface is somewhat worn with age and usage, stand rows of blue and green liquor bottles of many sizes and shapes, all authentically of the American pioneer period. Here, too, are old-fashioned jugs and demijohns and a collection of antique glassware. Over the big fireplace hang long-barreled pioneer rifles and a stuffed deer's head with spreading antlers.

In the kitchen may be seen early American cooking utensils of all kinds, as well as a spinning wheel. And to the rear of the tavern, among tall pines and wineglass elms, stands the big old Botsford barn, in which are displayed old-fashioned carriages and a stage-coach of the kind that a hundred years ago brought dusty travelers to the original Botsford Tavern.

Woodlawn

PATRICE MARANTETTE HOUSE. NEAR MENDON. BUILT 1840.

"ON THE south bank of the St. Joseph River, a mile-and-a-half southwestwardly from the present village of Mendon, where now stands his magnificent mansion, Hon. P. Marantette (then a young man) established his trading post. In the year 1833, after the Indians had become corrupted and degraded through the introduction of strong drink by the settlers, the writer first saw Mr. Marantette exerting an almost absolute control over the Indians, in which his chief aim was their prosperity and happiness, and, at the same time, indignantly inveighing against the inhumanity and heartlessness of those who introduced the poison into the wigwam."

These words are from an article on pioneer days in St. Joseph County, Michigan, read by S. C. Coffinberry at the annual meeting of the State Pioneer Society in 1878. They refer to Patrice Marantette, pioneer settler of lower Michigan, friend of the Indians, state legislator, and one of the last of the great line of French-Canadian fur traders.

Still standing, after more than a hundred years, is the old Marantette country seat, the "magnificent mansion" referred to by Mr. Coffinberry. Having been continuously occupied by four generations of the Marantette family, the house remains in sound condition on its original site close to the town of Mendon.

This house, called "Woodlawn" in its prime, was built by Patrice Marantette in 1840. At that time he had taken up agriculture and the breeding of fine horses, but earlier he had been a fur trader, one of the best known in the St. Joseph Valley. He was a native of Canada, born there in 1807, and it is said that his mother, Archange Marie Louise Navarre Marantette, was a descendant of the ancient royal family of France.

While still young, Patrice moved to Detroit, where he was educated by Father Gabriel Richard, who afterward became the only Catholic priest ever to serve as a representative in Congress. Upon reaching his majority, and while Michigan was still a territory under the governorship of General Lewis Cass, Marantette entered the fur trade in the wilderness country of lower Michigan between Detroit and Chicago.

Here in 1831 he became assistant to Colonel François Mouton, who had opened a trading post at Nottawa, near Mendon. Two years later young Patrice Marantette bought the Mouton trading post and set up in business for himself. He always refused to exchange liquor for furs, giving the Indians instead articles he had purchased in Detroit. And to Detroit he shipped his pelts, conveying them in pack saddles over the old Washtenaw Road, now State Highway 60 to Chicago.

For a few years business was good, and in 1835, Patrice married Frances Mouton, daughter of his former employer. The heyday of the trade had passed, though, and Marantette soon sold out his post, bought land, became a farmer, and built Woodlawn. Always a devout Catholic, he included a chapel in his new home, and in this chapel Father Edward Sorin, founder of Notre Dame University, celebrated the first Mass in St. Joseph County.

At Woodlawn Patrice Marantette reared a family of four sons and four daughters, and

MOOSE ELLET, WHITE PIGEON

The house that Patrice Marantette built in 1840, when he turned from
fur trading to farming, has been occupied continuously
by four generations of the Marantette family

his home was noted for "the unstinted hospitality and refined courtesy of its occupants." When he was elected to the state legislature, he led the successful fight to have Michigan's capital removed from Detroit to Lansing — on the grounds that Detroit was too vulnerable in case of war with England.

Marantette spent the remainder of his days at Woodlawn, and died there in 1878 at the age of seventy-one. Since then his house has been successively occupied by a son, a grandson, and a great-grandson.

In the fourteen rooms of this two-story Greek Revival house, which stands in a grove of maples overlooking the St. Joseph River, are to be found many quaint relics and family treasures from the days of Patrice Marantette. Within the house is the family chapel, where Father Sorin celebrated Mass. And just a few yards away is a granite marker which explains that Father Louis Hennepin, early missionary and explorer, stopped at this spot in 1680 to preach to the Indians of the St. Joseph River country.

A Michigan Farmhouse

WILL CARLETON HOUSE. NEAR HUDSON. BUILT 1840'S.

WHEN Hillsdale College celebrated the one hundredth anniversary of the birth of Will Carleton in 1945, one of the attractions for visitors was the nearby farmhouse in which the author of "Over the Hill to the Poorhouse" was born and reared. Here the Michigan "poet of the people" obtained the impressions of Midwestern rural and farm life that he later embodied in the colloquial ballads which made him the most popular American verse writer of the 1870's.

The modest country home in which Will Carleton was born is located some fifteen miles east of Hillsdale, on the outskirts of the village of Hudson. Here young Will met the rural types who came to visit the Carleton family and who were later to emerge as characters in his farm ballads.

Although Carleton left the farmhouse when he entered Hillsdale College, he returned often to it, even after he had graduated and had gone to work on the Hillsdale paper, to visit with his parents, sitting in a chair on the front porch during summer evenings.

It was after covering a divorce hearing for his paper that Carleton, in 1871, wrote the poem called "Betsey and I Are Out," which brought him his first fame. The story is that when he submitted the poem to a Toledo newspaper, it was thrown into the wastebasket by an assistant editor and was only accidentally found by the editor. After the Toledo editor published it, the poem was widely reprinted throughout the country.

When the editors of *Harper's Weekly* urged Carleton to write more verse in the same manner, he responded readily, drawing on the impressions he had received as a youth on the Hillsdale County farm. Then, in 1873, his first book, *Farm Ballads*, was published. Dealing with such themes as "Gone With a Handsomer Man," "Out of the Old House, Nancy," and "The House Where We Were Wed," this book was an instantaneous success and Carleton was soon receiving invitations to read his ballads from the lecture platform. His career as a platform poet eventually took him to all parts of the United States and even to Europe.

During the 1870's and 1880's it was a rare farm home that did not have a copy of *Farm Ballads*, or one of Carleton's later books, resting on the marble-topped walnut table in the front room. After *Farm Ballads* came *Farm Legends* (1875), *Farm Festivals* (1881), *City Ballads* (1885), *City Festivals* (1892), and *Rhymes of Our Planet* (1895). Carleton died in 1912 at the age of sixty-seven.

Of all Will Carleton's ballads, the most popular and longest remembered is "Over the Hill to the Poorhouse." With its familiar first stanza,

Over the hill to the poor-house I'm trudgin'
*   my weary way —*
I, a woman of seventy, and only a trifle gray —
I, who am smart an' chipper, for all the years
*   I've told,*
As many another woman that's only half as
*   old.*

this poem is said by students of Carleton's work to have stirred the nation, causing sons and daughters to reclaim their aged parents from poorhouses and giving rise to more than

Chicago Tribune

Practically unchanged stands the old white farmhouse where Will Carleton
was born more than a hundred years ago

one reform in institutions for the care of aged indigents.

A part of the poorhouse that Carleton made famous still stands in Hillsdale and is marked by a bronze plaque. This and the plain old farmhouse some fifteen miles away survive as memorials to the man of whom Elwood Corning, his biographer, wrote:

"Carleton lacked range. His imagination was limited and he often disregarded the laws of prosody. But in delineating the life of the farm he was most effective, and as that life, which he so sympathetically portrayed in his numerous ballads, becomes less and less a type, his verses will be cherished as true etchings of an earlier civilization which in all its realism formed so characteristic a part of our crude but developing nation."

In Greenfield Village

HENRY FORD BIRTHPLACE. DEARBORN. BUILT 1858. OPEN TO THE PUBLIC.

UNTIL a few years ago, there stood at the southeast corner of what is now Greenfield and Ford roads in the city of Dearborn, Michigan, a plain two-story farmhouse set back on a wide lawn and surrounded by a white picket fence. Spaced around the adjoining farmyard were a windmill and several sturdy barns and outbuildings. Beyond this farmstead in all directions, except to the south, stretched open country, the wheatfields and cornfields of other farms. In the sky to the south, however, loomed rows of tall smokestacks indicating a huge manufacturing plant.

There was a direct connection between that farmhouse and the awesome smokestacks to the south. For the man who founded the manufacturing plant was born in the plain farmhouse on Greenfield Road. His name was Henry Ford.

Having stood on its original site for more than three quarters of a century, the old Henry Ford birthplace was moved a few years ago to Greenfield Village, the unique historical community Ford had created near his factory. Here, in a quiet, peaceful setting reminiscent of an American village of fifty or seventy-five years ago, the small Ford birthplace, opposite the village green and still surrounded by its white picket fence, stands among a group of original American buildings and homes of historic value which have been transplanted from their original sites.

Among these are the birthplaces of Stephen C. Foster and William Holmes McGuffey, the Menlo Park laboratory of Thomas A. Edison, an Abraham Lincoln courthouse, and the early bicycle shop of Wilbur and Orville Wright. With its greenswards, shade trees, footpaths, curving driveways, and historic buildings, Greenfield Village is a part of a two-hundred-acre tract dedicated to the memory of Thomas A. Edison and known as the Edison Institute. It includes a large museum of American mechanical progress, housed in combined reproductions of Independence Hall, Congress Hall, and the old City Hall at Philadelphia.

When Henry Ford was born in the old farmhouse in 1863, it stood in the midst of a small crossroads settlement known as Greenfield. Not far away meandered the River Rouge, and some ten miles to the east, across flat country, was the thriving city of Detroit. To this city Henry Ford early turned his thoughts, for as a boy he did not like farming. While he helped his father and the hired hands to cultivate the three-hundred-acre family farm, he thought that much of the work he had to do could be done better by machinery.

During the winter months young Henry studied McGuffey's *Readers* and other books in the little red schoolhouse at Scotch Settlement. When Sunday came, he and his brothers and sisters were dressed in their best clothes by their neat, energetic Holland Dutch mother, the former Mary Litogot, and taken by her and her farmer-husband to the Episcopalian village church.

Henry Ford's liking for mechanical things increased as he grew older. He once dammed a creek near his schoolhouse and used the flow thus created to operate a water wheel he had made. About this time, too, he built a forge

The Henry Ford farmhouse and its front parlor

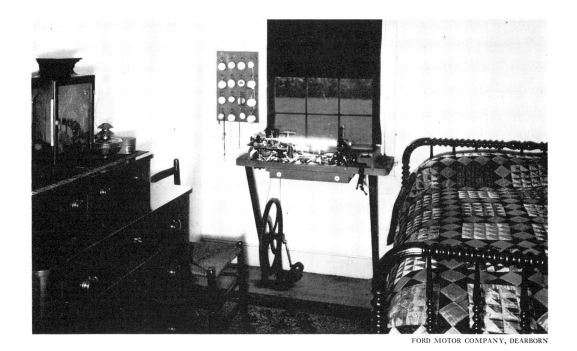

Ford's boyhood bedroom, with his first work table, and the sitting room

in the schoolyard and, using a blowpipe, melted some old glass bottles, reshaping them into new forms. When he was only eleven years old, he repaired a watch by taking it apart and putting it together again, using a filed shingle nail for a screwdriver. Small objects like watches and clocks continued to fascinate him and soon he was serving as watch repairer for the countryside.

When Henry Ford was fourteen, his devoted mother died, and he felt her loss deeply. In the succeeding months his interest in the farm lessened and his desire to work in a Detroit machine shop grew. Finally, in 1879, when he was sixteen, he left the Greenfield farm home, took the train to Detroit, and obtained a job there as a machinist's helper at two dollars and a half a week. He added to his small weekly salary by repairing watches at night for a Detroit jeweler.

Several years later, while young Ford was planning to establish a factory for the manufacture of fifty-cent watches, he received word that his father had injured himself on the farm. He returned to Greenfield, remained there three or four years, and during this time was married to Clara Bryant.

Soon, however, the spell of Detroit and its machinery drew him back to the city again. He worked first for the Dry Dock Engine Company and later as chief engineer for the Edison Illuminating Company. Then, after constructing several successful "horseless carriages," he organized the Ford Motor Company to manufacture low-cost automobiles. This was in 1903, when Ford was forty years old.

The growth of the Ford plant into the largest automobile factory in the world and the effects of its products on American life are an important story in the nation's industrial and social history. Although in his later years, Henry Ford surrendered control of the Ford company to his son and his grandson, he remained personally active in his shop at the River Rouge plant almost to the day of his death, at eighty-four, in 1947.

It might be said that the huge Ford plant, with its rows of smokestacks, its miles of factory buildings, its conveyor system, and its numerous smelters that light up the sky at night, had its origin in a small second-floor bedroom of the Greenfield farmhouse, where, at a table with a foot-operated lathe on it, the boy Henry Ford repaired watches for his Greenfield neighbors. That bedroom today contains all of its original furnishings, including Ford's boyhood tools. Similarly furnished are many of the other rooms in the old Henry Ford birthplace, and the total effect is that of a comfortable, typical Midwestern farm home of the 1860's.

On the Banks of the St. Joe

RING LARDNER HOUSE. NILES. BUILT 1860'S.

ONE of the earliest settlements on the famous old Chicago Turnpike between Detroit and the Windy City—a highway that once was part of the Great Sauk Trail and is now paved U.S. 112—grew into the present city of Niles, Michigan. Not only is Niles known as one of the few communities in the Midwest to have been, successively, under the flags of France, England, Spain, and the United States, but it is also the birthplace of a noted American author, Ring Lardner.

Although the house in which Ring Lardner was born and grew to manhood is privately owned and not ordinarily open to the public, it is receiving increasing attention from tourists each year as Lardner's literary stature grows with the passing of time. As a sometimes sympathetic, sometimes caustic, portrayer of naive American types, he seems likely to take his place with such other Midwestern humorists as James Whitcomb Riley, Ellis Parker Butler, and George Ade.

DEL MORGAN, NILES

Ring Lardner's Gothic-style home

A first glance at the old Lardner home, which stands at 519 Bond Street, tells one that the author of "Haircut" and "The Golden Honeymoon" was not reared in poverty. For the house in its prime must have been something of a showplace. It was built sometime in the late 1860's by R. C. Paine, the town's banker and later its mayor.

Paine chose the Gothic style for his residence, and this architectural mode is evident in some of the window casements and on parts of the exterior trim. The scrollwork dependent from the gables is an ornamental feature that marks the "Hudson River Gothic" style. The old house, set among tall cedars and maples, occupies an attractive position on a wooded bluff above the St. Joseph River — the "St. Joe" to those who live in its vicinity.

Henry Lardner, a successful basket manufacturer, had the means to purchase the big, fourteen-room house when Paine died in 1873, and the Lardners were living in it when Ring was born on March 6, 1885. Henry Lardner was a man of culture and spent much time in his library. Ring's mother was a daughter of the Episcopal minister in Niles and herself the author of two small volumes of verse.

In a rather bookish atmosphere, then, Ring Lardner was reared, receiving instruction from his mother and also from a private tutor. He read a good deal but he played more — fishing in the St. Joe, diving in the swimming hole above the paper mill dam, playing baseball or tennis or croquet, and tobogganing in winter.

After his graduation from the Niles high school in 1901, young Ring Lardner, although only sixteen and quite shy, set out for Chicago. He got a job at five dollars a week, first in the offices of the International Harvester Company and later in a brokerage office. Discharged from both places for "incompetence," Ring returned to Niles for a while, tried his luck in Chicago again, then took a job as a clerk in the Niles gas company.

It was there that his dry, humorous remarks about baseball games and ballplayers first attracted attention. He was urged to write them down and they were printed in the *Niles Sun*. And it was not long till the editor of the *South Bend Times* asked Ring Lardner to become that paper's sports writer. So the tall, shy, witty young man from Niles left his old Gothic home on the St. Joe for the last time.

Lardner won his first real fame as a humorous sports writer on the *Chicago Examiner* and later on the *Chicago Tribune*. Then, with the publication of his first book, *You Know Me, Al*, in 1916, he became a full-fledged short-story writer.

For many years the old Lardner residence was occupied by Ring's sister Lena, a Niles music teacher. Eventually she found it too large for her sole occupancy and decided to sell it. About 1940 it was converted, without too many alterations, into a rooming house. Except for these few alterations and the removal of a front porch, the old house remains much as it was when Ring Lardner romped through its rooms as a boy.

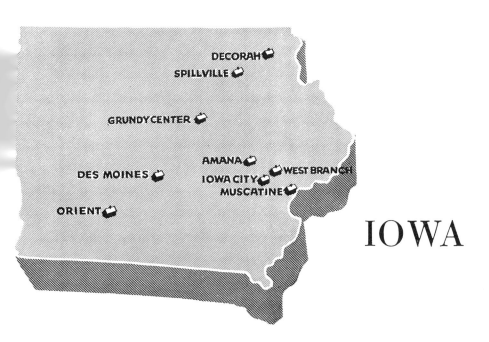

IOWA

As the settlements on the west bank of the Mississippi River – the towns of Dubuque, Keokuk, Burlington, and Davenport – filled with people, they asked for a territory of their own, asked to be set off from Wisconsin Territory. Chief Black Hawk and his tribesmen had been successfully subdued in 1832, and the United States had acquired by a treaty with the Sac and Fox Indians many acres of rich rolling prairie just west of the Mississippi. So the Territory of Iowa was set up in 1838. The westward tide of homesteaders continued to rise, and when immigrants came from the Old World to join it – from Scotland, Ireland, Sweden, Norway, Holland, Germany, Bohemia – there were soon enough people to form a state, and Iowa was admitted to statehood in 1846. In the years that followed, cornfields replaced the prairie grass, villages became towns, towns became cities. The transcontinental railroad appeared and opened new lands for settlement. Now there were schools, churches, colleges. Now Iowa was a representative Midwest state, worthy to be interpreted in art, in literature, in music.

Log Cabin Parsonage

ERIK EGGE CABIN. DECORAH. BUILT 1851-52. OPEN TO THE PUBLIC.

OF THE numerous foreign-born peoples who early settled in the Midwest, one of the most active today in preserving their American historical heritage is the Norwegian national group. One evidence of this is the collection of pioneer Norwegian-American houses and buildings which compose the outdoor section of the Norwegian-American Historical Museum at Luther College in Decorah, Iowa. Here, on the campus of the oldest Norwegian college in America, stand some of the original log cabin homes of the early immigrants from Norway who helped to build a thriving American civilization in the Upper Mississippi Valley.

One of these early Norwegian homes is the old Egge cabin, which occupies almost a central position in the Luther College group of historical buildings. It was built in 1851–52, shortly after the Winneshiek County Norwegian colony was established in northeastern Iowa. The cabin was constructed of squared and notched logs laid horizontally one above the other, in the manner introduced into the New World by the seventeenth-century Swedish settlers on the Delaware River. By the time the first Norwegians arrived in Iowa, the horizontal method of log house construction, rather than the vertical method of the French, was in general use on the frontier.

In this typical pioneer dwelling, Erik Egge and his wife, among the first to settle in the colony around Decorah, began their life in the New World. A year or so later their cabin became the first Norwegian Lutheran parsonage west of the Mississippi: The Reverend Vilhelm Koren and his wife Elizabeth lived with the Egge family when they first arrived from Norway.

Reverend Koren became one of the most prominent Norwegian Lutheran ministers in Iowa. A memorial to him today is the Koren Library of Luther College, which houses, in addition to books, a large collection of paintings by Norwegian-American artists.

A woman of considerable education and culture, Mrs. Koren kept a diary of her experiences as a preacher's wife. It was published at Decorah in 1914 and gives a fascinating account of the everyday life of ordinary folk when Iowa was frontier country. Describing the Egge cabin, Mrs. Koren writes: "The house was fourteen by sixteen feet, divided by curtains of calico into two rooms, of which the one afforded place for two beds which filled the one wall of the house and were separated from each other by a second curtain." The cabin was small but it was sturdy — ample protection against the cold of an Iowa winter.

The group of historical buildings at Decorah includes also a log schoolhouse, a primitive hut used for drying grain and malt before grinding, and the Little Iowa Cabin, another pioneer log dwelling. Among other exhibits in the museum at Decorah are numerous pieces of pioneer furniture, a variety of household articles, old Norwegian jewelry, national costumes, bridal gowns, tapestries, and a large collection of framed photographs of prominent Norwegian Americans. Many of these articles were personal belongings brought to Iowa from Norway in the chests and trunks of the immigrants.

Erik Egge's log cabin parsonage

In Old Amana

SOME of the growing number of foreign immigrants who helped to people Iowa after it became a state in 1846 came in groups to found religious or social utopias. The best known and most successful of these was the Amana Society, or Community of True Inspiration.

This pietistic communal organization of German origin settled on the Iowa River some twenty miles northwest of Iowa City. It prospered to such a degree that its holdings grew to some twenty-five thousand acres. Scattered over this large tract the society established seven villages, only a few miles apart: Amana itself, West Amana, South Amana, East Amana, High Amana, Middle Amana, and Homestead.

The Amana Society was composed of farmers and skilled craftsmen and their frugal, industrious wives. It was founded in Germany under the leadership of a tailor, a carpenter, and a servant girl. The carpenter was Christian Metz, and it was he who led the group, several hundred strong, to America. They established their first colony, called Ebenezer, near Buffalo, New York, in 1843.

In Germany the distinguishing features of the sect had been their rejection of the established church and their acceptance of the Bible as their sole religious guide. But in the New World they added communal organization to their doctrines, preaching and practicing the common ownership of all property except clothing and household goods.

It was Christian Metz who effected this change. He was not only a devout religious leader but a person of great administrative abilities. In *Amana That Was and Amana That Is*, Bertha M. H. Shambaugh wrote:

"Christian Metz seems to have been one of those rare leaders of men who under other circumstances might have led an unhappy people out of bondage or a faltering army to victory; whose magnetic personality and powers of persuasion might have drawn together the discordant factions of a Reichstag or a Parliament; and whose practical genius and gift as an executive might have guided a nation or directed an empire."

Under Metz's leadership, the Ebenezer settlement flourished, more members of the group came over from Germany, and by 1850 additional land was needed. Afraid that the distractions of Buffalo might tempt his people from their simple ways, Metz sent agents west to find a new location on the frontier. They chose the Iowa River site, and by 1859 the entire community had been transferred from New York to Iowa.

Many of the original buildings are still standing in old Amana, but chief among them, though little different from the others, is the house in which Christian Metz lived and from which he directed the affairs of the colony until his death in 1867.

The Christian Metz house is a plain, story-and-a-half gabled dwelling built of brown sandstone blocks with white trim and small-paned windows. The side and rear walls are of rougher masonry than the façade. A small front porch and rear addition are of later construction than the body of the house and somewhat mar it.

The sandstone blocks were quarried and

The Christian Metz house, center of a utopian experiment

shaped in the colony by Amana artisans, and Amana masons and carpenters built the house, as they did all the dwellings of the society. The furniture and other household equipment in the Metz house were made by Amana craftsmen.

During the years Metz occupied the brown sandstone house, the Amana Society lived simply and quietly and was almost entirely self-sustaining. All property was owned in common by the society and both its religious and temporal affairs were administered by a board of trustees. Men and women of the colony married, reared families, and carried on their appointed roles in the communal life. Income beyond their daily needs was obtained from the sale of the society's agricultural products and handicraft articles.

In all seven of the picturesque old villages are located various shops and small plants whose products have been sold throughout the Midwest for years. At Amana itself, for example, is the old woolen mill which turns out the famous Amana blankets, and the furniture shop where skilled craftsmen make tables and chairs from such woods as walnut and cherry. Another famous Amana product is their Westphalian-style hams.

Although after the Civil War there was a gradual decline in numbers and few new converts came in to replace the young people who left the community, the society maintained its distinctive way of life for more than three quarters of a century. Then the communal tie was dissolved, the property was divided among the members, and in 1932 the Amana Society was reorganized into a producing and marketing cooperative with a membership of fourteen hundred. Also the spiritual affairs of the colony were separated from the temporal by the formation of the Amana Church Society.

Otherwise the way of life in old Amana has not greatly changed. And in the center of the community, as an unofficial, unmarked shrine, stands the simple dwelling place of the man who founded it.

American Gothic

GRANT WOOD HOUSE. IOWA CITY. BUILT 1858.

IF THAT foremost of Iowa artists, Grant Wood, had wanted to paint a representative, middle-class, small-town residence of the Civil War period — something as old-fashioned and indigenous as the "cornfield Gothic" house in the background of one of his best known pictures, *American Gothic* — he could not have chosen a better subject to draw from than his own house in Iowa City.

This two-story residence of red brick, with gabled roof, stands behind a white picket fence, shaded by an old cedar and a tall weeping willow, its façade partly covered by English ivy. And it has most of the ornamental details of a typical, mid-nineteenth-century residence: ornate eave brackets, green shutters, lower-story windows reaching to the floor, and a doorway with arched fanlight and narrow sidelights. It even has the cast-iron "star" supports so conspicuous in the construction of brick dwellings of the old days. The exterior walls of the house are said to be twenty-six inches thick.

Before Grant Wood bought this house in 1936, it was an almost forgotten and run-down landmark of Iowa City's pioneer period.

It was built in 1858 by an early resident of the city, Nicholas Oakes, who established Iowa City's first brickyard and eventually made a fortune as a brickmaker. After the artist acquired the house, its address, 1142 East Court Street, became of national interest; many leading men and women of the arts and professions went there to visit one of America's outstanding regional artists — a painter who, like John Steuart Curry of Wisconsin and Thomas Hart Benton of Missouri, was finding fit subjects for his art in Midwestern landscapes and rural life.

After leaving his boyhood farm home near Anamosa, Iowa, Grant Wood lived in an old coach-house studio at the rear of a Cedar Rapids mortuary, supporting himself and his mother by doing interior decorating and making paintings for the mortician, David Turner. Later the artist helped to establish the Stone City art colony near his boyhood home on the Wapsipinicon River. Then fame came to him with the exhibition of his *American Gothic* in the Art Institute of Chicago, and soon he was a recognized American artist, with a comfortable income and a satisfactory position, including a studio of his own, at the University of Iowa.

In 1935 Grant Wood, at the age of forty-four, married Sara Sherman Maxon, an Iowa singer and choral director. And the next year the Woods moved into the eleven-room Oakes house at 1142 East Court Street, which the artist had purchased for thirty-five hundred dollars on a mortgage.

Thereafter Grant Wood continued his work, lecturing at the university, painting, writing, or with his own hands making many improvements in the Court Street house. Some earlier owner had built a porch across its front and Wood removed this as not architecturally in keeping with the rest of the house. The

artist also restored the ornamental eave brackets, which had previously been missing for many years.

Short, rather stout, his round face smooth-shaven and his reddish brown hair beginning to thin, Grant Wood, often with a cigarette in his mouth, was frequently to be seen in overalls working around the grounds of his mid-Victorian residence, tending rose or lilac bushes, planting pine trees, or making flag-stone walks. And often at night the lights would be bright in the old Court Street house as Mr. and Mrs. Wood entertained their many guests. Frequent visitors here were Carl Sandburg, Lawrence Tibbett, Paul Engle, John T. Frederick, Frank Luther Mott, and Clarke F.

Register and Tribune, DES MOINES

Grant Wood's house

Ansley. A guest in the house for an extended period was the English author, Eric Knight, one of the artist's close friends.

Grant Wood died on February 12, 1942, in his fiftieth year. A year or two later his Court Street house was acquired by E. C. Milt- ner, an Iowa City businessman. He and his wife, Dr. Pauline Moore, an Iowa City physician, take pride in the historical and artistic associations of their home and are keeping it as nearly as possible in the state in which Grant Wood maintained it when he was alive.

The House on Main Street

ANTONIN DVORAK HOUSE. SPILLVILLE. BUILT 1850's.

INTERESTING alike to music lovers and to Americans of Czech descent is a two-story brick-and-stone house in the small Iowa village of Spillville, on the winding Turkey River not many miles from Decorah. In this house Antonin Dvorak lived with his family during the summer of 1893, and it was here he composed two of his chamber music scores.

What brought the distinguished Bohemian composer to the little village of Spillville, more than a thousand miles from New York City, where he was then living, was a desire to visit a settlement of his fellow countrymen in the heart of America. Spillville, settled about 1854 by a group of eleven families from Moldautein in Bohemia, was a rural community of Czechs not unlike Dvorak's home village of Vysoká in Bohemia. One of Spillville's leading citizens at the time of Dvorak's visit was the village choirmaster, Johann Kovarik, and it was his son, Josef Kovarik, secretary to Dvorak, who induced the composer to visit the Iowa settlement.

Upon arrival in the village, Dvorak and his family — his wife, six children, a sister of his, and a housemaid — were given for their occupancy an eight-room house on Main Street. At that time the house was owned by a German, Herr Schmidt. Plain, square, standing flush with the sidewalk, it had been built many years earlier, of rough-faced sandstone blocks with finished bricks for the façade.

In this house, Dvorak, according to his biographers, spent three of the happiest months of his American sojourn. He enjoyed strolling along the banks of the Turkey River in the early morning, and often at Mass in the village house of worship, St. Wenceslaus Church, a reproduction of the cathedral at Kuttenberg, he played old Bohemian hymns on the organ, the congregation joining in, as was the custom in Bohemia. In the cool evenings he smoked his pipe, drank beer with the men villagers, or perhaps played a game of cards with them. Later at night, in his Main Street house, he would be heard playing old Bohemian folksongs on his violin. In time the villagers were calling him "Squire Dvorak."

At first there was no piano in the Main Street house, but the Kovarik family moved in their instrument for the composer's use, and during the succeeding midsummer days Dvorak wrote two pieces of chamber music embodying some of his reactions to America:

*Dvorak wrote two chamber music scores during the summer he spent
in this house on Main Street in Spillville*

the String Quartet in F Major, Opus 96 and the String Quintet in E Flat, Opus 97. A drum-like rhythm in the opening part of the quintet is said to express what Dvorak heard when three roving Indian medicine men sang and danced in Spillville. The folk songs of the American Indians, as well as of the Negroes, fascinated him.

Eager to hear his composition when it was finished, Dvorak formed an impromptu string quartet in the village, and his String Quartet in F Major was first played in the Main Street house.

From Spillville the Bohemian composer made short visits to three Midwest cities. In Chicago he was guest of honor for "Czech Day" at the Columbian Exposition; in Omaha he visited his friend, Mr. Rosewater, publisher of the *Omaha Bee;* and in St. Paul he called on another friend, Pastor Rynda. In the Twin Cities he saw again the great Father of Waters, which had so impressed him on his journey to Spillville from New York, and he also saw the lovely Minnehaha Falls of Longfellow's *Hiawatha.* While gazing at the falls, he is said to have penciled a theme on his starched cuff and this later became the slow movement of his Sonatina in G Major, Opus 100.

At the end of his summer in Spillville, Dvorak returned to New York, where he resumed his work as head of the National Conservatory and where, not long afterward, he wrote the popular *Humoresque*. Then in 1895 he returned to his native Bohemia. To-day, in commemoration of his three months in Spillville, there is a monument marking his favorite resting place on the bank of the Turkey River. And there are markers identifying the house in which the composer lived on Main Street.

Beside the Mississippi

ELLIS PARKER BUTLER HOUSE. MUSCATINE. BUILT IN 1860'S.

THE popular twentieth-century American humorist, Ellis Parker Butler, was born in a modest frame house at 607 West Third Street in the then boisterous steamboat town of Muscatine. Located in Iowa about two hundred and seventy miles north of Mark Twain's boyhood town of Hannibal, Muscatine is today a sizable manufacturing city and trading center, noted especially for its production of pearl buttons.

At the time of Butler's birth, December 5, 1869, the family home occupied the rear of the lot on Third Street. His father was Audley Gazzam Butler, who had married the former Adella Vesey of Muscatine. As a boy, Ellis lived the normal life of a Muscatine youth, with frequent adventures on the muddy banks of the great Mississippi. His imagination was aroused by the white packets on the broad river and by the activity of Negro stevedores on the Muscatine wharf. All of these youthful impressions are described in *Kilo*, a book about his boyhood days.

A few years after his graduation from high school Butler became a contributor of humorous articles to the *Midland Monthly*, the first of the many Iowa "little magazines" that have encouraged the creative spirit in the Middle West. It was established in 1894 by Johnson Brigham, state librarian of Iowa. Recognizing his young contributor's ability as a humorous writer, Johnson Brigham urged Butler to develop and perfect his sprightly talent.

After his marriage in 1899 and the birth of his first child, Butler left the Third Street house in Muscatine and went to New York to join the staff of a trade magazine. He eventually became editor and owner of the magazine, *Decorative Furniture*. It was at this period that his first book, and only serious one, was published, a volume on furniture entitled *French Decorative Styles*.

Meanwhile he continued writing humorous articles for national magazines and his talent as a humorist came to the attention of Ellery Sedgwick, then editor of the *American Magazine* and afterward the famous editor of the *Atlantic Monthly*. Encouraged by Sedgwick, the former Iowa resident wrote the story called "Pigs Is Pigs." In *The Happy Profession* Sedgwick tells about how the story came to be written.

"One morning a friend confided to me that coming to town on the train he had overheard

In Muscatine — the birthplace and boyhood home
of Ellis Parker Butler

a discussion between two railroad clerks as to the proper subclassification of guinea pigs as an item of freight. I knew the happiest humorist of my acquaintance would appreciate that. At the time, Ellis Parker Butler was editing a magazine devoted to the interest of wallpapers. Now there is little in life less congenial to the moods of humor than wallpapers, and I was forever prodding Ellis to turn to a more expansive vocation. This was my chance. I asked him to lunch, embellished the tale here and there with the slightest touches of fancy, and turned it over to him. Within a week he had transformed it into a thing of beauty and a joy forever. Three months later 'Pigs Is Pigs' was recognized as a classic."

After its publication in a book in 1906, it became a best seller and continued to be widely read for several decades.

His career as a humorist now launched, Butler turned out one book after another at almost yearly intervals. He published thirty-two in all. Among them were *The Incubator Baby*, *Perkins of Portland*, *The Great American Pie Company*, *Confessions of a Daddy*, and a whole series on the correspondence school detective, Philo Grubb. *Kilo*, the nostalgic recollections of his boyhood days in Muscatine, was published in 1907.

Although none of Butler's later books achieved the tremendous popularity of *Pigs Is Pigs*, they all won wide circulation and earned more than a comfortable living for their au-thor. During most of his writing years, But-ler's home was at Flushing, Long Island, but he was living in Williamsville, Massachusetts, when he died in 1937.

Although Butler's birthplace in Muscatine is now privately owned, it is often viewed by admirers of Butler's writings. The two-story white frame house – displaying a few interest-ing ornamental details like the fanlight under the cornice of the façade – was moved to the front of the old Butler lot in 1909 and since then has been remodeled into a two-family residence with a new porch added to the front. Of equal interest with the house is the collec-tion of Butler letters, manuscripts, and first editions on display in the P. M. Musser Public Library at Muscatine.

A Prairie Home

HERBERT QUICK HOUSE. NEAR GRUNDY CENTER. BUILT IN 1860's.

ALMOST in the center of Iowa, among wide rolling cornfields, red barns, tall silos, and black-top roads, stands the boyhood home of the novelist, Herbert Quick. Through the windows of this farmhouse, some six or seven miles northwest of the small town of Grundy Center, the boy Herbert saw covered wagons going west after the Civil War, observed prairie fires lighting up the night sky, and watched German immigrants breaking sod for new farms. Recording the experiences of his youth, Quick's trilogy of novels composed of *Vandemark's Folly*, *The Hawkeye*, and *The Invisible Woman*, is one of the better known fictional presentations of pioneer life on the great Midwestern prairies.

It was in 1869, when Herbert Quick was eight years old, that his father, Martin Quick, bought the farmhouse near Grundy Center which was to be the family home for the fol-lowing twelve years. Around it was an eighty-acre farm which the elder Quick bought for twenty dollars an acre.

Martin Quick was a New Yorker of Dutch extraction. In 1857 he and his bride, a woman of Irish descent, drove an ox-drawn wagon over the old Ridge Road through central Iowa and settled on a prairie tract near the village of Steamboat Rock on the Iowa River. In a crude frame house (no longer standing) on this tract, Herbert was born on October 23, 1861. By former marriages of both of his par-ents the new baby had two half-sisters and three half-brothers, as well as three full sis-ters.

Eight years later the Quick family was es-tablished in the new farmhouse near Grundy Center. Here, in a house shaded by cotton-woods and Lombardy poplars and surrounded by a lawn of blue grass, Herbert Quick grew to manhood. "We were poor," wrote the nov-elist in his autobiography, *One Man's Life*, "but we had more hope [than tenant farmers today]. And after we began to depart from wheat growing and depend more on live stock, we lived lives of rather restricted plenty. We had fruits, milk, eggs, and tables spread with everything that the appetite required."

The home of Herbert Quick, Iowa novelist

An attack of infantile paralysis when he was still a baby had left Herbert with a minor lameness. Unable, because of this, to participate fully in the play and work around the farm, he turned to the world of books. He was always first in his class in spelling, geography, and history at District School No. 9. It was in this schoolhouse that he was first attracted to literature through McGuffey's *Readers,* and as he grew older, he sought out what books he could find, having none in his own home. In time farmers around the countryside, whenever a stray book came into their possession, sent it over to the Quick place for Herbert to read.

When he was seventeen, Herbert attended a teachers institute in Grundy Center and received a certificate to teach country schools. But after a brief period of teaching, when he was still only a boy of nineteen, Herbert

Quick left his country home permanently and went to Sioux City. Here he studied and practiced law, entered politics, and in 1898 was elected mayor of Sioux City for one two-year term.

With the publication in 1901 of his first book, *In the Fairyland of America,* a volume of Indian folklore, Quick became more interested in literature than in law. Later he was named the editor of *Farm and Fireside* and joined the group of distinguished farm journalists from Iowa: Dante Pierce, Edwin T. Meredith, and the three Henry Wallaces.

After a successful career, not only as an author, but as an economist, traveler, and government adviser, Herbert Quick died of a heart attack on May 10, 1925, following a lecture at Columbia, Missouri. During his later life his home had been near Berkeley Springs, West Virginia.

Quaker Cottage

HERBERT HOOVER BIRTHPLACE. WEST BRANCH. BUILT IN 1860's. OPEN TO THE PUBLIC.

NOT only Germans of the Amana group, Norwegians of the Lutheran creed, and Bohemians of the Catholic faith established settlements in Iowa. Older American denominations, such as the Methodist, Baptist, and Presbyterian, were represented, of course, and so was that sturdy religious sect which had done so much to shape American history, the Quakers. And from one small Quaker settlement in Iowa came the thirtieth president of the United States. The plain cottage in which Herbert Hoover was born still stands on its original site, though its appearance has been somewhat altered by the building on of a two-story addition.

The Quaker settlement in which Herbert Hoover was born is West Branch, now a quiet farming village of about seven hundred population located twelve miles east of the university town of Iowa City. It was in 1853 that Hoover's great-grandfather, Jesse Hoover, and a few other members of the Society of Friends, went westward from Ohio in covered wagons and founded the settlement of West Branch in Iowa, building their modest homes around that focal point of all Quaker communities, the meetinghouse.

With Jesse Hoover when he helped to establish West Branch was his son Eli and Eli's son, also named Jesse. In his early twenties this second Jesse Hoover married Huldah Minthorn, one of the daughters of another Quaker household in West Branch. She was exceptional among the villagers because she had attended a young ladies' seminary and had studied for one year at the University of Iowa. After his marriage Jesse Hoover established

himself in business as the village blacksmith, and across the street from his shop the newly married couple set up housekeeping in a small, one-story frame house with a gabled roof. Like the other dwellings of that early Quaker community, it was severely plain, with simple board-and-batten siding, and with only two rooms.

Working hard in his hot smithy, Jesse Hoover won the business and respect of most of the Quaker villagers and farmers. When the threshing machine was invented, he was the first to introduce one into West Branch. Soon, in addition to his work as a blacksmith, he was selling threshing machines and other new agricultural devices as they appeared.

The Hoovers' first child, a boy they named Theodore, was born in 1871. Then early one August morning in 1874, Jesse slipped hurriedly from the little cottage and went to the nearby house of a woman relative known as "Aunt Ellen." Tapping on her window, Jesse told her: "Well, we have another General Grant at our house. Huldah would like to see thee."

The new baby was given the name of Herbert Clark Hoover. It was Aunt Ellen who recalled his birth years afterward, remembering what Jesse Hoover had smilingly said about "another General Grant." (General Grant was then president.) Her recollections are contained in a letter she wrote to her daughter in 1920, which was published in *The Making of Herbert Hoover* by Rose Wilder Lane.

"They then lived in a little house by the blacksmith shop," said Aunt Ellen in her letter. "It was a tiny house, but always so clean and neat, for Huldah was a nice housekeeper and kept house nice, whether it was small or large. It was, however, the kind of good housekeeping that does not destroy the family. Children always had a good time there. There was a hobby horse, and balls and tops, but there was a place for them when they were not in use. With Huldah, things were always *finished*. I can see that bureau drawer now, with everything ready for the coming event, all made by hand, for none of us had a sewing machine in those days."

At an early age the little boy Herbert was assigned simple tasks in the home and in his father's smithy, for both his parents adhered to the Quaker belief that children should learn to do constructive work as soon as possible.

When Herbert was six years old his father died and when he was ten his mother died. Thereafter he was reared by various Quaker uncles and aunts. Eventually he made his way to the West Coast and, after graduating from Leland Stanford University, became a mining engineer.

After Herbert Hoover became an important national figure, public attention was centered on the Iowa cottage in which he was born. When one of Grant Wood's notable Iowa paintings, *Birthplace of Herbert Hoover*

Register and Tribune, DES MOINES

Herbert Hoover's birthplace was a two-room cottage in the little Quaker village of West Branch

(painted in 1931 and now owned by the Des Moines newspaper publisher, Gardner Cowles, Jr.), was shown to President Hoover, he smiled and said it seemed "too glorified." But it brought back to him memories of the place of his birth, and in 1937 Herbert Hoover, accompanied by his son Allan, paid a visit to the little Iowa village of West Branch and there once more saw the cottage of his Quaker childhood.

Society Showplace

HOYT SHERMAN HOUSE. DES MOINES. BUILT 1877. OPEN TO THE PUBLIC.

DURING the last years of the nineteenth century, one of the social centers of Des Moines, the capital of Iowa, was the Major Hoyt Sherman mansion, located in a residential section just east of the city's central business district. This house, built by a younger brother of General William Tecumseh Sherman, is today a cultural and civic gathering place of the capital, and is widely known throughout Iowa as "the Hoyt Sherman place."

The old red brick residence, together with the spacious, landscaped grounds around it, was purchased in 1907 by the City Park Commission and was afterward leased to the Des Moines Women's Club with the stipulation that the club establish in it an art gallery to be open to the public at least three days a week. Accordingly the club constructed a one-story addition on the west side of the mansion to house the art gallery, and later a three-story wing was added on the east side to house the club's auditorium, which also is used by the people of Des Moines for civic meetings and rallies.

This old Des Moines landmark is situated in the center of the one-time Hoyt Sherman estate, almost a block-square landscaped tract on a slight rise overlooking the surrounding neighborhood. Curving driveways lead up to the arched Victorian doorway of the residence. Among newer trees on the grounds of the Hoyt Sherman place is an elm planted by the Abigail Adams chapter of the Daughters of the American Revolution to memorialize Henry C. Wallace, who, like his son, Henry A. Wallace, was at one time secretary of agriculture.

Some changes have been made on the exterior of the residence. A comfortable veranda that spanned the front and west side of the house has been removed, and the towering cupola, a distinguishing mark on so many late Victorian mansions, has been cut down to half its size, without, however, marring the general architectural effect. Inside the residence much has been left intact in the entrance hall and principal first-floor rooms. There are still, for example, the original walnut and oak paneled walls, the heavy staircase at the end of the entrance hall, and the ornamental marble fireplaces in parlor and living room.

When Hoyt Sherman first went to Des Moines in 1848, he was practically penniless, but when he died in 1904, he was one of the richest men in Iowa. Before the Civil War he and several others organized the Iowa State

Register and Tribune, DES MOINES

The Hoyt Sherman mansion, once a society showplace,
now a civic meeting place

Bank. After the war, he assisted in establishing the Equitable Life Insurance Company of Iowa, of which he later was president for fourteen years.

In *Pioneers of Polk County, Iowa*, L. F. Andrews tells the story that several years after Hoyt Sherman arrived in Des Moines, he wanted to acquire one of the five-acre tracts of the Pursely estate, which a local court had ordered to be subdivided and sold at auction. On the day of the auction Hoyt Sherman had only a hundred dollars to invest. When asked to serve as clerk of the auction sale for a fee of five dollars, he accepted the offer. On the point of losing the five acres he wanted when a bidder offered one hundred dollars for it,

Hoyt Sherman added his five-dollar fee to his bid and thus nudged out the opposing bidder. On this five-acre tract, twenty-seven years later, arose the imposing mansion known as the Hoyt Sherman place.

Major Sherman built his house on the hill at Woodland Avenue and Fifteenth Street in 1877. When the sloping grounds around it were planted with grass and shade trees, it took on manorial distinction and was considered one of Iowa's most magnificent dwellings — a fitting residence for one of the state's most prominent citizens. In the same year Major Sherman completed his Des Moines residence, his brother John was appointed secretary of the treasury by President Hayes, and John

Sherman was later an unsuccessful Republican candidate for the presidency on three occasions.

As a member of a distinguished family, then, Major Sherman was a person of consequence and his Des Moines home became a society rendezvous of the first rank. It is said that among the famous persons entertained at dinners and receptions in this house were President and Mrs. Ulysses S. Grant and Major William McKinley, then serving as a congressman from Ohio. Frequent visitors, too, were many who had been Major Sherman's fellow officers in the Civil War.

Adair County Farmhouse

HENRY WALLACE HOUSE. NEAR ORIENT. BUILT 1870'S.

IN SOUTHWESTERN Iowa stands a farmhouse that has been made historic by its associations with three of America's most famous agricultural journalists, all from the same family and all bearing the name of Henry Wallace.

The setting in which this house stands could be a Grant Wood landscape. It is located out in the rolling corn country some fifty miles southwest of Des Moines. More precisely, it stands near the tiny village of Orient, in Adair County. There is little to distinguish it, architecturally, from others in the vicinity. It is bare of architectural ornamentation — just an ordinary, story-and-a-half dwelling of frame construction with an ell addition. The shingled roof of the addition is continued outward, southern-style, to form a small porch which looks out on a conventional farmyard. Surrounding the house during the hot days of July and August each year are miles and miles of waving green corn, ripening under the powerful Iowa sun.

This setting was practically the same, except that the cornstalks had been shaped into shocks, when Henry Agard Wallace was born in the isolated white farmhouse on October 7, 1888. At that time his father, Henry Cantwell Wallace, was beginning his career as an Iowa farmer. He was not unknown to his neighbors in Adair County, for almost everybody in the countryside knew he was a son of "Uncle Henry" Wallace, one of Iowa's best known agricultural editors.

Born on a farm in western Pennsylvania, Uncle Henry had come to Iowa as a young man in the role of a home missionary of the United Presbyterian Church. He soon gave up preaching for reasons of health, and acquired land to become a farmer. Later he wrote agricultural articles for the *Iowa Homestead* and was editor of this journal for some years, until in the early 1890's he was discharged for attacking the railroads and advocating lower freight rates for farmers.

The third Henry Wallace was seven years old when his crusading grandfather founded *Wallaces' Farmer*, a farm paper that is still in existence. With its slogan "Good Farming — Clear Thinking — Right Living," *Wallaces' Farmer* grew rapidly in influence throughout the agricultural Midwest, and in time Uncle

*Henry Wallace's birthplace in the midst of Iowa cornfields is associated
with three generations of agricultural journalists*

Henry's advice on farm problems was sought by leaders of the Republican party. Eventually he served as a valuable member of President Theodore Roosevelt's Country Life Commission and as president of the National Conservation Commission. He also wrote a number of books that were widely read, among them *Trusts and How to Deal With Them* and *Letters to Farm Folks.*

Henry Cantwell Wallace, now coming to be called "Harry" Wallace, was associated with his father in the management of *Wallaces' Farmer*, and old Uncle Henry was a frequent visitor in the Adair County farmhouse. So as

young Henry Agard grew up, he heard much discussion of farm problems, agricultural journalism, and the general economic and political state of the Union. He learned much in those days about the effects of drought, the value of rotating crops, coping with destructive insects, the marketing of corn and hogs, and the compiling of agricultural statistics. And he continued this study of farming at Iowa State College in Ames, where his farmer-editor father was a member of the faculty.

Since 1897 the cabinet post of secretary of agriculture has been filled almost continuously by Iowans. The first appointment was that of

James Wilson, who was named to the post by President McKinley in 1897 and who held it until the year 1913. In 1920 another Iowan, Edwin T. Meredith, was appointed by President Wilson.

When Warren G. Harding became president in 1921, he appointed Henry Cantwell Wallace to succeed Meredith as secretary of agriculture. And in 1933 President Franklin D. Roosevelt named "Harry" Wallace's son, Henry Agard, to the same post. Eight years later the third Henry Wallace became vice-president of the United States.

Since that time public interest in the Wallace farmhouse in Iowa has increased. The house is privately owned and is not marked in any way, but it seems to represent in the minds of many Americans the typical home of "the common man," of whom Henry A. Wallace has consistently been the advocate.

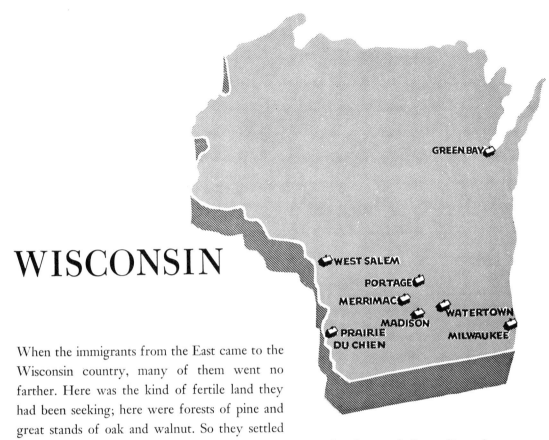

WISCONSIN

When the immigrants from the East came to the Wisconsin country, many of them went no farther. Here was the kind of fertile land they had been seeking; here were forests of pine and great stands of oak and walnut. So they settled on claims north and south of the Wisconsin River, on the shores of Green Bay, along the reaches of Lake Michigan. Here they mingled with the French Canadians who had established the fur trading villages of Green Bay, Prairie du Chien, and Milwaukee, and with the Southerners who had come up the Mississippi River in 1822 to mine lead in southwestern Wisconsin. In 1848 Wisconsin was admitted into the Union. Now a new element appeared in the population: Germans who had fled from their homeland after the revolutions of 1848. Many of these were of the professional and intellectual classes and they brought with them their books, their musical instruments, their artists' brushes. Soon other foreign groups arrived—Norwegians, Irish, Scotch, Welsh. And all these newcomers mingled with the older settlers and together they made Milwaukee, Racine, Madison, Kenosha, and Superior. They laid out great farms on the rolling land and cleared pastures and brought in Herefords, Holsteins, Durhams, and cattle from the Channel Islands. They made a state that has been a progressive force in Midwestern political, educational, and cultural life.

With Wattle and Daub

TANK COTTAGE. GREEN BAY. BUILT ABOUT 1776. OPEN TO THE PUBLIC.

BUILT by an early French-Canadian fur trader, later occupied by a justice of the peace who became the state's first schoolteacher, headquarters for British officers in the War of 1812, afterward the home of a Norwegian leader of the Moravian church, then the residence of a distinguished Dutch woman of considerable wealth and influence — such is the colorful history of an old house in Green Bay, Wisconsin, popularly known as Tank Cottage.

This cottage is the oldest house in Wisconsin and, like the Saucier house at Cahokia, Illinois, and the Vallé house at Ste. Genevieve, Missouri, it is a survival of the adventurous French Canadians who were the first white people to enter the wilderness of the Mississippi Valley. Besides this, Tank Cottage is of interest to architectural historians as one of the few wattle-and-daub houses extant in the Midwest.

When this cottage was built, probably in 1776, the British were still in control of the Great Lakes region and its highly profitable fur trade. One of the chief fur trading centers of that period was the old French settlement of La Baye, afterward to be known as Green Bay. Here, on the west bank of the Fox River, a *voyageur* and fur trader named Joseph Roi built for himself a crude cabin close to the water's edge.

In *Historic House Museums* Laurence Vail Coleman, director of the American Association of Museums, calls attention to the scarcity in the Midwest of early wattle-and-daub houses and describes Tank Cottage as one of the few such houses that are still standing. He refers, of course, to the central part of the present Tank Cottage, which is the original Roi cabin.

In building his cabin, Roi first constructed a rectangular framework of rough uprights, probably shaped with a portable whipsaw. Next he filled in the spaces between these with branches and twigs and leaves (the wattle) stuck together with mud and clay (the daub). Then he finished off the walls with crudely sawed wooden planking.

This method of filling in the space between inner and outer walls to provide extra protection against the cold is common among north Europeans and in New England houses of the seventeenth century. It is not often found in Midwest houses, nor is it characteristically French. Where Roi picked it up we do not know. His use of it in the original unit of Tank Cottage is, so far as we know, unique in Wisconsin.

Still to be seen today, too, is the big fireplace that Roi built into one side of his cabin.

Almost three decades after it was built, the Roi house entered the second phase of its history. This was in 1805 when Jacques Porlier, an amiable, educated French Canadian who, like Roi, was also a fur trader, bought the house and established himself in it to become one of Green Bay's important pioneer citizens. While serving as a justice of the peace on an appointment from the British authorities, Judge Porlier also taught the children of the settlement and so became Wisconsin's first schoolmaster.

At this time the British were still dominant in the Great Lakes region, although legally

147

the area belonged to the new American republic, being part of the Northwest Territory established by the Ordinance of 1787. During the War of 1812 officers of the British colonial army set up their area headquarters in the Porlier house. With the end of the war the British were finally driven from the Northwest Territory.

Judge Porlier continued to serve as a justice of the peace under the American regime, and he also became an agent of the new American Fur Company founded by John Jacob Astor. He died in his house by the river on July 18, 1839, at the age of seventy-four. "His death," wrote Deborah Beaumont Martin, historian of Tank Cottage, "and that of his old friend, Louis Grignon, which occurred soon after, marked the passing away of the French regime in Green Bay."

After an interval of about ten years, during which Wisconsin was admitted to statehood, the old Roi cabin became the home of Nils Otto Tank. A Norwegian by birth and education, Tank was a missionary of the Moravian church and, after his marriage to an aristocratic and well-to-do Dutch woman, he came with his wife to Green Bay and there settled in the Porlier house. He clapboarded the exterior of the house, plastered the interior walls, and added a wing on each side, that on the right to be used as a meeting place and prayer room for the church. Here Nils Otto Tank, leader of the Moravian church in Wisconsin, lived until his death in 1864. Thereafter the house was occupied by his widow, Madame Tank, until her own death in 1891 at the age of eighty-eight.

It was Madame Tank, more than any other

HENRY LEFEBVRE, GREEN BAY

Tank Cottage, Wisconsin's oldest house, has a long and colorful history

of its occupants, who gave a name and fame to Tank Cottage. A cultivated woman of independent means, appreciating and fostering the arts with great enthusiasm, she made her Green Bay home a storehouse of rare and valuable antiques inherited from her aristocratic Dutch forebears. She also presented to Green Bay the land that composes Union Park, in which Tank Cottage now stands, having been removed from its original riverside site in 1908 after it was deeded by George H. Rice to the Green Bay Historical Society. Open to the public as a museum, the cottage today contains many of the original Tank furnishings, including some of the family heirlooms brought from Holland by Madame Tank.

Fox River Cabin

ELEAZER WILLIAMS HOUSE. NEAR GREEN BAY. BUILT 1820'S.

TWELVE miles south of Green Bay, on the west bank of the historic Fox River, stands an old log cabin that was the home, a century ago, of a strange man who claimed to be Louis XVII, the lost dauphin of France. This man was Eleazer Williams, who, aside from his royalist claim, is identified in Wisconsin history as a missionary of considerable influence among the Indians of the Green Bay region.

Many scholars and historians now believe that the ten-year-old son of Louis XVI and Queen Marie Antoinette died of neglect while a prisoner in Paris during the French Revolution, yet the legend persists that he was secretly spirited away to America and grew to maturity there under an assumed name. As a result of this legend, a number of persons in Europe and America during the generation after the French Revolution claimed to be the romantic and tragic lost dauphin.

Eleazer Williams managed to gain a considerable measure of support for his assertion that he was actually Louis XVII of France. Several books have been published to advance his claim, and as recently as 1937 his story was dramatized in a movie short by the Metro-Goldwyn-Mayer Company under the title *A King Without a Crown*. But the latest and most authoritative volume on the legend of the lost dauphin, *The Son of Marie Antoinette* by Meade Minnigerode, issued in 1934, dismisses Eleazer Williams as being just another of the two dozen or more pretenders to the French crown.

Although it is not known exactly when Eleazer Williams built his cabin on the Fox River, many Wisconsin historians believe it was constructed sometime in the 1820's, soon after Williams settled in the Green Bay region and was married to Madeline Jourdain, daughter of a Green Bay blacksmith. It was in 1821 that Williams, a Protestant Episcopal lay reader and missionary, arrived in the Green Bay region from New York at the head of a large group of Oneida and Stockbridge Indians. Claiming he wanted to relieve overcrowded conditions in the Eastern reservations, Williams had secured the permission of President Monroe to move these New York Indians to Wisconsin, but his real purpose, it is said,

The log cabin of the "lost dauphin"

was to bring about the formation of an Indian monarchy, of which he would be the ruler. In any case, the Oneida and Stockbridge Indians were established on a reservation west of Green Bay after 1821.

It was no difficult task for Williams to lead these Indians; he could speak their tongue fluently and persuasively. Williams had been reared as one of the children of Thomas Williams, a chief of the Mohawk tribe, and his white wife, Mary Ann Williams. Because of this some people said Williams was actually a half-breed Indian, but others denied it, pointing out that his name is significantly missing among the names of the Williams children in the church register at Canandaigua, New

York. It was this circumstance, principally, that lent weight to his claim that he was the lost dauphin — added to the fact that he was born about the same year as the dauphin.

If Williams did hope to establish an Indian monarchy on the Wisconsin frontier, his dream was soon shattered. He and his Indian followers were in time at loggerheads over the purchase of suitable land, and the Indians expelled him from their councils. His activities for some years thereafter are not known.

There is no record that Williams met Louis Philippe, the exiled Duke of Orleans, when he visited the old French settlement of Green Bay during his American sojourn in the 1820's. The story is, though, that after being crowned king of France, Louis Philippe was troubled about his legal right to the throne in view of Eleazer Williams' claim.

In the course of time, the king's son, the Prince de Joinville, came to America and visited Green Bay, and while there is said to have had an interview with the Wisconsin missionary. According to Williams' story, the prince offered him a large sum of money to sign an official abdication of his right to the French throne, but when this version was repeated to the prince some years later, he vigorously denied it.

Surviving oil portraits of Eleazer Williams, painted by the Chevalier Fagnani and by the noted American pioneer artist, George Catlin, reveal a face that, according to Williams' supporters, is surprisingly like those of the Bourbons, with none of the characteristic features of an Indian. In *Wau-Bun*, a collection of reminiscences about the early days in the Northwest, Mrs. Juliette Kinzie described Williams as "a dark-complexioned, good-looking man" who appeared to her like a Spaniard or a Mexican. She added: "His complexion had decidedly more of the olive than the copper hue, and his countenance was grave, almost melancholy."

After returning to his native state of New York in 1850, Eleazer Williams devoted himself to study and writing, translating into the Iroquois language the Book of Common Prayer and producing a biography of the Indian chief who reared him, Thomas Williams. He died in 1858.

Today the cabin in which this self-styled lost dauphin of France lived is in the custody of the Wisconsin Historical Society. Built of squared logs with a stone chimney at one end, the story-and-a-half Williams cabin has been restored and some improvements have been made in its interior, including the lining of its walls with knotty pine boards. It is an interesting reminder of a historical mystery.

At the Portage

INDIAN AGENCY HOUSE. PORTAGE. BUILT 1832. OPEN TO THE PUBLIC.

ON THE custodian's desk in the Indian Agency House at Portage, Wisconsin, there is displayed for sale a book bearing the title *Wau-Bun, The "Early Day" in the North-West*. First published in Cincinnati in 1856 and long out of print, this book was recently issued in a new edition. It is now regarded as something of a classic of Midwestern frontier literature. And the reason it is on sale in the Indian Agency House at Portage is that it contains a full and entertaining account of the building of the old house and of life in it during pioneer times.

The author of this book was Mrs. Juliette Kinzie. A young woman of good education and a charming wit, Miss Juliette Magill was married to John H. Kinzie at her Middletown, Connecticut, home on August 9, 1830. And a year earlier, John Kinzie, son of one of the first settlers of Chicago, had been appointed government Indian agent at what was then known as "the Portage," in Wisconsin.

The Kinzies' house at the Portage was a center of pioneer social life

First used by Father Marquette and Louis Jolliet in 1673, the Portage long remained one of the most important and strategic points of water travel between the Great Lakes and the Mississippi River. Here the early traveler needed to carry his canoe only a mile and a half overland to get from the Fox River, the waterway south from Green Bay, to the Wisconsin River, which flows into the Mississippi. In 1829 the American government built Fort Winnebago at the Portage and John H. Kinzie was named Indian agent there.

Immediately after their marriage the Kinzies set out for their new home in the Western wilderness. At first they occupied rude temporary quarters at Fort Winnebago, waiting for the dwelling of their own they had been promised by the head of the Indian Department. But the government officials seemed to think more highly of the settlement's blacksmith than of the Indian agent. Mrs. Kinzie says in *Wau-Bun*:

"Permission was, however, in time, received to build a house for the blacksmith — that is, the person kept in pay by the Government at this station to mend the guns, traps, etc. of the Indians. It happened most fortunately for us that Monsieur Isidore Morrin was a bachelor, and quite satisfied to continue boarding with his friend Louis Frum, *dit* Manaigre, so that when the new house was fairly commenced we planned it and hurried it forward entirely on our own account."

This was the origin of the historic Indian

Agency House which survives today on the outskirts of the southern Wisconsin city of Portage. In the way it was built this house is an interesting contrast to the Roi cabin center of the Tank Cottage in Green Bay. Instead of wattle and daub between the inner and outer walls and between the studs, the Agency House has a fill of *solid brick* to serve the same purpose. This brick fill was covered outside with clapboard and inside with hand-split lath, and over the lath was spread a coating of pinkish plaster — pink because mixed with it were crushed mussel shells from nearby rivers.

Describing her new house Mrs. Kinzie wrote: "It was not very magnificent, it is true, consisting of but a parlor and two bedrooms on the ground-floor, and two low chambers under the roof, with a kitchen in the rear; but compared with the rambling old stable-like building we now inhabited, it seemed quite a palace."

Here the Kinzies lived comfortably — and after the Black Hawk War in 1832, peacefully — during the remainder of their stay at the Portage. To the Indians the agent was known as "Father" and to the French Canadians of the settlement he was "Monsieur John," while Mrs. Kinzie was "Madame John." John Kinzie, while in the employ of the American Fur Company under Robert Stuart at Mackinac Island, had learned the Winnebago language, and he was very popular among the tribesmen at the Portage because of his ability to speak their tongue. Mrs. Kinzie was equally popular for her patience, kindness, and friendliness.

"With an occasional dinner or tea-party to the young officers, sometimes given at the Major's quarters, sometimes at our own, our course of life passed pleasantly on," wrote Mrs. Kinzie in *Wau-Bun*. "At times I would amuse myself by making 'something very nice' in the form of a fruit cake or pie, to send to the quarters of the young officers as a present, it being supposed that possibly, without a lady to preside over their mess, it might be sometimes deficient in these delicacies." She also tells of importing a piano from the East for the Agency House and of the musicales held almost weekly thereafter, to the delight of both soldiers and Indians. When the Indians of the countryside gathered at the house to receive their government allotments from the hands of the "Father," the event was celebrated with ceremonial dances and gay festivities.

In 1834 the Kinzies moved to Chicago and there spent the remainder of their lives. The settlement at the Portage grew in population and became the home in later years of other writers of repute: Zona Gale, Frederick Jackson Turner, Marjorie Latimer, and Elinor Green. Here, too, as a boy, often came the naturalist, John Muir, and not far from Portage today lives the novelist, August Derleth. The old Indian Agency House — restored to its original appearance by the National Society of Colonial Dames under the supervision of Frank Riley, architect of Madison — is now open to the public as a museum of early American house furnishings.

Villa Louis

HERCULES L. DOUSMAN HOUSE. PRAIRIE DU CHIEN. BUILT 1843. OPEN TO THE PUBLIC.

MOST famous of Wisconsin's historic house museums, in fact one of the best known in the Midwest, is the commodious old mansion at Prairie du Chien called Villa Louis. This Northern "great house," like some of the old plantation dwellings of the South, has an open house celebration in the spring of each year, and this event annually attracts hundreds of visitors from cities and towns of the Upper Mississippi Valley.

The story of Villa Louis begins in the year 1843. In that year Hercules Louis Dousman, who had acquired a considerable fortune as an early Prairie du Chien fur trader, built a substantial, two-story brick house overlooking the Mississippi River. He named it the "House on the Mound."

Dousman had chosen for his house one of the most historic sites in Wisconsin. The grassy mound from which he named it was in reality an artificial hill built by the prehistoric Mound Builders and afterward used as a burial ground by the Fox Indians. This mound was observed by Father Marquette and Louis Jolliet when, coming out of the mouth of the Wisconsin River in 1673, they first saw the Mississippi River. After the French and British flags had flown over the little trading post of Prairie du Chien for many years, in 1814 the American flag was raised for the first time in Wisconsin over Fort Shelby, built that same year on what became the Dousman mound. A few months later Fort Shelby was captured by the British and renamed Fort McKay. When Fort McKay was evacuated at the close of the War of 1812, it was burned to the ground by the Indians. Then in 1816 the American government built another fort on the mound, naming it Fort Crawford, and this was occupied by troops until 1831, when a new Fort Crawford was built at another location.

It was about then that Hercules Dousman bought the historic mound and some forty-five hundred acres around it. At this time he was probably the most influential citizen of the old Northwest, respected alike by Indians and whites. His extensive fur trading operations in time made him the territory's first millionaire.

A year after his house was finished, Dousman married Jane Fisher Rolette, the attractive and vivacious widow of his partner in the fur trade, Joseph Rolette, known on the frontier as "King" Rolette. Mrs. Dousman, daughter of a Scottish father and a French mother, made the House on the Mound a beautiful and gracious home for her husband until his death in 1868.

Then in 1872 Mrs. Dousman rebuilt the house, making it much larger and much grander, in the florid post-Civil War style. The severely simple roof lines of the original were broken by a gabled elevation and ornate cornices and eave brackets. A great glass-enclosed porch was built to span the house on the east and south sides, and inside were added massive arched door frames, paneled ceilings, and heavy moldings. Because of these extensive changes, the house as it is today might properly be dated from the 1870's. It is generally mid-Victorian in feeling and retains little of the Classic Revival style of its original period.

Villa Louis, extensively remodeled in 1872 in the post-Civil War style,
is today a treasure house of mid-Victorian furnishings

The Dousman drawing room and dining room

*Portraits of Hercules Dousman I and Mrs. Hercules Dousman II hang
in the library of Villa Louis*

The House on the Mound was renamed when it became the property of Hercules Dousman II after the death of his mother in 1882. Young Dousman called the mansion Villa Louis after his own and his father's middle name — and also after St. Louis, the city in which he had been living since his marriage in 1873 to Nina Linn Sturgis, daughter of General Samuel Davis Sturgis of the United States Army.

When Nina Sturgis Dousman became the mistress of Villa Louis, the Prairie du Chien mansion took on renown as the scene of a long and brilliantly successful social life. Even after her husband's death in 1886, Mrs. Dousman maintained her reputation as a hostess while she raised to adulthood her five children.

Then for some years the old house was closed, until two Midwest historians, Dr. Joseph Schafer and Dr. Theodore C. Blegen, suggested that it be presented to Prairie du Chien as a memorial to one of the founding families of Wisconsin. This proposal was accepted by the Dousman heirs, and in 1935 the historic mansion and its estate, now reduced

The back parlor or morning room and the private chapel

Two Villa Louis bedrooms, furnished in rosewood and fine old mahogany

The southwest bedroom and the nursery

to eighty-four acres, were deeded to the city of Prairie du Chien and became Dousman Municipal Park.

In the midst of attractive grounds that contain a small lake, an old icehouse, a conservatory, the original office of the first Hercules Dousman, and a stone stable converted into a museum, Villa Louis stands today as an entrancing treasure house of Victorian interior furnishings: rosewood, mahogany, and walnut furniture, chandeliers of Waterford glass, rare oil paintings, velvet window draperies, china, silver, delicate glass stemware, and many family heirlooms. The interior of Villa Louis is probably the truest and most complete example of mid-nineteenth-century style to be found, not only in Wisconsin, but in the entire United States.

Octagon House

JOHN RICHARDS HOUSE. WATERTOWN. BUILT 1853. OPEN TO THE PUBLIC.

IT STANDS on a commanding site just at the edge of the city of Watertown — the House of Yesterday that inspired the House of Tomorrow. It is otherwise known throughout Wisconsin as the Octagon House.

This eight-sided Watertown house is a surviving example of an exotic style of domestic architecture that flourished briefly in America before the Civil War. Among all houses of this type still standing in Wisconsin, the Octagon House is by far the most elaborate, the most successful architecturally, and the best preserved.

It was Orson Squire Fowler of New York who proposed the odd design. In 1849 he published a book called *A Home for All; or, the Gravel Wall and Octagon Mode of Building.* "I kept asking myself," wrote Fowler in his introduction, "Why so little progress in architecture when there is so much in other matters? We continue to build in the same square form adopted by all past ages. Cannot some radical change for the better be adopted, both as to the external form of houses and their interior arrangements? Why not take our pattern from Nature? Her forms are mostly spherical!"

O. S. Fowler was also a well-known practitioner of phrenology, and some writers have tried to suggest a connection between his interest in that pseudo science and his unorthodox ideas about the shape of houses. This is an injustice to Fowler; there is no discernible connection between his two interests. He devised and advocated the octagon plan for housebuilding solely on economic and functional grounds.

In any case, there is no evidence that John Richards, the man who built the Octagon House in Watertown, had any interest in phrenology. He seems to have been a practical, realistic person of many talents, who was capable of designing his own house. He and his wife Eliza, both natives of Massachusetts, came to Watertown in 1837 when Wisconsin was still a territory. A very able lawyer, Rich-

John Richards' eight-sided house, as it originally appeared

ards became Jefferson County's first district attorney, later mayor of Watertown, and afterward the owner of a large saw and grist mill on the Rock River.

The Octagon House was occupied by successive generations of the Richards family for more than eighty years. Then in 1938 it was presented to the Watertown Historical Society by Mrs. Estelle Bennett Richards and her son, both of Oak Park, Illinois. With all its original furnishings intact, the Octagon House is open to the public as a museum and, like Villa Louis at Prairie du Chien, is the scene of an annual open house.

Just as interesting as the design of this house are its numerous mechanical features, all ap- parently innovations of the time and all the product of John Richards' talents. That he was a gifted house designer is shown by his original pencil sketches of the Octagon House, now on display in the dwelling.

The house stands at the top of Richards Hill, overlooking the beautiful Rock River valley. Its four stories are surmounted by a cupola-like lantern with four projecting chimneys. The walls are solid brick, thirteen inches thick – built of the famous cream-colored brick that gave Milwaukee its nickname, "Cream City." The brick for the Richards house is said to have been hauled from Milwaukee by ox cart.

When the house was built, narrow verandas constructed of wood completely encircled it at both the first- and the second-story levels. These were removed at some point in the past but they are to be restored. The front doorway is marked by an attractive fanlight and sidelights.

In the interior all four stories are planned exactly alike. There are eight rooms, four large and four small, on each floor — thirty-two in all, fourteen of which were designed as bedrooms. It was John Richards' express intention in 1853 to build the largest house in Wisconsin. Only the first three floors were to be used by the family; the fourth floor Richards intended for the accommodation of his millhands.

In all the main rooms of the house there are hot air and ventilating registers — to provide "central heating" in winter and "air conditioning" in summer. John Richards was a man of advanced ideas. Another unusual device for the time was the water system, whereby rainwater, caught on the sloping roof, flowed into a tank on the third floor, from where it was carried through lead pipes to the washstands and bathrooms on the lower floors.

In the basement may still be seen an elongated furnace for burning four-foot logs, a big brick Dutch oven that could hold two dozen loaves of bread, a cider room, and a cistern.

The most interesting feature of the interior, however, is the spiral staircase, of cantilever construction, which winds upward from the basement to the skylight cupola on the roof. This is one of the few such stairways in America.

The Richards house was definitely the inspiration for some of the basic ideas in the ultramodern House of Tomorrow that aroused so much interest at the Century of Progress Exposition in Chicago in 1933. George Fred Keck, the Chicago architect who designed the House of Tomorrow, was reared in Watertown, and early in his career he made a study of the design and mechanical details of the house on Richards Hill. Keck once wrote:

"To me the importance of the Octagon House lies in the inventive spirit the designer has displayed. This designer was so thoroughly versed in construction technique of the day that he could improvise and produce variations and improvements that were still sound construction."

Executive Mansion

GOVERNOR'S HOUSE, MADISON, BUILT 1854.

SITUATED on the wooded shore of one of Madison's four beautiful lakes, Wisconsin's Executive Mansion not long ago evoked these words from Mrs. Philip F. La Follette, one of its former occupants: "I know of no state that has a more historic home for its governors,

and although the house changes occupants according to the political trend of the day, it always maintains its personality and distinction."

The house was not always a governor's residence. It was built of brown Madison sandstone in 1854 by Julius T. White, who later in a home at Evanston, Illinois, entertained Abraham Lincoln. He was also a general in the Civil War. The land on which White built his Madison house was originally owned by James Duane Doty, a territorial governor of Wisconsin and brother-in-law of Mrs. White.

In his square, comfortable house beside Lake Mendota Julius White, according to a contemporary, "ensconced his fine collection of paintings and rare and costly bric-a-brac." Among the guests he and Mrs. White entertained here was the New York editor, Horace Greeley, who is quoted as having said: "Madison is the most beautiful of all inland towns and the homes are dignified and handsome.

Consider this house, for example, and its view of Mendota. Could aught be finer?"

The second owner and occupant of the mansion, George P. Delaplaine, who purchased it from White in 1857, had been secretary to the first and second governors of Wisconsin and was described as "a lover of literature and the fine arts and a man with a wide eastern and foreign acquaintance." During Delaplaine's occupancy, the house was a gathering place for authors, artists, and musicians.

Then in 1868 the house was purchased by the millionaire Eau Claire lumberman, J. G. Thorp. Elected to the state senate that year, Thorp set out to make his Lake Mendota resi-

UNIVERSITY OF WISCONSIN PHOTOGRAPHIC LABORATORY

The official home of Wisconsin's governors

dence the best known in Wisconsin. An artist from Chicago was brought in to paint scenic frescoes on the ceiling of the front parlor, which was to become a drawing room. Under the supervision of Mrs. Thorp new furniture was installed, including a parlor set of Egyptian design upholstered in purple brocaded satin. And in the music room was placed a grand piano specially designed by the Thorps' daughter Sara; it was ornamented with inlaid bronze medallion portraits of the great composers.

Shortly after the remodeling of their new house was finished, the Thorps had as their dinner guest Ole Bull, the Norwegian violinist, who was then on a concert tour of America. Two years later young Sara Thorp and the sixty-year-old violinist were married, and the wedding reception in the Thorp residence was the most brilliant social event the capital city had yet seen. Thereafter the famous violinist and his American wife divided their time between a home near Bergen, Norway, and the Thorp mansion at Madison.

About this time, too, the Thorps' son Joseph was married at Cambridge, Massachu-

setts, to Anne Longfellow, daughter of the poet, Henry Wadsworth Longfellow, and one result of this union was a poem by Longfellow, "The Four Lakes of Madison," in which he praised the setting of Wisconsin's capital city.

Among the distinguished guests entertained in the next few years at Lake Mendota by the Thorps and the Bulls were James Russell Lowell, Bayard Taylor, John G. Saxe, Bronson Alcott, and Carl Schurz.

In 1882 when Jeremiah M. Rusk was elected governor of Wisconsin, he bought the Thorp residence and made it his home. Three years later the state legislature voted to purchase the Thorp house for twenty thousand dollars and make it the official home of the state's governors, and this has been its role for more than half a century.

Still on its original site, but now crowded a little by other homes, the Executive Mansion, an American flag flying above its roof, is today maintaining "its personality and distinction" as ever. Among its interior furnishings are some of the pieces of furniture Ole Bull imported for it from Europe.

In Durward's Glen

BERNARD DURWARD HOUSE. NEAR MERRIMAC. BUILT 1870. OPEN TO THE PUBLIC.

SOMETIME after he came to America in 1845, the Scottish-born artist, Bernard Isaac Durward, who had taken up residence in Milwaukee, painted a portrait of Bishop John Martin Henni of the Milwaukee diocese, first German Catholic bishop in the United States. While at work on this painting, Durward was

converted to the Roman Catholic faith, and in 1861 he left Milwaukee with his family and established a home in a pine-shaded glen of the Baraboo hills of south-central Wisconsin, there to occupy himself with religious devotions and the painting of natural scenes.

This was the origin of the most unusual of

Bernard Durward's cottage, winter and summer

Wisconsin's many combined scenic and historic sites, a place now known throughout the state, and even beyond its borders, as Durward's Glen. Still in its wild, natural state, except for the buildings erected by the Scottish artist, Durward's Glen each year attracts an increasing number of religious pilgrims, nature lovers, art devotees, and students of Wisconsin history.

The simple frame house in which Durward in 1862 set up housekeeping with his wife and two children adds one more to the historic houses strung along the winding Wisconsin River. On this historic waterway one finds not only Durward's home but the Indian Agency House at Portage, Villa Louis at Prairie du Chien, and more recent landmarks such as Taliesin, home of the architect, Frank Lloyd Wright, at Spring Green, and Arkam House, home of the writer, August Derleth, at Sauk City. Also on the Wisconsin River, not more than thirty miles north of Durward's Glen, is the most popular of all scenic spots in the state, the Wisconsin Dells.

Durward and his family lived quietly in their plain cottage at the bottom of the solitary glen. When the house was finished, Durward chose another spot on his forty-acre tract and built a studio in which to work. In Milwaukee he had specialized in portrait painting, and two of his portraits of Milwaukee pioneers now hang in the Wisconsin Historical Museum at Madison. But in the glen Durward turned to painting and sketching the wild beauty of the rocky gorge in which he lived — "making his inks from the berries which abounded there, and his drawing pens from quills."

In 1887 a new rough stone studio was built near the family cottage, and here today may be seen Bernard Durward's paintings and drawings, as well as samples of the work of his artist-son, Charles Durward.

Another son, Wilfred, grew up to be a naturalist, and the other two, John and James, became priests of the Roman Catholic church. The stone monument to the memory of Mrs. Durward in the family cemetery bears the inscription: MOTHER OF PRIESTS.

In 1866 Durward and his sons, selecting a suitable site among the evergreens at the top of the glen, built there a small chapel out of native stone. They called it St. Mary's of the Pines. And in this chapel both John and James sang their first Masses. Later the family cemetery was laid out next to the chapel and a series of steps was made along the rocky sides of the gorge leading up to the chapel and its burying ground.

A decade or so later the Reverend John Durward, upon returning from a visit to Palestine, supervised the construction of Stations of the Cross in the glen, mixing the pathway soil with earth he had brought from the original Stations in the Via Dolorosa at Jerusalem. For many years Father John, as he was known, served as pastor of St. Joseph's Church in nearby Baraboo. He was the author of a widely read Catholic book, *Holy Land and Holy Writ*. He died in 1918 and was buried in the family cemetery at the glen.

With the passing of the years, Durward's Glen has become a shrine of art as well as of religion. Because of the annual increase of tourists, a parking lot was laid out some years ago just outside the glen and from here posted foot trails lead to the various buildings and other objects of interest in the ravine. A new building is the log structure housing the chapel and living quarters of novitiates of the Order of Camillian Fathers, a Catholic order whose members care for sick or infirm men of any race or creed. But perhaps of greatest interest to sightseers is the plain clapboarded cottage with the steep roof in which the Durwards lived.

Millionaire's Mansion

ALEXANDER MITCHELL HOUSE. MILWAUKEE. BUILT 1870'S.

SITUATED near the cultural center of Milwaukee, which includes the Court of Honor, Marquette University, and the Milwaukee Public Library and Museum Building, is the city's most famous old house: the Alexander Mitchell mansion. It has been standing here for almost three quarters of a century, and as the home of the Wisconsin Club, the old residence still plays an important role in the civic life of Milwaukee. The man who built the house was one of the founders of Milwaukee and the progenitor of a family that attained great prominence. His grandson was the "fighting prophet" of the Army Air Forces, Brigadier General William ("Billy") Mitchell.

Son of a well-to-do farmer of Ellon, Aberdeenshire, Scotland, where he was born on October 18, 1817, Alexander Mitchell studied law and served as a bank clerk in Aberdeen before coming to America at the age of twenty-two. An invitation to serve as secretary of the Wisconsin Marine and Fire Insurance Company took young Alexander west to Milwaukee, then a frontier village.

When the insurance company began issuing money, as a clause in its charter permitted, the banking interests of the town started a fight against it. This was the day of wildcat banks, however, and Mitchell's company gained the upper hand because its certificates were sound and could be instantly redeemed. It was young Mitchell who led this fight and in time he gained control of the insurance company. And it was "Mitchell's money" that served the currency needs of Wisconsin after its admission to statehood in 1848.

Eventually Mitchell went into the banking business himself, became one of the founders of the Chicago, Milwaukee, St. Paul and Pacific Railroad, and entered politics; serving two terms in Congress.

Now one of the Northwest's foremost citizens, Alexander Mitchell built for himself the mansion in Milwaukee that survives today. It is located at 900 West Wisconsin Avenue, just west of Milwaukee's central business district. At the time the house was built, this neighborhood was an exclusive section for wealthy families, and Mitchell's architect, E. Townsend Mix, built him a millionaire's dwelling—solid, imposing, ornate, and set in the midst of landscaped grounds. Here are the steep mansards, bays, dormers, and tower that one finds on nineteenth-century millionaire's residences in New York, Chicago, and other large American cities.

In this great town house, Alexander Mitchell, a stout man with a beard, who smoked cigars and always wore a red carnation in his lapel, resided as Milwaukee's first citizen. His wife ruled the city's social life. She was long remembered for having staged one of Milwaukee's most lavish society events: the Grand Ball of All Nations in 1884. She was also known for her interest in American history, having been one of the three founders of the women's organization that bought and restored George Washington's home, Mount Vernon.

Alexander's son, John Lendrum Mitchell, was reared in the Wisconsin Avenue mansion. Instead of taking up a business career as his father had done, John became a scholar, scientific farmer, and public official. In the early 1880's he served as president of the Milwau-

168

kee school board and a few years later helped to establish the College of Agriculture at the University of Wisconsin. He was elected to represent Wisconsin in Congress, first in the House and then in the Senate. And one of the best known scientific farms of the Great Lakes area at the time was Senator Mitchell's estate, Meadowmere, just outside Milwaukee.

This was not the birthplace of General Mitchell, however. A bronze plaque in front of an ancient dwelling opposite the Place Grimaldi in Nice, France, reads: "Here was born William Mitchell, General, U. S. Army Air Service, December 29, 1879." His parents were visiting on the Riviera at the time of his birth.

After the return of the family to Milwaukee, little Billy Mitchell was often in his grandfather's large mansion on Wisconsin Avenue, and here he early heard talk of public affairs and met outstanding men and women of the state and the nation. From the master of this house, as well as from his father, General William Mitchell undoubtedly acquired many of the characteristics that made him one of America's pioneers of the air.

Milwaukee Journal

In their great town house, the Mitchells ruled Milwaukee's social life

Middle Border Home

SOON after his books had begun to earn him some money, Hamlin Garland bought for his aging parents a small but comfortable house in the village of West Salem, Wisconsin, some twelve miles northeast of La Crosse on the Mississippi River. West Salem was the writer's own birthplace and a town in which his parents had had pleasant experiences years earlier, before their futile attempts at farming in the "middle border" country of Wisconsin, Iowa, and Dakota Territory.

Hamlin Garland spent his summers in the West Salem house in the years that followed, writing and obtaining from his parents much of the material that later went into his great trilogy of Midwestern pioneer life, *A Son of the Middle Border*, *A Daughter of the Middle Border*, and *Back Trailers of the Middle Border*.

This old West Salem house still stands on its original site at the west end of the village, and because it was for more than three decades Garland's summer home, it is generally known as the Hamlin Garland house. Although it is privately owned and not open to the public, it is an object of interest to many tourists passing through this Mississippi River "coulee country."

Garland was born in West Salem (his birthplace no longer stands) on September 14, 1860, but when he was about four years old, his parents moved to a farm at Green's Coulee, not far from West Salem. There the boy got his first experiences of farm life.

His father, Richard Garland, was a native of Maine who, brought west to Wisconsin by his parents, had worked as a lumberjack in the Badger State's pine forests. Not too successful at farming, he thought more and newer acres might help, and in 1869 moved his family to a big farm near Osage, in northern Iowa.

Here the boy Hamlin began to help till the soil, and here he attended the district school and made the acquaintance of McGuffey's *Readers*. Liking books and school better than farming, he continued his studies at Cedar Valley Seminary at Osage. Having, as the custom then was, to deliver an oration when he graduated, he appropriately chose for his topic, "Going West."

In 1881 Richard Garland caught the "Dakota fever" and decided to homestead on a still larger piece of land near Ordway in Dakota Territory. So the hard work of pioneer farming, the gamble with weather and soil, began all over again for the Garlands.

But not for Hamlin. He was now of age and knew he did not want to be a farmer. He intended to be a professor, perhaps a writer. So when his family moved to Dakota, he went east to Boston. There he spent his time reading and going to concerts, plays, and art galleries. He also went on a walking tour through New England with his young brother, Franklin Garland, who afterward became an actor.

Hamlin Garland began his career as a writer in Boston, but he did not find his principal theme as a novelist until after a vacation visit in 1887 to his parents and the scenes of his boyhood — West Salem and Green's Coulee in Wisconsin, the farm on the Iowa prairie, and the homestead his parents were now living on in Dakota Territory. This visit convinced him that he should write about the things he

MRS. JOHN MEYER, WEST SALEM

The home of Hamlin Garland, novelist of the Middle Border

knew best, about pioneer farm life in the vast "middle border" region of America. And a few years later, in 1890, his first book was published, *Main-Traveled Roads.* It was with money earned from this volume of realistic Mississippi Valley farm stories that he bought the house in West Salem.

After his parents were settled in this house, Hamlin Garland took up residence in Chicago. There, among other things, he helped to found the Cliff Dwellers Club, which is still in existence. By now he was married to Zuline Taft, sister of the well-known sculptor, Lorado Taft, and the aunt of Mrs. Emily Taft Douglas, in 1946 congresswoman from Illinois.

After the death of his parents, Hamlin Gar-

land and his wife continued to spend their summers in the West Salem house until 1915, when they moved permanently to the East. The author of the Middle Border series died in 1940 at the age of eighty.

The old, two-story Hamlin Garland house is much as it was when Garland lived there and as he described it in "The Homestead in the Valley," the last chapter of *A Son of the Middle Border.* The present owners of the house hope someday to convert it into a Hamlin Garland museum, since there are still in the house numerous books from Hamlin Garland's library as well as several heirlooms and some personal belongings of the eminent author.

ELK RIVER
MINNEAPOLIS ST. PAUL
MENDOTA
HASTINGS
LE SUEUR FRONTENAC

MINNESOTA

Some of the immigrants pouring into the vast Mississippi Valley went north into the Big Woods of the Minnesota country, the Sioux country of "sky-tinted water." There the newcomers found a few scattered fur trading stations that had survived from the old French days of Radisson, La Salle, Hennepin, Nicolet, and Le Sueur. They also found vast forests of conifers and hardwoods, great tracts of fertile prairie country, many watercourses and azure lakes, and soldiers at Fort Snelling to protect them from the Sioux and the Chippewa. Near the fort two settlements grew up around a steamboat landing and a grist mill on the banks of the Mississippi, and these in time became the "twin cities" of St. Paul and Minneapolis. Now men of vision and ability asserted themselves, and the new country became Minnesota Territory in 1849. This brought another wave of settlers from the East to people the additional lands opened to settlement through treaties with the Sioux, and in 1858 Minnesota became a state. Then came the Germans and the Irish, the Swedes, Norwegians and Danes, the Czechs and the Poles and the Finns. And working together to make homes where the wilderness had been, to grow wheat for the flour mills and dig ore from the iron mines, the many peoples slowly in succeeding generations fused into one strong, proud American people.

Fur Trade Capitol

HENRY HASTINGS SIBLEY HOUSE. MENDOTA. BUILT 1835. OPEN TO THE PUBLIC.

EACH year several thousand school students and grownups from Minnesota and adjoining states visit an old stone house in a quiet village just south of St. Paul, at the confluence of the Mississippi and Minnesota rivers. Here lived, more than a hundred years ago, the "Father of His State," Henry Hastings Sibley.

This simple old limestone residence in the historic village of Mendota, just across the Minnesota River from Fort Snelling, was built in 1835. At that time Sibley was a young fur trader. A native of Detroit, where he was born on February 20, 1811, Sibley, after a good education, including two years' study of law, had decided to enter the fur trade and for five years worked under Robert Stuart of the American Fur Company at Mackinac Island. When Sibley became a partner in the company in 1834, he took charge of the Minnesota country, while his friend and fellow trader, Hercules L. Dousman, assumed control of the Wisconsin country, with headquarters at Prairie du Chien.

As chief company agent in the Minnesota region, then, Henry Sibley arrived at Mendota in the fall of 1834 and the following year built a two-story stone house to serve in the dual role of dwelling place and fur trading station. He built his house with limestone quarried and shaped in the vicinity with the aid of about one hundred trappers, *voyageurs*, and Indians. All timbers used for joists, beams, and braces were hand-hewn and fitted together with wooden pegs, and the interior walls were finished with a plaster made of mud and clay mixed with straw, applied over laths of inter-woven willow sticks. The house contained six rooms and an attic and basement.

From this house Sibley directed the operations of the fur company throughout a great wilderness area including the present states of Minnesota and North and South Dakota and the Canadian province of Saskatchewan. Here he dealt with the Indians and the trappers, the traders, and fellow company officials. And here he dispensed bachelor hospitality to the officers of nearby Fort Snelling and any visitors who came.

At one time or another the personable and cultivated Sibley was host to General Lewis Cass, Henry Rowe Schoolcraft, General John C. Frémont, George Catlin, Senator Stephen A. Douglas, and the French engineer, Joseph N. Nicollet. His Mendota house was the social center as well as the business headquarters of the area — especially after his marriage in 1843 to Sara Jane Steele, sister of Franklin Steele, the sutler at Fort Snelling. In time, though, as his family grew, he found it necessary to move his office into a new addition at the east end of the house.

It was in this office, now known as the Capitol Room, that Sibley and others formulated plans for the organization of Minnesota Territory. (The name *Minnesota*, which in the Sioux language meant "sky-tinted water," was chosen at Sibley's insistence.) His office became the territorial capitol in 1849 when the territory's first governor, Alexander Ramsey, lived temporarily with the Sibleys after his arrival in the new country. And from this office, when Minnesota became a state in 1858,

*The house of Henry Hastings Sibley, the "Father of His State," was
Minnesota's first territorial capitol and first state capitol*

The parlor and Sibley's office, now called the Capitol Room

A bedroom in the Sibley house

Henry Hastings Sibley directed its affairs as the new state's first governor.

Among articles on display in the Capitol Room today is Sibley's portable writing desk of Circassian walnut. Here, too, over the fireplace, is a large equestrian oil painting of General Sibley reviewing his troops when, as commanding officer of the military district of Minnesota, he led expeditions against the Sioux Indians in 1862–63.

In 1862 the Sibleys established a new home in St. Paul and there, in his later years, General Sibley lived a quiet life, writing articles, attending meetings of the Minnesota Historical Society, and serving for a time as president of the board of regents of the University of Minnesota. He died on February 18, 1891, at the age of eighty years.

After the Sibleys left the old house at Mendota, it was used for several years as a Catholic school and convent, then as a studio by the Minnesota artist, Burt Harwood, and finally as a run-down lodging place for homeless wanderers. It was rescued from this state in 1910 by the St. Paul chapter of the Daughters of the American Revolution and, after being restored and refurnished, was opened to the public as a museum.

In outward appearance the house resembles somewhat the early stone houses of Pennsylvania. A small portico over its front entrance and an outside stairway at one end are its only noticeable exterior features. Legend says the stairway was built so the Indians and trappers could come and go from the second floor without disturbing Sibley downstairs. Inside, the rooms have been completely restored and furnished in the style of Minnesota's territorial period, many of them containing original Sibley pieces.

The yellow-gray gabled house sits behind a white picket fence in a landscaped setting at the base of a bluff, facing the skyscrapers and grain elevators of the Twin Cities to the north. It is the principal unit of a group of restored historic buildings, including the Sibley icehouse and smokehouse, the Jean Baptiste Faribault house, home of another early trader built not long after the Sibley house, and the De Puis house, built in 1854. This last has been converted into a dining place known as the Sibley Tea House.

In Minnehaha Park

JOHN H. STEVENS HOUSE. MINNEAPOLIS. BUILT 1849. OPEN TO THE PUBLIC.

FEW American cities the size of Minneapolis retain within their borders today even one house built before they became cities. Minneapolis has managed to preserve three.

One is the Alex Cloutier house at 915 Second Street Northeast, which, according to Cloutier family records, was built in August 1848, and is believed by some to be the first frame house built in Minneapolis. Another is the Godfrey house at Central and University avenues Southeast. This house, too, was built in 1848 but, according to some city historians, not until a few months after the construction of the Cloutier house. Its builder was Ard Godfrey, a master millwright from Maine and foreman for Franklin Steele, the sutler at Fort Snelling. The house was moved from its original site at Main and Pine (now Second) streets to its present location in Richard Chute Square.

But perhaps the most unusual of the three old Minneapolis dwellings is the Stevens house, located in Minnehaha Park along with the falls that Longfellow made famous in *Hiawatha*. The house has a number of "firsts" to its credit. It was the first frame house built in that part of Minneapolis lying west of the Mississippi River. In it Hennepin County was organized, its first officers were elected, and its first court sessions were held. Its builder and owner, Colonel John Harrington Stevens, helped here to establish the settlement's first agricultural society, school district, singing club, and literary society. Within the walls of this house the name Minneapolis had its origin, and under its roof was born, on April 30, 1851, the first white child on the city's west side: Mary Stevens.

At this time the Stevens house stood near the present site of the Great Northern Depot in downtown Minneapolis, and there it remained as the city grew up around it. Then in 1896 the house was acquired by the Minneapolis Board of Park Commissioners, plans

*Colonel John H. Stevens' home was a center of political
and social life in early Minneapolis*

were made to preserve it as a historic landmark, and its removal to Minnehaha Park was
made a civic event. Mounted on wheels, the
old house was pulled through the streets of
Minneapolis by relays of school children.

When this happened, the man who built
the house and gave it distinction was still alive.
He had seen the Twin Cities grow from a few
log houses each into one of the country's big
metropolitan areas.

Colonel John Stevens, having come west
from Vermont, was mining for lead in Wisconsin and Illinois when the Mexican War
broke out. He had made the acquaintance of
Henry Dodge, governor of the Territory of
Wisconsin, and the governor got a commission

for him in the army. When the war was over,
Stevens set out for Texas, intending to settle
there, but on the way he fell in with a north-
country booster who persuaded him the Upper Mississippi had more to offer him.

Before Stevens could build his house, he
had to secure a permit from the secretary of
war because the west bank of the Mississippi
was then part of the Fort Snelling military
reservation. On the east bank, just opposite the
new Stevens home, stood the little settlement
of St. Anthony, consisting of a few houses and
a sawmill for which the power came from the
Falls of St. Anthony. From this sawmill Stevens obtained planed lumber for his house. It
was small and simple, a story and a half high,

with suggestions of the prevailing classic mode in its plain lines.

To this house, in 1850, Colonel Stevens brought his bride, Frances Helen Miller of Westmoreland, New York. She bore him six children. Soon after settling on the west bank, John Stevens purchased one hundred and sixty acres of land around his house and this he later subdivided into lots which he sold to newcomers. As the settlement around him grew, however, Stevens, who had the soul of a pioneer, became dissatisfied, sold his holdings, and moved with his family to new frontier country at Glencoe, Minnesota. It is said that he realized only a modest sum from the sale of his land, which in the twentieth century became part of downtown Minneapolis.

After editing a newspaper at Glencoe for some years, Colonel Stevens returned to Minneapolis and there, after the Civil War, engaged in various occupations, principally the promotion of agriculture. He edited several farm papers, served as president of the Minnesota State Agricultural Society, helped to establish the agricultural department of the University of Minnesota, and wrote several books, including *Personal Recollections of Minnesota and Its People* — in which he "seems to have remembered everybody but himself." He died in 1900 at the age of eighty.

St. Hubert's Lodge

ISRAEL GARRARD HOUSE. FRONTENAC. BUILT 1855.

IN A delightful account of "The 'Fashionable Tour'" in *Grass Roots History* Theodore C. Blegen tells about the early steamboat tours on the Mississippi and how interest in these trips was first aroused by large panoramas of the river country exhibited in Eastern cities.

"Even before the Civil War," writes Mr. Blegen, "large numbers of people from the South flocked to Minnesota as a summer resort; and the habit was resumed not long after Appomattox. Folk from the east and west joined in exploiting the vacation and tourist attractions of Minnesota. The day of the 'Fashionable Tour' on the upper Mississippi passed when steamboating declined in the face of railroad competition."

One man who took this "fashionable tour" in pioneer days remained in Minnesota and established there a baronial estate that was perhaps the best known such place in the Upper Mississippi Valley in the years following the Civil War. The man was Israel Garrard and the house was St. Hubert's Lodge.

It was in 1854 that Israel Garrard, a graduate of Harvard College and of a Cincinnati law school, made the boat trip up the Mississippi which first brought him to Minnesota Territory. He was a person of some wealth, and when a beautiful wooded tract near the small settlement of Frontenac, on the widening of the Mississippi known as Lake Pepin, caught his fancy, he immediately bought it as a site for a hunting lodge. Later he added more and more acres until his holdings stretched for three miles along the Minnesota side of the river.

Israel Garrard's hunting lodge stands on a bluff above the Mississippi

General Garrard lived like a feudal lord on his large estate

Here in 1855 Garrard built St. Hubert's Lodge — importing some of its woodwork and furnishings by steamboat from Cincinnati — and here he spent his summers hunting, fishing, riding his blooded horses, sailing, entertaining guests, and watching the Mississippi packets going by.

Although a native of the North — he was born in Cincinnati in 1825, and reared there — Garrard favored the way of life of his Southern ancestors, landowners in Virginia and Kentucky. When the Civil War came, however, he supported the North, raised a company of troops in Cincinnati, served as colonel of the Seventh Ohio Regiment in some important battles, and at the close of the conflict emerged as a brigadier general.

After the war General Garrard took up permanent residence in his Northern hunting lodge. Having brought with him from Cin-cinnati numerous relatives and retainers, all of whom built houses on the Garrard estate at Frontenac, the general in the years following lived the life of a feudal lord. He not only served notable game dinners to guests of distinction but provided the counterpart of a modern soup kitchen for hungry Sioux tribesmen of the region.

From his twenty-two horse stable Garrard brought out thoroughbreds each summer for races on his private course. It is said he also hired a balloonist to entertain his guests by going aloft over Lake Pepin and staging false crashes into the water, then swimming back to shore. When not entertaining or hunting, General Garrard spent much time in his large, well-stocked library.

Among well-known people who were guests in St. Hubert's Lodge at various times were the actor, Joseph Jefferson, the mural painter, John La Farge, and the general's fellow Cincinnatian, Henry Ward Beecher. While guests at the lodge in 1883, the two architects, Christopher Grant La Farge and George L. Heins, visited the nearby quarries and were so impressed with the creamy color of the Frontenac limestone that they later used this stone for the interior of the sanctuary and apse of the Cathedral of St. John the Divine in New York City.

Some idea of what life was like in St. Hubert's Lodge during its heyday may be gained from the opening pages of a novel, *House of Vanished Splendor*, by the Minnesota writer, William McNally. In this story the lodge is identified as "St. Antoine's," and Garrard as "Jefferson Baldwin."

The pleasant, generous host of St. Hubert's Lodge died in 1901. One of the last acts of his life was to force a railroad to detour its riverside tracks inland around his estate. He gave the land for the railroad stop, around which grew up a new village called Frontenac Station. Earlier, although the general was not a Catholic, he had offered a group of Ursuline nuns their choice of several sites for a convent. Today on the wooded knoll they chose, some three miles from the lodge, stands the plain, gray building of Villa Maria.

Although now the summer home of a Minneapolis businessman and not open to the public, the old lodge at Frontenac is an object of considerable interest to tourists. It is a white, rambling building of board-and-batten construction, with long Southern-style galleries across a part of its front, looking out over Lake Pepin to the distant green bluffs of Wisconsin. Few changes have been made in the interior of the lodge since General Garrard's death, and still to be seen in it are some of the original furnishings and the insigne of St. Hubert, patron saint of hunters.

Doctor's Office

WILLIAM J. MAYO BIRTHPLACE. LE SUEUR. BUILT 1859. OPEN TO THE PUBLIC.

ONE of the greatest of Minnesotans was born in one of the smallest and plainest of the state's historic houses. Hardly a more unassuming cottage could be found than the one in which Dr. William James Mayo was born in the small Minnesota River town of Le Sueur.

In *The Doctors Mayo* (1941) Helen Clapesattle says of this house: "It was not pretentious, just a small, two-story, gabled cottage. The largest room was the kitchen, which served also as a dining room, and upstairs under the gables, in a room so low ceiled as to give away the small stature of its builder, Dr. Mayo arranged his medical books, his massive rolltop desk, overlarge for the space, and his equipment for mixing medicines. That was his office."

With his own hands Dr. William Worrall Mayo, father of the renowned Mayo brothers, built this modest frame house at Le Sueur in 1859. At that time he was a "horse-and-buggy doctor" on the Minnesota frontier, to which he had come some five years before from England by way of New York, Indiana, and

St. Paul. Making a living by professional service was not easy in that time and place, and Dr. Mayo supplemented the meager fees he received from his patients with odd dollars from a variety of other occupations — from steamboating and ferrying to newspaper publishing. That he should plan and build his own house was quite in keeping.

It was in character, too, that the house should have a Greek Revival doorway and incongruous Gothic gable ends, and that the arrangement of its rooms should be a bit irregular, for Dr. Mayo was a man of positive opinions which did not always follow the rules.

In this simple Le Sueur cottage, William James Mayo, the older of the famous brothers, was born on June 29, 1861, and here he spent his first three years.

These were Civil War years, and Dr. W. W. Mayo, denied a commission as a regimental surgeon, was acting as medical examiner for the Le Sueur County draft board when the Minnesota Sioux took to the warpath in 1862. The men of the Minnesota Valley had to leave their homes and take up arms against the redmen. Dr. Mayo joined them, and Mrs. Mayo was left to protect her two little daughters and baby son in the Le Sueur cottage. To stay there took courage, for the whole community was in terror lest the Indians should appear in their midst. As Mrs. Mayo told it later:

"Will was a baby in arms and safe enough, and I scared the other two children into staying indoors. When it was necessary for me to go to the barn or the well, I'd put on a pair of overalls and tuck my hair under one of the

The birthplace of William J. Mayo

Doctor's old hats. . . . With a gun in my hand what a figure I must have cut in those overalls! I often think of it. So brave and manly; and my heart in my mouth."

But she helped to take care of the settlers from the countryside who fled to Le Sueur for safety. Eleven families took shelter in the Mayo cottage and barn, and blankets were spread out for them in every room. In one day Mrs. Mayo baked an entire barrel of flour into bread to feed her guests.

It was not until two anxious and dangerous weeks had gone by that the danger passed and Dr. Mayo returned to Le Sueur.

In 1863 President Lincoln appointed Dr. Mayo chief examining surgeon for the southern half of Minnesota, with examining headquarters in Rochester, and the following year the Mayos moved to a new home in that town. The second son, Charles Horace Mayo, was born there on July 19, 1865, but the house of his birth is no longer standing.

What the Mayos did in Rochester — how they built a country doctor's practice in a "little town on the edge of nowhere" into one of the world's great medical centers "to which men come from the ends of the earth for treatment and instruction" — is one of America's truly great stories.

The Old Doctor was important in the beginning of this development and he lived long enough to know that his sons were brilliant and world-famous surgeons, though not long enough to see the giant Mayo Clinic building of today rise on the site of his first Rochester home. He died in 1911 at the age of ninety-one.

The Mayos sold the Le Sueur house when they moved to Rochester, and little is known of its subsequent history until 1932, when the Le Sueur newspaper urged that steps be taken to preserve it. In November of that year the house was marked as a historic site by joint action of the Minnesota Historical Society and the Minnesota Highway Department. Two years later the Mayo brothers bought the house and gave it to the city of Le Sueur.

The house is now open to the public as the quarters of the Le Sueur library. In its rooms may be seen some mementos of the Mayos, including the Old Doctor's medical instruments and some of his books. And in the entryway stands the heavy old rolltop desk with bookshelves above, which he used when the room under the gables was his office. On the walls are autographed pictures of the two Mayo brothers, who died within a few months of each other in 1939.

Hudson River Gothic

WILLIAM G. LE DUC HOUSE. HASTINGS. BUILT 1860. OPEN TO THE PUBLIC.

DISTINCTIVE both for its style of architecture and for its historical associations is the old General Le Duc mansion in Hastings, a thriving manufacturing town and farm trading center some twenty miles below St. Paul. The Le Duc house is said to be the first one in Minnesota built in the architectural style known as Hudson River Gothic.

The William Gates Le Duc house in Hastings

The vogue for this style, which flourished in America before the Civil War, was fostered by the architectural handbooks of A. J. Downing, a landscape gardener, rural architect, and proprietor of a country estate on the Hudson River that was much admired in its time. Downing, in association with Charles Vaux, designed many of the houses and estates along the Hudson during this period, and it is possible that General Le Duc had seen one of the Hudson River estates and wanted to duplicate it on his Minnesota property. For inspiration he could have turned to a popular book by Downing, *Architecture for Country Houses*, which was published only a few years before Le Duc began the construction of his residence.

At this time General William Gates Le Duc

was a man of wealth and one of Minnesota's most prominent citizens. He had come to St. Paul from Ohio, where he had attended Kenyon College and studied law. Minnesota Territory was then in its first year and St. Paul was still a frontier town. Le Duc opened a law office and also a book and stationery store.

Soon he was actively promoting the development of the new territory. In 1851 he published the *Minnesota Yearbook* from his bookshop, and in 1853 the territorial legislature appointed him to arrange the Minnesota exhibit for the Crystal Palace Fair in New York.

The legislature allowed him only three hundred dollars for expenses, but he made the most of the sum. To give Easterners an idea of what Minnesota was like, he took to New York an Indian canoe, some wild rice, furs, a sample of grain from Minnesota farms, and a live buffalo. He had quite a time getting the buffalo to New York, and then the officials at the fair would not allow him to exhibit it and he had to sell it to a side show. But the rest of the exhibit was enough to attract favorable comment from Horace Greeley in the *New York Tribune*.

Upon returning to St. Paul, William Le Duc obtained the first charter for a railway in the territory and formed a company to build a line from St. Paul to Duluth. Later he helped organize the company which constructed the Wabasha Street Bridge in St. Paul, one of the first bridges across the Mississippi River. Having purchased considerable land in the meantime, Le Duc next laid out the section known as West St. Paul.

Now a man of some fortune, Le Duc decided to move to Hastings and build a residence suitable to his station. He had earlier acquired a flour mill at Hastings, and in this mill he began manufacturing flour from Minnesota spring wheat. He is said to have been the first miller to market this type of flour.

On a sizable tract of land in what later became the south end of Hastings, Le Duc immediately began the construction of his stone Gothic home, but work on it was interrupted by the outbreak of the Civil War. During this conflict Le Duc served in the army quartermaster department, at first as a captain. He was later advanced to lieutenant colonel and served under a boyhood friend, General William Tecumseh Sherman. At the end of the war Le Duc was brevetted a brigadier general of volunteers.

Upon General Le Duc's return to Hastings, his Hudson River Gothic mansion was completed and became the country seat of the Le Duc family.

Tall, wiry, black-eyed, a man of great energy and quick decisions, General Le Duc was soon engaged in a variety of enterprises. He helped to form the Hastings and Dakota Railroad and was its president until 1870. He also had a part in designing the Remington typewriter. Then in 1877 he became a national figure when President Rutherford B. Hayes appointed him commissioner of agriculture in the cabinet. It was while President Hayes was making a tour of the West in 1880 that General and Mrs. Le Duc entertained the president and Mrs. Hayes in their Gothic residence at Hastings.

After completing his service in Washington, William Le Duc returned to his Minnesota home and there spent the remainder of his days in retirement, although he was occasionally active in affairs of the Minnesota Historical Society. He died in his home in Hastings in 1917. He was then in his ninety-fifth year.

Both its exterior and interior unchanged since the days of its prime, the old Le Duc residence, still in its grove of pines and elms, is today an antique shop and, as such, preserves much of its Victorian atmosphere. The three-story, gabled house is made of cream-colored limestone blocks and has, without preponderant ornamentation, the familiar details of the Hudson River Gothic style: arched doorway, spacious bays, a tower, dormers, and scrollwork trim under the gable ends. An eclectic note is apparent in the Italianate eave brackets of the tower.

There are fifteen rooms in the house, opening off a center hall on each floor. A beautiful stair rail of glowing cherry wood leads to each floor landing. In the drawing room and the dining room on the first floor hang bronze chandeliers said to have been made in England but obtained by General Le Duc from an old church at Batavia, New York.

In a Ghost Town

"MINNESOTANS of a generation ago," wrote John D. Hicks in 1921, "could boast that their state was the home of three men of nation-wide fame — Archbishop Ireland, the forward-looking churchman; James J. Hill, the railway-builder; and Ignatius Donnelly, the apostle of protest. Each was a western type."

Of these three men, Ignatius Donnelly was by far the most colorful, daring, eccentric, and gifted. In the last decades of the nineteenth century he was like some flashing comet in the American sky. Through his books, his orations, his newspapers, and his leadership in political movements he earned the designation, locally and nationally, of the "Apostle of Protest."

The house from which Donnelly carried on his turbulent career still stands — in a state of neglect and disrepair, however, that does little credit to the state of Minnesota. It is viewed each year by an increasing number of tourists who leave their names in the guest book on Donnelly's old desk.

Square, two stories high, and of frame construction, the Donnelly house, which once had such architectural embellishments as verandas, shutters, and a cupola, is the principal building in Nininger, a small settlement on the Mississippi River just outside the town of Hastings. When Ignatius Donnelly lived in this house, which was then surrounded by landscaped grounds that sloped down to the river, he was widely known as the "Sage of Nininger."

Even in those years, however, Nininger was a ghost town. It represented the collapse of one of the earliest of Donnelly's many dreams.

Although identified as a Westerner, Donnelly was a product of the East. His parents had come to this country from Ireland in 1817 and had settled in Philadelphia. There Ignatius Donnelly was born on November 3, 1831, and there he was educated in the free Quaker schools. After practicing law in Philadelphia for a short time, he became interested in the westward movement and made his way to Minnesota Territory. Moving to the townsite of Nininger, he entered real estate speculation with other Philadelphia lawyers and businessmen, realized a goodly profit, and built himself a comfortable residence overlooking the Mississippi.

In the dreams of its promoters Nininger was to become the metropolis of the Northwest. And for a good many months by no means all its promise was on paper. It had a newspaper, Donnelly's *Emigrant Aid Journal*, a hotel, a dance pavilion, several sawmills, a flour mill, and a number of substantial homes. It was a place of gay parties, of lyceum lectures and concerts, and of long political debates.

In all this Ignatius Donnelly was the moving spirit. At twenty-six, the bright young Irishman is said to have wondered, with such success already his, what was left for him to do the rest of his life!

Then came the panic of 1857 and almost overnight Donnelly found himself virtually penniless. The boom in Nininger collapsed, its residents moved away, and one by one its buildings, including Donnelly's own house, were moved to nearby Hastings. Only Donnelly himself remained.

Choosing to stay in Nininger, Donnelly set

The Donnelly house in the 1870's

about recouping his fortunes and a decade later was able to build himself another house on the Mississippi shore. This is the house in which Donnelly lived for the remainder of his long and exciting life, the house to which many people, rich and poor, came to seek the counsel of the Sage of Nininger, the house that still stands almost alone in its deserted village.

With the failure of his townsite project, Donnelly, a man of unusual oratorical ability, entered politics, was elected lieutenant governor of Minnesota in 1859 under Governor Alexander Ramsey, and afterward was sent to Washington as congressman from his district during the Civil War.

Defeated for re-election to Congress in the late 1860's, Ignatius Donnelly broke with the Republican party and became an independent in politics. For the succeeding three decades he was a reformer and crusader in the cause of the common people against the privileged classes. He was an outstanding leader in the successive phases, before 1900, of what has been called "the agrarian crusade" or "the agrarian revolt" — that is, the attempt of Midwestern farmers to correct their grievances through organized action, political or otherwise.

Though they did not often succeed in putting their candidates in office, their efforts were by no means futile. Many of the reforms they sought were in time incorporated into the programs of the established parties and enacted into law. And a share of the credit for this must go to the brilliant polemics, in speech and in writing, of Ignatius Donnelly.

The Sage of Nininger was no mean prophet. Sitting in the library of his residence on the Mississippi more than half a century ago, he wrote: "We should throw the gigantic moral influence of this great republic into the scale in favor of every effort of the people of

Today the Donnelly house, once a center of political and intellectual
life, stands in a state of disrepair and neglect on the
deserted townsite of Nininger

Europe to improve their condition and strike down their tyrants. The cowardly policy of non-interference, which might have been wise in the days of our youthful imbecility, is no longer necessary. . . . The time may come — it may be near at hand — when America, to preserve free institutions for her own people, will be compelled to carry the banner of liberation across the waters of the Atlantic, and advance towards the rising sun, until every despot is swept from the face of Europe."

From 1874 to 1879 Donnelly edited and wrote leading articles for the weekly *Anti-Monopolist*, and in his latest years he was editor of the *Representative*, a Populist organ.

It was as an author of books, however, that Ignatius Donnelly won his widest fame, in England and France as well as in America. In the intervals between political campaigns he would retire to his Nininger study to earn his living by writing. His first book, *Atlantis*, the story of the supposed lost continent, was published in 1882. Then came *Ragnarok*, which dealt with the beginnings of the earth, and *The Great Cryptogram*, in which Donnelly tried to prove that Bacon wrote Shakespeare's plays. Donnelly's last book before his death in 1901 was *Caesar's Column*, a novel setting forth his idea of utopia in a classless society.

These books have perhaps little more than historical interest today, but they were enormously popular when they were published. *Atlantis* went through twenty-one editions, and the sale of *Caesar's Column*, at home and abroad, is said to have reached seven hundred thousand copies.

House below the Hill

ALEXANDER RAMSEY HOUSE. ST. PAUL. BUILT 1872.

AT WALNUT and Exchange streets in St. Paul, in an old residential section that spreads out "below the hill" on a Mississippi River flat, there stands an austerely dignified stone mansion, now gray with age, which the city planning board of St. Paul has voted to acquire and preserve as a municipal museum. At the same time this action was taken, the state legislature authorized the gathering of funds for the erection of a suitable statue on the grounds of the state capitol to the memory of Alexander Ramsey, the man who lived in the mansion below the hill.

A striking contrast to the modern skyscrapers "on the hill" to the north, the gray old Ramsey mansion retains almost the same atmosphere of grandeur, inside and out, as when it was Ramsey's home during the last decades of the nineteenth century. Built in 1872, the square stone house, two and a half stories high, is characterized by such late Victorian architectural features as a mansard roof, dormers, bays, a commodious veranda, an English basement, and tall, narrow windows. It stands on an ample lot, shaded with trees and surrounded by an ornate cast-iron fence.

When Ramsey built this house, he had been living in St. Paul for almost twenty-five years. Born near Harrisburg, Pennsylvania, on September 8, 1815, Alexander Ramsey was or-

phaned at the age of ten, later worked in a
great-uncle's store, was employed for a time
as a carpenter, and then began studying law.
After being admitted to the bar in 1839, he
joined the Whig party and early showed his
aptitude as a political leader. He was elected
to Congress for several terms, and in 1849
President Taylor appointed him the first governor of Minnesota Territory.

From that time on Minnesota was Ramsey's
home and he was one of its most sagacious
leaders. He served as territorial governor until
1853, then retired for a short time to private
life in St. Paul, making judicious investments
in real estate there. Several years later he was
elected mayor of St. Paul, and after Minnesota
Territory was admitted to statehood in 1858,
he succeeded Henry Hastings Sibley as gov-

ernor for two terms. Then in 1863 Ramsey
was elected to the Senate from Minnesota and
he continued to serve as senator for the next
twelve years.

In 1879 President Hayes named Alexander
Ramsey his secretary of war. After two years
in this position Ramsey withdrew permanently
from politics, except for occasional periods of
service on one or another national commission.
He had built his stately stone residence during
his years as senator, and to this he now retired
to live a pleasant and tranquil life. In the last
few years before his death in 1903 he was for
a second time the president of the Minnesota
Historical Society, over whose beginnings he
had presided from 1849 to 1863.

The Ramsey house is now owned and occupied by Mrs. Charles Furness, Alexander Ram-

*The Ramsey house has the architectural features of the late Victorian
period — dormers, mansard roof, tall windows, ornate cast-iron fence*

sey's daughter. When it becomes the property of the city of St. Paul, the intention is to make it both a memorial to one of Minnesota's founders and a repository of late nineteenth-century household furnishings. For in the spacious, lofty rooms of this old St. Paul mansion one may see the same gilt French mirrors, walnut and mahogany chairs and tables, brocaded draperies, marble statuettes, crystal chandeliers, and other interior furnishings that were here when Senator and Mrs. Ramsey occupied the house.

House that Flour Built

JOHN S. PILLSBURY HOUSE. MINNEAPOLIS. BUILT 1877.

Minneapolis Star-Journal

The hallway of the remodeled Pillsbury house is decorated with rare scenic wallpaper

ALMOST every day during the 1890's, an elderly, dignified man would emerge from the large brick mansion at 1005 Fifth Street Southeast in Minneapolis, walk a few blocks to the campus of the University of Minnesota, and there consult with the president or with members of the faculty, or sometimes with groups of students. And what he had to say on these daily visits was listened to with respect, for he had proved himself over a period of many years a good and wise friend of the university.

John Sargent Pillsbury had come to Minnesota from his native New Hampshire as a young man of twenty-eight in 1855. He had managed to save up a few dollars, and these he invested in a hardware store in partnership with Woodbury Fisk, also from New Hampshire. A year later Fisk's sister Mahala became Mrs. Pillsbury.

Adding an interest in public affairs to his business activities, John Pillsbury was serving in the state senate in 1864 when a crisis arose in the affairs of the state university. Its lands were heavily mortgaged, and the mortgagees were about to foreclose. Pillsbury took the lead in finding ways and means to prevent this disaster and put the university on its feet financially. From this timely intervention stemmed his unflagging interest in the institution and his title, at the hands of Minnesota historians, of "Father of the University."

The John Sargent Pillsbury house as it looks today

It was in 1872 that John Pillsbury, along with his brother George and nephew Charles, organized the Pillsbury milling company which contributed so substantially toward making Minneapolis "the mill city" — the flour milling capital of the world. The famous Pillsbury "A" Mill, built a few years later, is still, after half a century, the world's largest single producer of flour, and its product is known to almost every housewife in America.

In 1876 the Republican party asked John Pillsbury to run as its candidate for governor. He agreed, was elected, and then re-elected for two more terms. As the state's chief executive he was more the businessman than the politician, insisting on the elimination of waste and corruption. He called in experts to get rid of the grasshoppers that had been the scourge of the prairie farmers, and when the legislature failed to appropriate funds enough to maintain the state penitentiary, he drew on his personal bank account to keep the institution going. But his major achievements as governor were a series of measures designed to improve the public school system and strengthen the university.

The brick mansion on Fifth Street in Minneapolis was built while John Pillsbury was governor, and when he had finished his terms in office he retired to private life with his family in this house near the university campus.

One of the best known and most distinctive buildings on that campus is Pillsbury Hall, for which Mr. and Mrs. J. S. Pillsbury provided the money. It is notable both as a building designed by the distinguished Minneapolis architect, LeRoy S. Buffington, and as an excellent example of "Richardson Romanesque" architecture.

John Pillsbury died in 1901. His Fifth Street house was occupied by the family until 1911, when they offered it to the university for a rental of one dollar a year. It served as the home of the university president on these terms until it was deeded to the institution outright in 1945.

Until that time the house had remained as it was built—a great, square dwelling of cream-colored brick with high-pitched roofs, towerlike chimneys, dormers, a porte-cochere, roomy verandas, and ornamental details in modern Gothic. But when ownership passed to the university, the old mansion was transformed, under the supervision of Johns H. Hopkins, consulting designer of the university, into an attractive early nineteenth-century New Orleans style residence, largely by the removal of the Gothic-ornamented porches. Its exterior is now painted a bland off white with gun-metal trim.

Appropriate interior changes also were made. The woodwork is now white and the wall colors in the dining and reception rooms repeat colors and shades of the original Oriental rugs in those rooms. The rare scenic wallpaper in the entrance hall was a gift to the university from Mr. Hopkins.

This university president's house, then, though somewhat changed from its original form, stands as a living and useful reminder of the "Father of the University."

Home of the Empire Builder

JAMES J. HILL HOUSE. ST. PAUL. BUILT 1887.

STANDING on a commanding eminence overlooking downtown St. Paul, the old James J. Hill residence remains today as sound and firm as the great railroad empire its occupant built in the Northwest in the 1870's.

Located at 240 Summit Avenue, on the edge of St. Anthony Hill, the great stone mansion, somewhat hidden in summer by the trees and shrubbery of its landscaped grounds, faces northwest—for this house a symbolic direction. For it was in the Northwest that "Jim" Hill made his fortune—the great north-central domain whose development was, paradoxically, both cause and result of Jim Hill's Great Northern Railway system.

It was this system that opened up to settlement the prairie land and mountain country of the Northwest. It was this system that carried immigrants from the East and from Europe into the new states of North and South Dakota, Montana, Idaho, Wyoming, and Washington. And it was this system that afterward transported the grains, ores, lumber, and other products of these same immigrants to markets in the East and in faraway China and Japan.

The home of James J. Hill on St. Paul's Summit Avenue

It may be, as the government geologist, John Wesley Powell, prophesied at the time and as the events of the 1930's seemed to prove, that Jim Hill's vision of the Northwest as an agricultural Eden was a mirage and his plans and policies for its development a grievous mistake. But his intentions were of the best and his efforts were certainly successful in achieving his purpose, whether that purpose was right or wrong.

James Jerome Hill was born in a crude log house not far from Toronto, Canada, in September 1838, of a hard-working father and mother, both of whose parents were Irish immigrants. Coming to St. Paul in 1856, just eighteen and without funds, young Hill secured work as a warehouseman on the St. Paul wharf. Then he became consecutively a steamer agent, representative of Canadian

trappers and traders, a coal dealer, and finally owner of a steamboat line. Soon he was organizing the Red River Transportation Company, which inaugurated service by rail, stage, and steamboat between St. Paul and Winnipeg. Then in 1878 he obtained control of the failing St. Paul and Pacific Railroad and, with the aid of Canadian capital, restored it to a sound condition and extended its right of way. This railway became the parent road of the Great Northern system, which, when organized in 1890, reached to Seattle, Washington.

By that time the Empire Builder, as James J. Hill is often called, was already established in his stone mansion on St. Anthony Hill. This massive dwelling was built in 1887 at a cost of two hundred thousand dollars. It is designed in the heavy Richardson Romanesque style, and its walls of rough-faced red sandstone blocks look stern and fortresslike. Especially noticeable is the solid stone porte-cochere, with semicircular arches, at the front of the residence, a unit typical of the architectural style developed by H. H. Richardson. This three-story mansion, with high-pitched slate roof and many dormers, occupies the center of a good-sized plot of ground behind a low cast-iron fence and a row of thick shrubbery.

In this house James J. Hill lived with his family, entertaining his business associates and his influential friends, and devoting his leisure time to his art collection or his library. While living here, Hill, whose wife was of the Catholic faith, contributed fifty thousand dollars toward the building of the Cathedral of St. Paul, and here he made arrangements to establish and endow the Hill Reference Library, now one of the Midwest's outstanding research libraries.

Death came to James J. Hill on May 29, 1916, in his seventy-eighth year. Today his impressive, thirty-two room residence is the home of the Saint Paul Diocesan Teachers College. Although some remodeling has been done, the interior remains much the same as in Hill's day. From the center of the magnificent, paneled reception room, lighted by crystal chandeliers and warmed by great stone fireplaces, a grand staircase leads upward past leaded, stained-glass windows to the ballroom, dining room, and other rooms on the second floor, all retaining their original woodwork and lighting fixtures. In the first-floor reception room hangs an oil portrait of the Empire Builder by the French artist, Henri Caro-Delvaille.

Shrine of the Grangers

OLIVER HUDSON KELLEY HOUSE. NEAR ELK RIVER. BUILT 1896.

ABOUT three miles southeast of the small Minnesota town of Elk River, alongside highway U.S. 10, there is embedded in an attractive setting of blue limestone blocks a bronze historical tablet which explains that the farm nearby was the early homestead of Oliver Hudson Kelley, founder of the Grange in the United States. Beyond this marker may be seen the old Kelley home, a square, white-painted frame dwelling of two stories with green trim and low-pitched roof. The side toward the highway is the rear of the farmhouse, which faces toward the Mississippi River only a few hundred feet away at the base of a gentle slope.

Oliver Hudson Kelley was born in Boston on January 7, 1826. His father was a tailor. After being educated in the Boston public schools, Kelley, at the age of twenty-one, took the westward trail and arrived in Chicago in 1847. He secured a position there as clerk in a drugstore, working at the same time as a reporter for the new *Chicago Tribune*. After six months in Chicago, however, young Kelley went to Peoria, where he became a telegraph operator, and then in 1848 was transferred by

Minnesota farm home of Oliver Hudson Kelley, founder of the Grange

the telegraph company to Bloomington, Iowa. A year later, he went north to the new territory of Minnesota to take up a claim on government land near Elk River.

At first young Kelley engaged in the Indian trade at the Elk River post established by the now almost legendary half-breed woodsman, Pierre Bottineau, but soon he turned to clearing and farming his land. At that time a new village, called Itasca, was developing near the Kelley tract, and the founder of the Grange sometimes identified his home as being at Itasca. But in later years this village declined and finally disappeared altogether.

From the very first, Kelley was ardently enthusiastic about the future possibilities of Minnesota. In the intervals of tilling his acres and tending his livestock, he wrote letters to Eastern newspapers lauding the future prospects of the North Star state. Then in 1863 he was called upon to write an article on Minnesota for inclusion in a report by the United States commissioner of agriculture.

This article led to Kelley's appointment in 1864 as an agent in the Department of Agriculture at Washington, and it was after an official tour of the West and South that Kelley conceived the idea of organizing the farmers of the country into a fraternal group for their social and economic betterment. Soon he had others interested in his idea, and on December 4, 1867, in a Washington office, the National

Grange of the Patrons of Husbandry was formally organized, with Oliver Hudson Kelley as its secretary.

Kelley resigned from the Department of Agriculture and started out as an organizer for the new agrarian association with, it is said, "a railroad ticket to Harrisburg and $2.50 of Grange funds in his pocket." He earned his way westward by selling charters in the new order. Farmers were quick to respond to such an organization, but even so there was scarcely enough income for the secretary to pay his train fare and living expenses, and at Madison, Wisconsin, he was forced to borrow money for the rest of the trip to his farm home in Minnesota. But he was undismayed and, establishing headquarters in his farmhouse near Itasca, continued the work of organizing the Grange movement.

Although the Grange, of course, became an important national organization that did a good deal toward righting some of the worst economic wrongs of distressed farmers, its greatest strength and probably most effective membership developed in its founder's home state of Minnesota.

After the panic of 1873, however, Kelley seemed to lose interest in the Grange movement as he became more absorbed in Florida land speculation. But before moving to Florida and founding the town of Carrabelle, he completed his authoritative *Origin and Progress of the Order of the Patrons of Husbandry*, which was published in 1875.

When Kelley's Florida venture proved a failure, he returned north to Washington and there spent the remainder of his days. Often, however, he spent the summer months at his Minnesota farm home, a dwelling built in 1896 which replaced an earlier house on the same site. He died in 1913 in his eighty-seventh year and was buried in Rock Creek Cemetery, Washington. There in 1926 the National Grange erected a monument over his grave. His memory is kept more actively alive, however, through the annual picnics held by the State Grange of Minnesota on the grounds of the Oliver Hudson Kelley homestead.

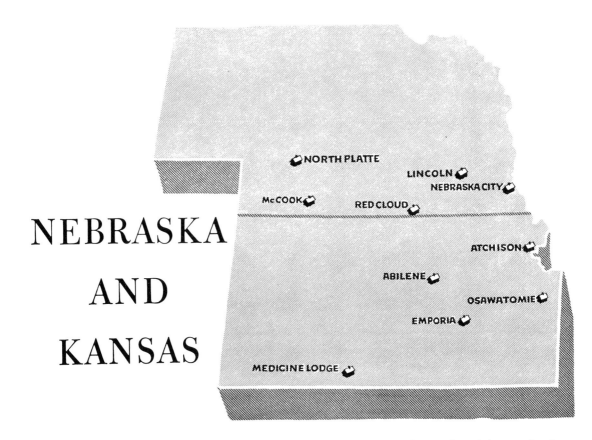

NEBRASKA
AND
KANSAS

Where once the buffalo and the Indian roamed, where long ago Coronado vainly sought the golden Seven Cities of Cibola, immigrants from the East and the South staked out their claims and tilled the prairie soil. When Congress passed the Kansas-Nebraska Bill, guerrilla warfare flared red along the Kansas-Missouri border until the slavery question was settled by the Civil War. Into free Kansas then came ex-Union soldiers to settle on the shortgrass lands opened up by the Santa Fé and Union Pacific railroads. Cowboys from the Southwest drove Texas long-horns up the dusty Chisholm Trail to the yards at Dodge City and Abilene. The villages grew into towns, the towns into cities: Topeka, Kansas City, Lawrence, Leavenworth, Wichita. And outside the cities stretched fields and cattle ranges, with a forest of oil derricks towering above.

The settlers poured into Nebraska, too, a little later. Some of them, living at first in sod houses, broke the prairie soil in the fertile valleys. Others, venturing farther westward to the Great Plains, brought in cattle and established ranches. At intervals there came the grasshopper plague, the prairie fire, the searing drought, or the blinding blizzard to ruin the crops and destroy the herds. But the farmers and the cattlemen, and the businessmen, too, found ways of overcoming natural disasters, and so in time erected a new state on the Western prairie.

Cabin of a Martyr

JOHN BROWN CABIN. OSAWATOMIE, KANSAS. BUILT 1854. OPEN TO THE PUBLIC.

THE John Brown cabin, enclosed in a protective superstructure, is the principal object of interest in the John Brown Battleground Memorial Park at Osawatomie, Kansas. A small town on the Marais des Cygnes River, Osawatomie lies in the center of the bloody border warfare country of pre-Civil War days, not more than fifteen miles west of the Missouri border and some forty miles south of Kansas City.

John Brown was not the owner of the cabin in which he lived during the guerrilla warfare days; it was the property of his brother-in-law, the Reverend Samuel Lyle Adair.

The historic cabin, built of squared logs chinked with plaster and containing a main room and a loft, was built in 1854 by a squatter named Samuel Glenn.

In that same year Congress passed the fateful Kansas-Nebraska Bill, setting up the two new territories of Kansas and Nebraska but leaving the question of whether these should be slave states or free for the settlers themselves to decide. It was not long after the bill was passed that the Reverend Mr. Adair brought his wife and children to the new Kansas Territory and bought for two hundred dollars the Glenn cabin and a tract of land around it on the outskirts of Osawatomie.

The next year, in 1855, Mrs. Adair's five nephews, the five sons of John Brown, arrived to take up claims near the Adair cabin. They all immediately became active in the antislavery, or Free Soil, movement. Seeing some of the proslavery Southerners from Missouri brandishing firearms, the Brown brothers wanted shotguns and pistols, too, and they wrote home to their father to send them weapons and ammunition.

John Brown was then living in North Elba, New York, a small Negro community in the Adirondacks. He decided at once to join his sons in Kansas. He would take them firearms so both they and he could fight to keep Kansas free of slavery.

The fanatical old abolitionist arrived in Kansas Territory in October 1855 and established his home with his sister in the Adair cabin. He helped his brother-in-law add a lean-to kitchen to the cabin, and here a few years later eleven Negro slaves were hidden after John Brown had brought them out of Missouri.

From the Adair cabin, a month after his arrival, John Brown rushed to the defense of the Free Soil town of Lawrence with a small band of antislavery men including his five sons and a son-in-law. An invading force of Border Ruffians, as the proslavery Southerners were called by their opponents, had threatened to destroy Lawrence.

Brown's side won out in this contest, but when more and more Free Soilers were killed by Border Ruffians, and when his own life and the lives of his sons were threatened, John Brown decided on a drastic act. There followed, on the night of May 24, 1856, the Pottawatomie Massacre, in which five proslavery men were killed on the banks of the Pottawatomie Creek, near Osawatomie.

Then came the last act of John Brown's turbulent career in the Territory of Kansas—the Battle of Osawatomie. This was fought August 30, 1856, on a low-lying hill within

John Brown's cabin in Osawatomie

thirty rods of the Adair cabin. In this encounter Brown and some thirty or forty of his followers met General John W. Reid at the head of two or three hundred Border Ruffians. Five of Brown's followers were killed, including his son Frederick, and several more were wounded. What the casualties were on Reid's side has never been ascertained, although one report states there were seventy killed or wounded. After the battle the Border Ruffians sacked and burned Osawatomie.

Some months later John Brown returned to the East and there evolved the plot that led to the sensational debacle at Harpers Ferry and to his execution for treason in 1859 — less than two years before the Territory of Kansas was admitted into the Union as a free state. Brown was now a martyr, and the song "John Brown's Body" was soon on the lips

of almost every Union soldier in the Civil War.

Saved from destruction during the Battle of Osawatomie because of the reluctance of a proslavery man to set it on fire while several sick women were under its roof, the John Brown cabin, as it is now called, continued to serve as a home for the Adair family for many years. In 1910 it was removed from its original site and set up in the John Brown Battleground Memorial Park, the scene of the Battle of Osawatomie. Near it today stands a life-size bronze statue of the bearded, bushy-haired martyr. In addition to trundle beds, spinning wheels, candle molds, and other relics of pioneer days in Kansas, the John Brown cabin contains a cherry wood table on which the fiery abolitionist wrote many letters during his brief stay in Kansas Territory.

Scouts' Rest

BUFFALO BILL CODY RANCH. NORTH PLATTE, NEBRASKA. BUILT 1870.

AS THE last and most glamorous of America's frontiersmen and Indian fighters, William F. (Buffalo Bill) Cody performed the feats that brought him fame in a region that is today part of the settled and peaceful Midwest. It was within the present state of Nebraska, on the western boundary of mid-America, that Cody first made his reputation as a plainsman, scout, and buffalo hunter.

In the 1870's the wide prairie country partly included by Nebraska was the "Wild West," but with the coming of civilization into this plains region, the frontier was pushed farther and farther westward until today the "West" is generally understood to be the Rocky Mountain country. And it was in the Rocky Mountain country that Buffalo Bill spent his last days, having moved on to that rugged region when Nebraska became too settled and civilized for him.

As a survival of Buffalo Bill's early Nebraska days, there stands at North Platte a sturdy ranch house that was Cody's home for nearly two decades. The former plainsman called his place Scouts' Rest, and such, indeed, it was, for he entertained here many other famous scouts of the plains, including Kit Carson, the North brothers, Pawnee Bill, Dr. W. F. Carver, Death Valley Scottie, and Buck Taylor. Another intrepid fighter entertained at Scouts' Rest was General Phil Sheridan, under whom Cody had served as an Indian scout.

But the most interesting fact about this North Platte ranch house is that here Buffalo Bill originated the Wild West Show, which he eventually took to all parts of the United States and Europe, thus, perhaps, spreading abroad an idealized and glamorized concept of the Western frontier of America. It was on the grounds of his ranch, adjacent to Scouts' Rest, that Cody staged a round-up, or rodeo, during the Fourth of July celebration of 1882 at North Platte, and from this he evolved, in the following year, the first "Round-up of Western Sports."

Located some three miles northwest of North Platte, on·the flat bottom land of the Platte River valley, Scouts' Rest was acquired by Buffalo Bill in 1877. At that time Cody was in possession of considerable means, having made a successful tour of America during the previous three years in a theatrical production called "The Prairie Waif," which starred Wild Bill Hickok as well as Cody.

After establishing himself at Scouts' Rest, which included a large tract of farming and grazing land, Buffalo Bill, in partnership with Major Frank North and Captain Luther North, bought a vast ranch in the sand-hill country some fifty miles north of North Platte. In the years following, when not on the road with his Wild West Show, Cody divided his time between Scouts' Rest and the North and Cody Ranch.

As host to other plainsmen in his North Platte ranch house, Buffalo Bill often reminisced about his younger years as an Indian scout and buffalo hunter during Nebraska's territorial period. When Cody was a boy of seven, in 1853, his family moved to Weston, Missouri, from LeClaire, Iowa. At that time Weston was a frontier settlement on the Missouri River opposite Leavenworth, in the Kansas country. Seeing long wagon trains leaving Leavenworth for the West, young Cody wanted to join them, and at the age of eleven he became an outrider for one of these trains.

A few years later he became a stagecoach driver and in 1860 rode the famous Pony Express across the Nebraska country and through the Rocky Mountains. With the coming of the Civil War, he enlisted in the Union army, and then, when the war was over, he became an Indian scout in Nebraska Territory, serving chiefly under General Sheridan and General George A. Custer.

There was an interval at this period, however, in which young Cody engaged in the activity which first earned him from his quasi biographer, Ned Buntline (Edward Zane Carroll Judson), his nickname of Buffalo Bill.

This was when he shot buffalo on the plains of Nebraska to provide meat for workers who were building the Union Pacific Railroad across the state. It is said that in seventeen months he delivered 4280 buffalo to the railroad company.

Another of Cody's exploits occurred in 1872, when he served as guide on a buffalo hunting expedition in Nebraska organized for the Grand Duke Alexis of Russia. Still another was his singlehanded duel with the Cheyenne chief, Yellow Hand, in the Sioux War of 1876, with Buffalo Bill the victor.

All these Western adventures, along with the flood of dime novels about him which appeared from the pen of Ned Buntline, enhanced his appeal to the American public when he became a showman — the handsome,

The ranch house of Buffalo Bill Cody

long-haired buckskin-wearing star of the spectacular Wild West Show. And a showman he remained to the end of his days. He died in Denver on January 10, 1917, and his body lies where he wanted it to — on the top of Lookout Mountain in Colorado.

Although called a ranch house, Scouts' Rest seems to an Easterner rather like an old-fashioned Ohio farm home. It is a white-painted "Queen Anne villa," with most of the bays, dormers, porches, and gingerbread trim of an Eastern country home of the same period. It is now the private home of a leading Nebraska cattle raiser. Inside the big red barn may still be seen, though slightly faded and frayed, some of the big colorful posters that advertised Buffalo Bill's Wild West Show to an older generation.

Arbor Lodge

J. STERLING MORTON HOUSE. NEBRASKA CITY. BUILT 1870. OPEN TO THE PUBLIC.

SOME forty miles south of Omaha tourists may find one of the most beautiful historic estates in the Midwest. This is the sixty-five-acre wooded tract at Nebraska City now known as Arbor Lodge State Park. This once private estate that is now public property was the home of the foremost of American tree lovers, J. Sterling Morton, the founder of Arbor Day in America.

At Arbor Lodge J. Sterling Morton patiently created, over a period of almost fifty years, a country estate that is in reality an arboretum, a beautiful park containing practically every type of tree and shrub, as well as many kinds of flowers, native to the temperate zone. In addition, Morton was prominent in public life as a journalist, as an official of the territorial government of Nebraska, and as secretary of agriculture in the cabinet of President Cleveland.

The origin of Arbor Lodge State Park, which in normal times has an average of thirty thousand visitors annually, is to be found in the old mansion that stands almost in the cen-

ter of the park. It was in the original unit of this mansion, built in 1855, that Julius Sterling Morton first dreamed of beautifying the grounds around his house with trees, shrubs, flowers, and vines. He and Mrs. Morton had come to Nebraska City from Detroit in 1854, the year of the Kansas-Nebraska Bill. Morton immediately became the editor of the *Nebraska City News*, the second newspaper in the new territory. He also entered politics and, after serving in the territorial legislature for several terms, was appointed secretary of the territorial government in 1858, remaining at this post until 1861. After the territory became a state in 1867, Morton served in various positions with the State Board of Agriculture and was elected its president in 1872.

In this position Morton persuaded Governor Robert W. Furnas to issue the first Arbor Day proclamation. Then in 1885 the Nebraska legislature made Arbor Day a legal holiday and established April 22, Morton's birthday, as the day on which tree planting is carried out each year in Nebraska. Later other states

Sixty-five acres of gardens and woods surround the Mortons'
Southern colonial mansion

proclaimed Arbor Days until the custom became universal throughout the United States and its possessions.

Meanwhile Morton had been realizing his ambitions for his own home. Originally the house was a four-room, L-shaped dwelling of frame construction. With a family of four growing sons, the Mortons needed more room, and they enlarged the house in 1871 and again in 1879. In the second remodeling they added a large two-story porch across the front. And all the while they had been planting and landscaping the grounds as they had planned when they began to build.

In 1881 Mrs. Morton died. Mr. Morton lived on at Arbor Lodge until 1893, when he left it temporarily to serve as secretary of agriculture during President Cleveland's second administration. Returning to Nebraska City at the end of his Washington service, he established the *Conservative*, a weekly journal, which he continued to publish until his death in 1902.

Arbor Lodge then passed into the posses-sion of the eldest son, Joy Morton of Chicago, who in 1885 had founded the Morton Salt Company. A nature lover like his father and mother, Joy Morton made Arbor Lodge his summer home and continued to maintain its sunken garden, rose arbor, pine grove, and arboretum. The son once again remodeled and enlarged the old house, and as he made it then it may be seen today—a white, dignified, Southern colonial mansion notable for its stately two-story porticoes on three sides.

After it had served as his summer home for twenty years, Joy Morton presented Arbor Lodge and its grounds to the state of Nebraska, and in 1923 it became Arbor Lodge State Park. The splendid old mansion is now open to the public and guide service is available. There are fifty-two rooms in the house and almost all of them contain original pieces of Morton furniture. On the grounds of the park is a life-size statue of Morton, and nearby are a pioneer's log cabin, a picnic grove, and the old Morton coach house, containing a stagecoach and various family carriages.

Crusader's Cottage

CARRY NATION HOUSE. MEDICINE LODGE, KANSAS. BUILT 1870's.

IN THE small prairie town of Medicine Lodge, a trim community out in south-central Kansas where many blue-overalled wheat farmers, sombrero-hatted cowpunchers, and leather-jacketed oil men from nearby Oklahoma forgather on Saturday afternoons, there stands a modest cottage of yellow-painted brick that has become an object of national interest.

That interest began almost fifty years ago when, one Saturday afternoon in the summer of 1899, a sturdy, determined, middle-aged woman walked out of the brick cottage, set up a hand organ in front of a saloon on Main Street, led a small group of women in singing a few hymns, and then, armed only with a stout umbrella, advanced with her band to wreck the saloon. The umbrella-wielder was

Mrs. Carry A. Nation, who in a few years' time attracted international attention for her arduous, hatchet-swinging fight against what she considered the evils of the liquor traffic.

Before the episode in Medicine Lodge, Mrs. Nation, who was then in her fifty-third year and slightly gray-haired, had been living quietly in the brick cottage with her husband, David Nation, for ten years without attracting any special attention, and her life in earlier years had been even more normal.

A native of Kentucky, where she was born in a Garrard County farmhouse on November 25, 1846, Carry Amelia Moore, whose father was a well-to-do slaveowner of Irish extraction, was taken at the age of nine to Belton, Missouri. Here, when she was twenty-one, Carry Moore married Dr. Charles Gloyd, who died a few years later as a result of excessive drinking. Left with a baby daughter to support, the widow taught school at Holden, Missouri, for four years and then in 1877 married David Nation, who was nineteen years her senior. Nation was a lawyer, a Union veteran, a newspaper editor, and a minister of the Christian Church.

After unsuccessful attempts at farming and hotelkeeping in Texas, the Nations moved to Medicine Lodge, Kansas, in 1889. Located on the Medicine River, the site of Medicine Lodge was believed by the Indians to be sacred to the Great Spirit, and here the redmen had always maintained a medicine lodge.

Medicine Lodge was then a lively cow town of the Western country, with seven saloons on its Main Street. The saloons greatly disturbed Carry Nation, for one of the main reasons she had wanted to come to Kansas was

HOMER VENTERS, SUN CITY

Carry Nation's little brick house in Medicine Lodge

because of its prohibition law. On her first day in Medicine Lodge, however, she found that the prohibition law was being flouted, that "joints" operated by "jointists" (as the saloons and their proprietors were then called) were going full blast on Main Street.

This weighed on her mind as she sat reading the Bible in the basement of her cottage home, for it was in the basement that she usually prayed, meditated, or read. She soon organized a local chapter of the Woman's Christian Temperance Union, but it was not until late in the 1880's that Carry Nation, while reading the Bible in her cottage one day during a severe electrical storm, received that "Baptism of the Holy Ghost" (as she later wrote) which caused her to become a militant temperance crusader. The immediate result was the umbrella attack on the saloon.

Although unsuccessful in wrecking the saloon, having been forcefully ejected by the white-aproned proprietor, Carry Nation remained with her singing group in front of the place until the saloon-keeper resigned himself to closing up for the day. The next day he left town.

Encouraged by this degree of success and backed by many housewives of the town whose husbands were heavy drinkers, the energetic, thin-lipped Carry Nation began a public attack on the town officials and within a few weeks all seven of the Main Street saloons were closed.

Having closed the saloons of Medicine Lodge, Carry Nation a year later singlehandedly attacked a "joint" in the nearby town of Kiowa, almost completely wrecking it with rocks wrapped in newspapers. Then she went on to Wichita, second largest city in Kansas, and it was there she first used the hatchet with which she was identified for the rest of her career. In Wichita, too, she was arrested for the first time and this added to her fame as a militant crusader. She sometimes called herself the "John Brown of Prohibition." Her unrestrained temperance activities eventually caused David Nation to divorce her.

After a brief but extraordinary career, during the latter part of which she lectured widely in America and Europe, the Kansas crusader died in 1911 and was buried beside the grave of her mother at Belton, Missouri. A granite shaft above her grave contains the words:

CARRY A. NATION
FAITHFUL TO THE CAUSE OF PROHIBITION
"SHE HATH DONE WHAT SHE COULD"

Although not open to the public, the old Carry Nation cottage at Medicine Lodge is identified by a historical tablet placed there by the Woman's Kansas Day Club. The house, plain, gable-roofed, and with a small porch at its front, is located at the southeast corner of Oak and Fowler streets. In its basement there is still an old-fashioned table said to be the one Carry Nation used as a desk while reading her Bible.

Editor's Home

AS OHIO is known for its presidents and Indiana for its authors, Kansas can claim distinction as the home of more prominent newspaper editors than any other state in the Midwest. One of the earliest and most famous of the Kansas journalists was Ed Howe, founder and, for more than a third of a century, editor and publisher of the *Atchison Daily Globe.*

It was as much through his books, though, as through his newspaper editorials that Howe won renown from coast to coast. His first and best known book, *The Story of a Country Town,* was published in 1883 and not a few literary critics regard it as a minor American classic. When it was completed, however, no publisher would take it because of its uncompromising realism. Only after Ed Howe had printed the book himself was its merit and importance recognized, especially by Mark Twain and William Dean Howells.

A faithful account of life in a small Midwestern town, *The Story of a Country Town,* together with Joseph Kirkland's *Zury: The Meanest Man in Spring County* (1887), began a tradition of bitterly satirical American realism that was amplified some three decades later by two books of similar background, *Winesburg, Ohio* and *Main Street.*

Contrary to popular belief, *The Story of a Country Town* does not portray life in Atchison, Kansas. It is based on what Ed Howe saw and experienced in the small Missouri town of Bethany, located some eighty miles from Atchison. The Howe family had settled in Bethany after an overland journey in a covered wagon from Treaty, Indiana, and in the Missouri town, Ed Howe as a boy of twelve began his newspaper career, helping his father, Henry Howe, print a local journal. Besides being a newspaper proprietor, the elder Howe was also a farmer, schoolteacher, and Methodist circuit rider.

After wandering through the West as a tramp printer, young Ed Howe came to Atchison and there in 1877 established the *Atchison Daily Globe.* In a few years he had made enough profit from this venture to build a comfortable residence for himself and his family on the old Doniphan Road. At that time the site Howe had chosen for his house was out in the country, with only a few homes in the vicinity. Now it is 1117 North Third Street, in the midst of a rolling, wooded residential section overlooking the Missouri River.

In this house the lean-faced editor and author, wearing his customary black sack suit and shoestring tie, a pipe in his mouth and perhaps with a favorite dog at his feet, wrote the essays and aphorisms that made his reputation as an editor. He entertained a good deal, his guest list over the years including such persons as Senator John J. Ingalls, Mrs. Elbert Hubbard, Amelia Earhart Putnam, H. L. Mencken, and William Allen White.

During the years, too, Howe turned out about a dozen more books, but most of these were written at his country estate, Potato Hill, outside Atchison. After turning over the *Globe* to his two sons in 1911, the Atchison editor established *E. W. Howe's Monthly,* which he continued to publish until his death in 1937 at the age of eighty-four.

Three years after he founded the Atchison Daily Globe, *Ed Howe was
able to build himself a square, roomy, red brick house*

Large, square, two stories high, and built of red brick with white stone trim, the old Ed Howe residence, standing on a green bluff among elms and maples planted by the editor-philosopher himself, is today the home of his niece, Adelaide Howe, who served for many years as her uncle's secretary. The interior of the house, with its fourteen comfortable rooms, remains unaltered since the days when Ed Howe lived there. Undisturbed, too, are his books, prints, pipes, old Corona typewriter, and other personal belongings. Still other mementos, including Howe's desk and an oil portrait by N. R. Brewer, are on display in the *Globe* editorial office in downtown Atchison.

Red Rocks

WILLIAM ALLEN WHITE HOUSE. EMPORIA, KANSAS. BUILT 1880's.

WHEN William Allen White was a young college student in Emporia, there was built in the town's residential section a substantial house that aroused his admiration. The builder of the house was a prominent and successful Emporia citizen, Judge Almerin Gillett; the material used for part of it was red sandstone blocks from that strangely romantic place, the Garden of the Gods in the Colorado Rockies; and the name the judge gave the house when it was done was Red Rocks. The young college student liked all these things about the house and dreamed that someday he would own one like it.

After studying in the College of Emporia for two years, young White left Emporia in 1885 to accept his first newspaper job in the nearby town of El Dorado. Although born in Emporia (February 10, 1868), William White had spent his boyhood in El Dorado, his family having moved there when he was a child. His father, Dr. Allen White, was of New England stock, and his mother was of Irish extraction. When the elder White died William was still a boy, and the widowed

Mrs. White managed to complete her son's education by keeping boarders and serving as a private tutor. It was to relieve his mother of this burden that White, at the age of seventeen, decided to leave school and go to work.

After a few years' experience on the El Dorado papers, young White went to Lawrence and enrolled at the University of Kansas, earning his own and his mother's expenses by working part time on the *Lawrence Journal*. Subsequently, after working on various big-town newspapers, including the *Kansas City Star*, where he came under the beneficial influence of the distinguished publisher, Colonel William Rockhill Nelson, White decided he wanted to be a small-town editor. So in 1895, two years after his marriage to Sallie Lindsay, a Kansas City schoolteacher, White returned to the town of his birth, Emporia, and there, with three thousand dollars he had borrowed, he bought the *Emporia Gazette*.

It was an early editorial, "What's the Matter with Kansas?" that brought the *Gazette* its first fame. About the same time White pub-

Emporia Gazette

The house of the "Sage of Emporia"

lished his first book, a volume of short stories called *The Real Issue,* and this and succeeding books, as well as numerous magazine articles, added to the renown of both the *Emporia Gazette* and its proprietor. In time William Allen White became known throughout the country as the "Sage of Emporia."

Back in Emporia, White renewed his admiration of Red Rocks, the Gillett home, and a few years later, when the house was offered for sale, it became the home of Will and Sallie White.

Here the Sage of Emporia lived for the rest of his life; here he and his wife reared their two children, Bill and Mary; and here the Whites welcomed, with the same pleasure and hospitality, both their Emporia neighbors and some of the greatest men and women of their time. Just after World War I the interior of the house was slightly damaged by fire and the first floor was restored from a new design by Frank Lloyd Wright.

When William Allen White died in 1944, newspaper editorials throughout the country regretted the passing of "one of the truly great Americans of this age." His death, however, did not greatly diminish the number of callers at Red Rocks, for Mrs. White, who continues to live there, is as highly esteemed as was her husband.

Located at 927 Exchange Street, on a large corner lot shaded by stately elms, the White residence presents an English half-timbered effect above its solid first floor walls of red Colorado sandstone. The most notable of the rooms in the three-story residence is the living room, with its low, beamed ceiling, paneled walls, rows of books, Chinese tapestries, and a capacious stone fireplace. In the windows of the dining room are displayed collections of rare Venetian, Bohemian, and Russian glass stemware which the Whites ob-tained in Europe on their numerous travels abroad.

On the second floor there are two rooms of particular interest: the editor's study and the room of his daughter Mary. This second has remained untouched since the day in 1921 when young Mary White left it to go for a horseback ride and was killed in an accidental fall. It was her death that inspired William Allen White to write, with his wife beside him, the most famous of his editorials, entitled simply "Mary White."

Home of the Great Commoner

WILLIAM JENNINGS BRYAN HOUSE. LINCOLN, NEBRASKA. BUILT 1880'S.

SHORTLY after moving into his house at Lincoln, state capital of Nebraska, William Jennings Bryan came home one morning at daybreak after traveling all night on a train. Then a young lawyer newly arrived from Illinois, he had filled a speaking engagement the previous evening in western Nebraska. Waking his wife, the young lawyer told her of a curious experience he had had while talking to his audience the night before. "Mary, I have had a strange experience. Last night I found that I had power over the audience. I could move them as I chose. I have more than usual power as a speaker. I know it. God grant that I may use it wisely."

This incident marked the beginning of Bryan's career as one of America's outstanding political leaders and orators. The house in which these words were spoken still stands on its original site in Lincoln. Though unmarked and somewhat altered, and with its once-familiar front porch now gone, the old Bryan residence at 1625 D Street continues to attract many sightseers. It was, before being altered and modernized, a substantial frame residence, two stories high, its roof surmounted by a single, suitably proportioned tower, and its façade spanned by a restful veranda.

Bryan and his family lived here for fifteen years, from 1887 to 1902. It was during this period that the "Great Commoner" first achieved national fame as an orator, Chautauqua lecturer, political leader, and presidential nominee of the Democratic party.

A legal mission first brought Bryan to Lincoln in 1887. Born at Salem, Illinois, on March 19, 1860, he had been practicing law in Jacksonville, where he had a few years earlier been graduated from Illinois College. After visiting Nebraska in his twenty-seventh year, Bryan decided to settle in Lincoln and practice law there. One reason for his decision was that he had been offered the opportunity to conduct a legal-aid column in one of the Lincoln newspapers, an offer which he readily accepted. He then brought his wife and baby daughter, Ruth, to Lincoln and there the Bryan family took up residence in the D Street house.

A few months afterward, Bryan began holding political conferences in his parlor with local Democratic leaders. It was at this period, while he was serving as a Democratic speaker, that he had the revelation of his unusual oratorical ability. From then he transferred his chief interest from law to politics.

HISTORIC AMERICAN BUILDINGS SURVEY

1625 D Street, Lincoln

A year and a half after settling in the D Street house, Bryan entered the national political scene by being elected congressman from his district. This was something of an accomplishment for a Democrat in an overwhelmingly Republican district. It was said that he had won this victory through his oratorical powers. Bryan was re-elected to the House once. In 1894 he failed to win election to the Senate and for several years he edited the *Omaha World-Herald*.

About this time he became a regular Chautauqua speaker, and almost every year for the rest of his life he spent a season on the road, arguing for causes and reforms that were close to his heart.

In 1896, when he was a delegate to the Democratic National Convention in Chicago, Bryan delivered his famous "Cross of Gold" speech. His triumphant oratory so swayed the convention that he was given the Democratic nomination for president, though he was only thirty-six.

Advocating free and unlimited coinage of silver as a solution to the farmers' and workers' economic problems, William Jennings Bryan staged a spectacular campaign through the country but lost the election to William McKinley. In 1900 he was again given the

presidential nomination by his party and was once more defeated by McKinley. Defeat came to him a third time in 1908 when he lost the presidential race to William Howard Taft. In the intervals during those years, however, he kept his ideas before the public by editing his own weekly newspaper, the *Commoner*.

Bryan was no longer living in the D Street residence, but on the outskirts of Lincoln in his country house, Fairview, when in 1912 he became secretary of state in the cabinet of President Woodrow Wilson. He had already given up Fairview, too, and was living in Florida at the time he helped to prosecute J. T. Scopes, a Tennessee schoolteacher, for teaching the theories of evolution in the public schools. This famous trial, held in 1925, marked the high point of the great controversy between fundamentalists and liberals over the interpretation of the Bible, in which Bryan had militantly championed the cause of the fundamentalists.

Five days after the close of the trial, William Jennings Bryan died quietly in his sleep. He was buried in the national cemetery at Arlington, Virginia.

In Red Cloud

WILLA CATHER HOUSE. RED CLOUD, NEBRASKA. BUILT 1880'S.

IN THE flat, fertile valley of the Republican River, a stream that takes its course leisurely through southern Nebraska, is the pleasant, prosperous, farming village of Red Cloud. Here lived, in her girlhood, a distinguished American novelist, the late Willa Cather. It was in Red Cloud, and before then on a Nebraska ranch, that Willa Cather received those impressions of prairie life, and especially of life among the early Bohemian settlers on the prairies, which she later embodied in her Nebraska novels, *O Pioneers!*, *The Song of the Lark*, and *My Antonia*, and in her famous short fictional work, *A Lost Lady*.

Except for the broad porch spanning two sides of it, the Cather house in Red Cloud remains practically the same as when young Willa lived here during her teens. It is the sort of small-town Nebraska house one might find described in a Cather novel — neat, white-painted, and set back on a lawn ornamented by lilac bushes and shaded by a few elms and maples. From the restful porch of this house, which stands at the southwest corner of Sixth Avenue and Seward Street, one may observe across the street the First Methodist Church and in the center of a square the Webster County courthouse.

Willa Sibert Cather was born near Winchester, Virginia, on December 7, 1875, and spent her early childhood in the conventional Southern home of her Anglo-Irish parents. When she was nine years old, her father, Charles F. Cather, decided to emigrate to the newly opened Western country. Thus Willa Cather grew up on the Nebraska prairie, and she has always seemed more a Midwesterner than a Southerner, in spite of her Virginia birth and ancestry.

The Cathers moved first to a Nebraska ranch. Here the small girl Willa became acquainted with the sturdy German and Czechoslovakian immigrants who were establishing homesteads on the prairies. She played with their children, rode horseback with them, and learned their customs and folkways.

In the late 1880's Charles Cather took his wife and children to the small county seat town of Red Cloud and went into the real estate business. Young Willa continued her interest in music and in the English and Latin classics which she had learned to appreciate from her two cultured grandmothers, both of whom lived with the Cather family.

By now almost a young lady, slightly plump, with reddish brown hair and bright blue eyes, Willa Cather entered the Red Cloud high school and was soon showing exceptional ability as a writer. She was passionately fond of music, and during her high school years she decided she wanted to live in a large city, where she could find concerts as well as intellectual companionship. When she left Red Cloud after graduating from the high school and becoming a student at the University of Nebraska at Lincoln, Miss Cather never returned, except for brief visits, to the town of her girlhood.

However, she must often have thought of the two-story frame house on Sixth Street and about her life in Red Cloud among the hardworking Czechs and Germans, as she later advanced from newspaper work in Pittsburgh to the editorship of *McClure's Magazine* in

MRS. DOROTHY KOENIG, RED CLOUD

Willa Cather's girlhood home

New York. It was during these busy years in the East that, in what leisure time she could find, Miss Cather wrote *O Pioneers!*, which was published in 1913. It was followed by *The Song of the Lark* and by *My Antonia*. In these novels Miss Cather portrayed the struggles of foreign immigrant girls in the Western prairie country, telling their stories with great insight and sympathetic understanding.

In her later work, Willa Cather transferred her fictional backgrounds to other regions — the Southwest in *Death Comes for the Archbishop* and French Quebec in *Shadows on the Rock* — but it is agreed by most literary critics that in the future she will be best known for her Midwestern novels: the books that describe the kind of pioneer life she knew as a girl on a ranch and in the small Nebraska town of Red Cloud.

Senator's Home

GEORGE W. NORRIS HOUSE. MC COOK, NEBRASKA. BUILT 1890'S.

FEELING in his democratic way that he was a neighbor among neighbors, the late Senator George W. Norris, one of Nebraska's and one of America's most distinguished citizens, lived in a conventional, middle-class house no more pretentious than any other in the small western Nebraska town of McCook. Since the death of Senator Norris in 1944 at the age of eighty-three, and especially since the publication of his widely read autobiography, *Fighting Liberal*, the Norris home at McCook has become the town's principal object of interest, although it is unmarked and is still a private residence.

To this house at 706 Main Street the former Nebraska senator retired in 1943 after having served for forty years in both houses of Congress. During that long period, as James E. Lawrence points out in his introduction to *Fighting Liberal*, the independent Nebraska senator stood out more prominently as a far-sighted public figure than any of the numerous presidents who came from Norris' birth state of Ohio. Having settled permanently in his McCook home after the close of his public career, Norris immediately began work on his autobiography. In this task he was assisted by his long-time friend, James E. Lawrence, editor of the *Lincoln Star*, and by his wife, Ellen, who before her marriage to Senator Norris was a McCook schoolteacher. Fortunately, the autobiography was completed before Norris died in 1944.

George W. Norris was born in 1861 in the characteristically Midwestern town of Clyde, Ohio, which later provided the background of Sherwood Anderson's book, *Winesburg,*

Ohio. Norris worked as a farm hand in order to obtain money for his college and law education. After finishing his law studies at Valparaiso University — an Indiana institution then known as the "poor man's Harvard" — and after a short stay in Washington Territory, young Norris went to Nebraska, at first settling in Beaver City, where he began the practice of law. He became active in Republican party politics, was elected county attorney and, later, district judge.

In a few years Judge Norris moved with his family to McCook and there he built the house on Main Street which was to be his home for the rest of his long life. It was in 1903 that Judge Norris first entered the scene of national politics, when he was elected to the House of Representatives. He served continuously in the House until 1913. After that he was elected continuously to the Senate and remained there until his retirement from public life in 1943.

As congressman and senator in Washington for forty years, George W. Norris was much of the time away from his McCook home. But he returned to this home as often as he could between sessions of Congress. Here, the "fighting liberal," long-time leader of the independents in the Senate, rested and relaxed between battles in Congress. Here, the man who consistently advocated ownership of power facilities by the public and who almost singlehandedly fought for the creation of the Tennessee Valley Authority, sat on his front porch during hot summer evenings, smoking a pipe or cigar, and often chatting with his McCook neighbors. During these summer va-

The Nebraska home of George W. Norris — for forty years the
"fighting liberal" of Congress

cations Norris would frequently work about his house or grounds, wearing overalls. One might see him repairing a bench, pruning his lilac bushes, or watering the lawn. During these intervals, too, Senator Norris would spend some time each day answering mail in a McCook office he shared with his old friend, Carl Marsh.

Since the death of Senator Norris, his Main Street home continues to be the residing place of Mrs. Norris. The house, which faces City Park, has been somewhat altered since it was first built, a front porch, for one thing, having been removed. It is a gabled, two-story dwelling, modestly Tudor in style, with a stucco exterior, paneled doors, and a suggestion of half-timber construction. This house has within it a large collection of material associated with the career of Senator Norris — letters, records, photographs and newspaper clippings, as well as a few Norris family heirlooms, including the spinning wheel used by his Pennsylvania Dutch mother in making clothes for her husband, herself, and her twelve children.

National Shrine

DWIGHT D. EISENHOWER HOUSE. ABILENE, KANSAS. BUILT 1890's.

WHEN General Dwight D. Eisenhower returned to the United States after leading the Allied forces to victory in Europe in World War II, he announced that one of the first places he wanted to see was his boyhood home in Abilene, Kansas. And to Abilene he went, following the great and joyous welcomes extended to him in Washington, New York, West Point, and Kansas City.

In Abilene, a small Kansas town in the center of the wheat country, General Eisenhower hurried to the inconspicuous, two-story, white dwelling in which he had spent his boyhood and young manhood, and there, in the old-fashioned parlor, he once more greeted his mother, eighty-three years old now.

Although Dwight Eisenhower was born in Denison, Texas, on October 14, 1890, both his parents and his paternal grandparents were early settlers of Kansas. It was in 1876 that his grandfather, the Reverend Jacob Eisenhower, with a group of other Pennsylvania Germans, established a farming colony on the open prairie just south of Abilene. Here Reverend Eisenhower tended his one-hundred-and-sixty-acre farm and on Sundays preached to the colonists.

At that time Abilene, located at the north end of the famous Chisholm Trail, was just achieving law and order after a violent period as one of the most riotous cow towns in the West. On its downtown streets the saloons and dance halls and gambling places that had become symbols of its lawlessness were giving place to general stores and churches — to the satisfaction of solid settlers like the Eisenhowers.

Instead of becoming a farmer, David Eisenhower, the minister's son, attended Lane University at Lecompton, Kansas, and then went into business. At Lane he met Ida Elizabeth Stover, a former Virginia girl, whom he married in 1885. With cash from a small inheritance, the bride bought for herself, among other things, an ebony piano which is still a cherished possession in the Eisenhower family.

After an unsuccessful attempt at conducting a general store, David Eisenhower moved his family to Denison, Texas, where he obtained work on a railroad. And it was there that Dwight was born. The Eisenhowers remained in Denison only two years, returning in 1891 to Abilene, where David Eisenhower secured work as a mechanic in the Belle Springs Creamery plant. He later became an engineer there. Though he never earned more than one hundred dollars a month in this position, he and his wife managed on this small income to rear seven healthy boys.

During the first eight years of their residence in Abilene, the Eisenhower family lived in a rented house on Southeast Second Street. In 1899, however, when the boy Dwight was nine years old, the family moved into the two-story frame house at 201 Southeast Fourth Street, on Abilene's humble south side. This house was originally owned by Dwight's uncle, Abraham Lincoln Eisenhower, who was on weekdays a veterinarian and on Sundays a minister of the River Brethren. When Abraham went to California, he sold his house, together with a three-acre tract east of it, to his brother David.

"Ike" Eisenhower's boyhood home

As a boy in this Fourth Street house, Dwight Eisenhower, who was early called "Ike" by his schoolmates, listened one night a week to the reading of the Bible by his mother, fought with his brothers, felt the difference between his family and the rich families living "on the other side of the tracks," hoed the potato patch and fed the chickens, peddled vegetables in a buggy with an older brother, and read dime novels and played "Wild West."

In high school Dwight Eisenhower continued his average record as a student, became especially interested in history, starred on the baseball and football teams, and loafed some hours away at the soda fountain in Joner Callahan's café. Then, when he was approaching his twentieth year, he applied for an appointment to West Point, passed the examinations, and soon thereafter left Abilene for the military academy in the East.

In the years that followed, while "Ike" was advancing to responsibility and power as a general in the army, Mr. and Mrs. David Eisenhower continued to live unpretentiously in the white house on Fourth Street. The elder Eisenhower died in 1943, two years before his illustrious son returned from the great victory in Europe, but present with Mrs. Eisenhower in the Abilene home on that June day in 1945 were the general's four living brothers: Milton, president of Kansas State College; Arthur, a Kansas City banker; Edgar, an attorney in Tacoma, Washington; and Earl, a power company official in Charleroi, Pennsylvania.

In June 1947 the Eisenhower house, left intact since the death of Mrs. Eisenhower in 1946, was officially dedicated as a national shrine, to become part of a million-dollar memorial to all men and women who served in the armed services of the United States during World War II.

NORTH AND SOUTH DAKOTA

Now there was a new region for the westward migrants to occupy — the Territory of Dakota, created in 1861. Now they could settle on a huge, Great Plains territory out of which were later to be formed the states of North and South Dakota, most of present Wyoming, and much of what is now Montana. But the movement of peoples into the new Dakota Territory was slow at first. Not until the discovery of gold in the Black Hills by General Custer's military expedition in 1874 did the Easterners come in a rush. Then appeared the rough mining towns of Custer and Deadwood, and with them such characters as Wild Bill Hickok and Calamity Jane.

Gradually the gold rush dwindled, then stopped, and slowly the Indians were suppressed, after the dramatic episode that has become legend as Custer's Last Stand. Then the great grasslands of Dakota Territory, east of the Black Hills and north of the Bad Lands, turned into big farms and broad cattle ranges. Frontier settlements grew into towns and cities, and immigrants from northern Europe came to join the settlers from earlier American frontiers. By 1889 the territory was ready for division into states. North and South Dakota were created simultaneously, the only twins in the Union. No one knows which proclamation of statehood President Cleveland signed first; the "Sister States of the North" are together the Union's thirty-ninth and fortieth members.

On the Old River Road

JOSEPH HENRY TAYLOR CABIN. WASHBURN, NORTH DAKOTA.
BUILT 1870'S. OPEN TO THE PUBLIC.

IN THE days when overland freighters creaked along the River Road that led from Bismarck to settlements and military posts farther up the Missouri River, there lived in a log cabin not far from the village of Washburn an unusual frontier character. This man was Joseph Henry Taylor — soldier, trapper, hunter, printer, editor, and author.

Joseph Henry Taylor built his cabin in the scattered little settlement of Painted Woods in the early 1870's. He had come there by a roundabout route from Chester County, Pennsylvania, where he was born in 1843 of Quaker parents. Soon after his schooling was finished, Taylor served as a Union soldier in the Civil War and then drifted westward, riding on horseback through the wilds of Iowa, Nebraska, Colorado, and New Mexico.

In 1867 he arrived in Yankton, the capital of Dakota Territory, and there established the

RUSSELL REID, BISMARCK

Taylor lived a bachelor's life in his log cabin at Painted Woods

227

territory's first Democratic newspaper. There, too, according to legend, he suffered disappointment in love. His letters to the girl of his choice were either lost or intercepted and she married another man. Hearing this, so the story goes, Taylor gave up his newspaper post and sought the solitude of a bachelor's life in the log cabin at Painted Woods.

This settlement is said to have derived its unusual name from a woods nearby in which rival Indian tribes painted the trees with symbols of their victories and defeats. As postmaster of Painted Woods, Taylor did not use his cabin for the letter office; a large hole cut in the trunk of a tree served that purpose.

When not occupied with his official duties, Taylor hunted and trapped along the Missouri River, visited with the Indians, or talked with the drivers of the overland wagons that hauled supplies from Bismarck, then the western terminal of the Northern Pacific, to upriver settlements and military posts as far as the mouth of the Yellowstone River.

After living for many years at Painted Woods, Taylor returned to civilization in the county seat town of Washburn. Here he became editor of the *Washburn Leader* and wrote four books about his earlier days in the woods along the upper Missouri River. Since he was a printer as well as an editor, Taylor printed his own books in the *Leader* shop, setting them in type as he composed them. In this unusual manner he wrote *Sketches of Frontier and Indian Lives on the Upper Missouri and Great Plains, Beavers and Their Ways, Twenty Years on the Trap Line,* and *Kaleidoscopic Lives.*

A bachelor to the end of his days, Joseph Henry Taylor died in the *Washburn Leader* print shop on April 8, 1908. He was then in his sixty-fifth year.

Long forgotten, the simple log cabin that Taylor occupied during his Painted Woods period was found a few years ago to be fairly well preserved. It was therefore removed from its original site and set up in Washburn as a memorial to one of the town's early citizens. Located on East Main Street, the Taylor cabin is now open to the public as a museum. It contains numerous mementos associated with Joseph Henry Taylor and the early days of McLean County. The cabin is in the care of the newspaper which Taylor once edited, the *Washburn Leader.*

Oldest in the Hills

WAY CABIN. CUSTER, SOUTH DAKOTA. BUILT 1875. OPEN TO THE PUBLIC.

SURVIVING from the year of the sensational gold rush to the Black Hills is a solid, well-built log cabin in Custer that is said to be the oldest dwelling in the Black Hills. It originally stood on the bank of French Creek near the point where gold showings were first discovered on July 27, 1874, but it has been removed from its original site and is now the principal object of interest in Way City Park, a small recreational area just off Custer's main business street.

Open to the public as a museum, this gold

O'NEILL PHOTO COMPANY

Log cabin built during the gold rush of '75

rush cabin contains hundreds of relics from pioneer days in the Black Hills. There are also displayed here natural history specimens, including cleverly mounted birds and animals, minerals, and rare botanical exhibits. Most of the material displayed in the cabin was originally collected by Judge Harry E. Way, pioneer resident of Custer. It was Judge Way who removed the cabin to its present site, installed in it his historical collection, and donated both the cabin and the ground around it to the city of Custer.

The famous gold rush into the Black Hills was set in motion by General George A. Custer, who was in command of an expedition sent in to the region to explore its mineral resources. The actual discovery of gold on French Creek was made by Horatio N. Ross, a prospector attached to the expedition, but it was General Custer who announced the find

to the world. In the log cabin museum there is displayed an issue of the *Chicago Inter-Ocean* from 1874 which headlines the discovery in one word: GOLD!

The rush to the French Creek area began at once. But the Black Hills were still a Sioux reservation, and troops were ordered into the Hills to clear out the gold seekers. It was a unit of these soldiers, troops of the Fifth Cavalry, who built the log cabin that is now a museum in Custer.

One of the first groups of gold seekers to arrive at French Creek was the so-called Gordon party from Sioux City. They built a stockade and lived in it for one winter, but the entire group was placed under arrest in the spring of 1875 and taken to Fort Laramie in Wyoming. A full-size reproduction of the Gordon stockade may be seen today on the original site just outside Custer.

When a new treaty was signed with the Indians in which they ceded the Black Hills to the whites, the military withdrew and squatters rushed into the region in greater numbers than before. A mining town grew up near the place of Ross's find two years before, and when General Custer was killed in the Battle of the Little Big Horn in Montana, his name was given to the new French Creek town. The cabin nearby which the soldiers had built now became the home of one of the army of prospectors that invaded the Hills country.

When a new gold strike was made in Deadwood Gulch, some fifty miles to the north, most of the prospectors left Custer to set up a new mining town, Deadwood, which became in a year or two one of the most turbulent towns of the Old West. But Custer soon recovered from the depletion of its population, new settlers arrived, mica was discovered in its vicinity, and in 1890 it was connected with the outside world by a railroad. Since then Custer has become one of the principal tourist centers of the Black Hills.

After the exodus to Deadwood, the old log cabin on French Creek became the home of a permanent Custer settler until its historic value attracted the attention of Judge Way. Made of hand-hewn logs, the cabin is twenty feet long and sixteen feet wide and is roofed with shingles. A fireplace was added sometime after the original construction.

Standing there in Way City Park, the old cabin is equally reminiscent of the exciting gold rush days and the less exciting days described in the old Western song:

Oh there's two old tramps, boys,
A-marching along.
They're not very gay, boys,
They're singing no song;
They're just from the West, boys,
Their fortune's been told —
They're stragglers from the Black Hills,
Been digging for gold.

Then don't go out West, boys,
Stay home if you can;
I'm just from the West, boys,
I'm a broken-down man,
And old Sitting Bull and Comanche Bill
Will raise up your hair
In those dreary Black Hills.

In Way City Park, too, is displayed an old stagecoach that was used on the road between Deadwood and Sydney, Nebraska, during the "Days of '76." At that time Custer was a halfway station on this mountain road. Abandoned on the ice at Sylvan Lake one winter many years ago, the Sydney stagecoach sank to the bottom of the lake in the following spring and lay there until it was discovered by a swimmer a decade or so ago and was brought to the surface and placed in the park.

Another exhibit in Way City Park is a small rock monument placed there in 1921 by the Association of Black Hills Pioneers and dedicated to the memory of Horatio N. Ross — who, in spite of his famous gold strike, died a pauper.

Frenchman's Folly

CHÂTEAU DE MORES. MEDORA, NORTH DAKOTA. BUILT 1883. OPEN TO THE PUBLIC.

OUT on the wide, windy plains of western North Dakota, not far from the Montana border, there stands perhaps the strangest historic house in the Midwest. The man who built it was not a Westerner, nor was he an American. He was a French nobleman, the Marquis de Mores. And the house he built for himself, though outwardly it looks like a long, two-story ranch house, inside has many of the arrangements and appointments of a medieval European castle. It is known throughout North Dakota as the Château de Mores.

It was a great dream of power and fortune that brought the handsome, dashing young French nobleman to Dakota Territory. Born in Paris in 1853, the Marquis de Mores — whose full name was Antoine-Amedée-Marie Vincent Manca de Vallombrosa — was educated by private tutors, in a Jesuit college, and then in several outstanding French military academies.

It was during a brief period of service as an officer in the French army that the young marquis met and married, in Paris, Medora von Hoffman, the beautiful red-haired daughter of a New York banker. Restless and ambitious, the Frenchman was stirred to action by his wife's stories of the splendid opportunities to be found in the great American West. He conceived the idea of establishing a gigantic meat-packing industry there near the source of supply in the cattle country. He believed that by using the new refrigerated railroad cars to transport the meat to Eastern cities, he could capture a major portion of the market from Eastern packers.

A quick trip through the plains country convinced the marquis his idea was practicable

— and also introduced him to the weird beauty of the Dakota Bad Lands. They fascinated him and he chose them as the site for his new enterprise.

In 1883 the Marquis de Mores arrived in Dakota Territory, bought forty-five thousand acres of grazing land, and built a house for his wife — a house on the pattern of the French châteaux to which he was accustomed. He made of his ranch a kind of feudal estate, with such accessories to the château as a carriage house, coachmen's quarters, servants' lodgings, large stables, and barns. And here he and his personable marquise, for some three years, lived a gay and gracious life that was remarkable for the time and place. At their big château, staffed by a retinue of French servants, they entertained Eastern aristocrats and foreign gentry, hunting, riding, dancing, and dining.

Across the Little Missouri River from the château, De Mores platted a new town which he named Medora after his wife. There, along with houses, stores, and a hotel, he built a slaughter house and a packing plant, conveniently near the newly laid tracks of the Northern Pacific Railway. He also established a stage and freight line between Medora and the booming gold mining town of Deadwood, in what was later to become South Dakota. And he entered the field of agriculture and began experimenting in methods of irrigating the arid Bad Lands.

By the summer of 1884 the marquis was shearing fourteen thousand sheep and grazing tens of thousands of cattle. At his abattoir hundreds of animals were slaughtered a day.

*The Château de Mores in western North Dakota is all that remains of
a wild dream of financial conquest*

*In the dining room are the De Mores silver, wine service,
and set of Minton china*

His refrigerated meat was selling at prices which threatened to ruin his Eastern competitors. It looked as though his fabulous scheme to corner the meat-packing industry would succeed.

Within three or four years, however, all these ambitious ventures of the imaginative, impulsive nobleman had collapsed. Among the reasons given for the failure of his enterprises were his lack of business experience and the local friction that developed between the aristocratic Frenchman and democratic cattlemen of the region. It is said that some of these cattlemen resented the marquis' special car on the Northern Pacific Railway, his lavish life at the château, and especially his attempt to fence in his ranch in a land given to the open range.

This latter project led to a gun battle between De Mores' men and his neighbors, and one of the outsiders was killed. The marquis was arrested for murder and after a dramatic trial was found innocent by the territorial court in Bismarck in 1885.

By this time, however, De Mores had decided to abandon his great cattle-raising and meat-packing project in the Bad Lands. The following year he returned to France with his wife and two small sons. After later adventures in India and China, the Marquis de Mores was killed by natives in North Africa in 1896. He was then in his forty-third year.

Although the marquis' meat-packing project at the source of supply was a failure, the idea proved essentially practical, for such plants now exist in West Fargo and Grand Forks. And his pioneer experiments in irrigation, as well as his founding of the town of Medora, lend credit to his name. It was, incidentally, a hotel he built at Medora, called the

Rough Riders Hotel, which provided the name for Theodore Roosevelt's famous cavalry regiment in the Spanish-American War. As a neighboring rancher of the Marquis de Mores, young Roosevelt was a frequent guest in the château.

Inherited by the marquis' son, the Duke de Vallombrosa, the curious old Château de Mores was turned over to the North Dakota State Historical Society in 1936, largely at the suggestion of the society's superintendent, Russell Reid.

All the buildings of the ranch still survive and are included in a state park known as the De Mores Historic Site. The interior of the château, with its twenty-eight rooms, includes a salon, a hunting room, a great hall, and a wine cellar, and the glass-paneled doors of many of the first-floor rooms have a simulated stained-glass effect.

In the hunting room may be seen stuffed big game specimens, mementos of hunts by the marquis and marquise. On display in the dining room, in addition to the original furniture, are the De Mores wine service, silver articles, and a fine collection of Minton china. Most of the rooms are furnished as they were in the beginning, with some rare and exotic household pieces. From the windows of the château one can view the winding Little Missouri River and the distant houses of Medora. The De Mores packing plant was destroyed by fire in 1907 and all that survives of it today is a tall, brick smokestack. In Medora, occupying the center of a small park, there is a life-size bronze statue of the Marquis de Mores.

RUSSELL REID, BISMARCK

The bedroom of the Marquise de Mores, with its lacy bed canopy
and simulated stained-glass door panels

Bad Lands Ranch House

THEODORE ROOSEVELT CABIN. BISMARCK, NORTH DAKOTA. BUILT 1883. OPEN TO THE PUBLIC.

ONE of the principal historic sights in Bismarck, the capital of North Dakota, is the rough log cabin in which Theodore Roosevelt lived when he was a rancher in the Dakota Bad Lands. The Roosevelt cabin, removed from its original site, is now located on the grounds of the state capitol and is open to the public as a museum. Before being permanently established here, it was exhibited at the St. Louis world's fair in 1904 and at the Lewis and Clark Centennial Exposition in Portland, Oregon, in 1905.

In its landscaped setting on the capitol grounds, the squat old cabin forms a striking contrast to the new state capitol, a white, modernistic structure that rises nineteen stories into the blue North Dakota sky.

It was on a September day in 1883, we are told by Herman Hagedorn in *Roosevelt in the Bad Lands* (1921), that young Teddy Roosevelt, who was then twenty-five years old and not in the best of health, first arrived on the Little Missouri River. He had finished his studies at Harvard and at Columbia University Law School and was already a member of the New York legislature.

After his first buffalo hunt, young Roosevelt decided he liked the Bad Lands country so well that he wanted a ranch of his own where he might spend the summer months living the rugged life of a Western cowhand. And he wanted it in the Bad Lands — that arid, starkly beautiful region of buttes, mesas, canyons, and hills forming the valley of the Little Missouri River in western North Dakota and eastern Montana.

Exercising squatter's rights, like most of the ranchers in the Dakota country, young Roosevelt, during his first summer in the area, acquired a large tract of land which he named "Chimney Butte Ranch," because of its location near the butte of that name. It was situated on the Little Missouri River some seven miles south of Medora, the town platted that same year by the Marquis de Mores.

From the one-story log house on his new ranch, Roosevelt rode out early each morning with his cowhands, took part in round-ups and branding operations, went on hunting expeditions, and traced the lonely trails among the fantastic buttes. Soon his health improved, and eventually, as he came each summer to this North Dakota region, he acquired a hardy constitution that was to remain with him for the rest of his life. But in spite of his efforts to become an authentic Western cowman, Roosevelt was never considered anything but a greenhorn by the real cattlemen of the region — he always remained "the four-eyed dude from New York."

It was natural that Roosevelt and his nobleman neighbor, the Marquis de Mores, should become friends, and the New Yorker was often a visitor at the Château de Mores. For a time, though, relations between them were strained. Convinced by suspicious circumstances that Roosevelt was aiding his enemies in their plots against him, the marquis lost his temper and challenged Roosevelt to a duel. When the future president promptly replied that he was ready at all times to answer for his actions, the Frenchman withdrew his challenge and invited Roosevelt to discuss the trouble over dinner at the château. Satisfac-

Teddy Roosevelt's ranch house in the Bad Lands

tory explanations were exchanged and their friendship was resumed.

By this time Roosevelt was operating a new and larger ranch, the Elkhorn, located some miles north of the Marquis de Mores' property. Still retaining his original Chimney Butte Ranch, the young New York legislator divided his time between the two places during his summer visits to the Bad Lands. He continued these visits until 1886, when his expanding political career in New York put an end to them.

When the Spanish-American War came, Roosevelt resigned as assistant secretary of the navy, rounded up his former companions on the Western ranches, and formed a cavalry regiment which became famous in the war as the Rough Riders. During subsequent steps in his rise to the presidency, Roosevelt continued his interest in the Western country, which had earlier led him to write a four-volume history, *The Winning of the West.* As chief executive, President Theodore Roosevelt only once found time to pay a return visit to his former ranching country, and on that occasion he said: "The romance of my life began here. Looking back to my old days here, I can paraphrase Kipling and say, 'Whatever may happen, I can thank God I have lived and toiled with men.'"

Standing today behind a handsome hand-wrought iron gate, designed by Haile Chisholm, the old Roosevelt cabin contains numerous bits of Rooseveltiana, among them guns, books, photographs, and manuscripts. On display, too, are an old-fashioned cook-stove and some substantial furniture of the type used in Western ranch houses.

The Governor's Mansion

ASA FISHER HOUSE. BISMARCK, NORTH DAKOTA. BUILT 1884.

AN AMPLE white residence at the north-west corner of Fourth Street and Avenue B in Bismarck has been the home of all of North Dakota's governors for the past half century. This official residence, however, was originally a private dwelling, the home of a wealthy and respected pioneer businessman.

That man was Asa Fisher. Arriving at Bismarck in the late 1870's, when Yankton, far

below on the Missouri River, was still the territorial capital, Asa Fisher entered the brewing business and in time became a man of means. At first he and his family lived in a modest cottage, but with his rise in the business world of Bismarck, the pioneer brewer decided to build a home suitable to his station. So in 1884, one year after Bismarck became the territorial capital, Asa Fisher built for himself the com-

The Asa Fisher house was a famous social center in territorial days

modious residence which survives today as the Governor's Mansion of North Dakota.

From material on this house gathered by Russell Reid, superintendent of the State Historical Society of North Dakota, it would appear that the Fisher home was a social rendezvous almost from the beginning of its existence. During its earliest years, when Bismarck was crowded with legislators, officials, land speculators, and homesteaders, the Fisher residence was the scene of many social functions attended by territorial officials and their wives, and also by officers and their wives from nearby Forts Abraham Lincoln and Yates. Mr. and Mrs. Fisher entertained many of Bismarck's religious and cultural groups, sponsoring church socials, charity events, reading clubs, and musical programs.

Soon after Dakota Territory was divided in 1889, the question of acquiring a suitable home for North Dakota's chief executive came up, and the legislature quickly decided on the Fisher residence. It was available at the time, was appropriate architecturally for its intended use, and was a landmark of the state's territorial days. Thus, in 1893, it became the official residence of the governor of North Dakota and has continued as such since that year.

The first chief executive to occupy the mansion was Governor Eli C. D. Shortridge, who had been elected to office on a fusion ticket composed of the Farmers' Alliance, the Democratic party, and the Populist party. Shortly after Governor Shortridge and his family were established in the former Fisher residence, some improvements were made on the house, including the addition of a two-story front porch. At this time, too, the ground around it was landscaped, a flagpole was erected, and elm and box elder trees were planted by two Bismarck veterans of the Civil War, James Kenyon and "Farmer" Wallace.

Now shaded in summer by the elms and elders planted almost fifty years ago by the veterans, the Governor's Mansion, except for the porch, remains largely as it was during the period of the Fisher occupancy. It is a square, three-story frame residence, white-painted, and with numerous gables and bays. Still here are some of the ornamental details, especially on its upper portion, which characterized such "Queen Anne" residences of the 1880's.

East River Landmark

ARTHUR C. MELLETTE HOUSE. WATERTOWN, SOUTH DAKOTA.
BUILT 1885. OPEN TO THE PUBLIC.

AMONG the few historic houses in South Dakota — the state is still too young to have many — none is better known than the Mellette residence in Watertown. This house, recently converted into a public museum, was for many years probably the most important social center in that part of South Dakota known as "East-river" — that is, east of the Missouri River, which divides the state in half. When the Mellette residence was built, the gold rush into the Black Hills — the "West-river" area — had already subsided, farms and cattle ranches

MELLETTE MEMORIAL ASSOCIATION, WATERTOWN

The old mansion on Mellette Hill

were spreading out over the prairies, and residents were making plans to have their territory admitted to statehood.

Arthur Calvin Mellette was a native of Indiana, where he was born in Henry County on June 23, 1842. He graduated from Indiana University in 1863 and completed his law studies after the close of the Civil War. Then, following his marriage to Margaret Wylie in 1866, he settled at Muncie, Indiana, where he became editor of the *Muncie Times* and also a leader in county and state politics. In 1879 Mellette and his family moved to Watertown in Dakota Territory, and there the lawyer at once opened an office and also became active in territorial affairs. By 1885 he was able to build his impressive brick house on what later became known as Mellette Hill.

When Arthur C. Mellette was appointed governor of Dakota Territory, his new residence in Watertown took on increased social prominence, although Governor Mellette himself was often away from home attending to his official duties in the territorial capital at Bismarck. Then came 1889 and the admission of the "twins" to statehood. And Arthur C. Mellette was the first governor to be elected by the people of South Dakota.

After completing his term as state governor at Pierre, the new capital, Mellette returned to Watertown, resumed the practice of law, and once more took up residence in his mansion on Mellette Hill. Here he continued to live until his death in 1896, when he was only fifty-three. He was buried in Watertown.

The Mellette house was occupied thereafter by a succession of families. Finally it was abandoned and in the course of time began to show signs of neglect. When, several years ago, the city authorities declared it a fire hazard and ordered it torn down, a civic-minded Watertown woman, Mrs. F. J. Scholtz, took steps to preserve it as a historic landmark. The Mellette Memorial Association was organized to acquire and restore the old mansion and to maintain it as a public museum.

Saved by the association, the Mellette home, which stands at Fifth Street and Fifth Avenue Northwest, is a two-story brick dwelling with a three-story tower surmounting the low-pitched roof. Like so many similar mansions of the 1880's, it has wide cornices ornamented with fanciful eave brackets. Having restored the exterior of the residence, the Mellette Memorial Association began the refurbishing of its interior and by 1946 had already completed and opened to the public the first-floor rooms.

Twelve Mile Ranch

JOSEPH HEUMPHREUS HOUSE. NEAR CUSTER, SOUTH DAKOTA. BUILT 1890.

MOST unusual of South Dakota's historic dwellings, and one of the best known in the Black Hills, is the solid old log house that forms the focal point of Twelve Mile Ranch, twelve miles southwest of Custer on the historic Cheyenne Trail.

Here is a typical early Western ranch, with its cowhands, corrals, and chuck wagons, which at the same time is a cultural center that attracts scientists, artists, and writers who are interested in the Black Hills. It has nothing about it of the dude ranch, however. Guests at Twelve Mile Ranch take an active part in its operation and live the rough life of cowhands.

All the activities of Twelve Mile Ranch, a two-thousand-acre tract located in Harney National Forest, are directed from the comfortable, two-story log ranch house which has been standing on this site since 1890. From its windows one can look out over the pine-covered reaches of Pleasant Valley, along the bottom of which winds the old stage trail from Custer to Cheyenne, Wyoming. It was the attractiveness of this location that caused Joseph Heumphreus, a cattleman from Texas who had come to Dakota Territory in 1877, to settle here, stake out a ranch, and build a large house for himself, his wife, and his four children. Among the evergreen stands on the valley slopes, he found many good-sized tracts of cleared land suitable for cattle grazing, and in time, he had one of the largest cattle ranches in the Black Hills.

But when Joseph Heumphreus first arrived in Dakota Territory, he lived in the mining town of Deadwood, then at the height of its turbulent early history. It was not until 1884 that he established Twelve Mile Ranch and, a few years later, built his sturdy ranch house. From the very first, the Heumphreus place became a center of hospitality, especially for passengers on the stages traveling between Custer and Cheyenne. Among its early promi-

*Joseph Heumphreus' ranch house stands near the old stage
trail between Custer and Cheyenne*

nent guests was Captain Seth Bullock, organizer of Theodore Roosevelt's Rough Riders and for many years United States marshal for South Dakota. For a time during this period, too, Joseph Heumphreus served as a county commissioner, dividing his time between the ranch and the county seat in Custer.

With the death of Joseph Heumphreus in 1917 his ranch was taken over by his three sons and daughter. Under their management, Twelve Mile Ranch, without losing its Old West atmosphere, became a seat of scientific and cultural activities relating to the Black Hills. This development at the ranch has been fostered by the Heumphreus daughter, Mary, a former teacher, government official, and county superintendent of schools. Many

groups of college students have stayed at Twelve Mile Ranch, studying the minerals and rock formations of the Black Hills under the direction of their geology instructors. The ranch has also been a gathering place for scientists in other fields and for artists and writers attracted by the scenery and the legends of the Hills.

What all these guests find at Twelve Mile Ranch is in reality a natural history and art museum of the Black Hills region. In the old ranch house Miss Heumphreus has installed one of the largest libraries in the Hills, noted especially for its volumes on the botany and geology of the area. Here, too, is a sizable collection of art objects and antiques, including American pressed glass, Indian relics, pioneer china, paintings by artist-guests at the ranch, and a group of seventy colored drawings of Black Hills wild flowers.

There is also on display a collection of one thousand mineral specimens and fossils from the surrounding mountain country, all properly identified. This collection was largely gathered by Miss Heumphreus' brother Mont, a geologist and former state mining inspector for South Dakota. Another brother, Ford Heumphreus, an expert cattleman, operates the ranch itself and its half-dozen guest cabins and supervises field trips for the guests to various points of interest in the Black Hills.

Home of Deadwood Dick

RICHARD CLARKE CABIN. NEAR DEADWOOD, SOUTH DAKOTA.
BUILT 1890'S. OPEN TO THE PUBLIC.

TWO miles north of Deadwood, once one of the most melodramatic of Western frontier towns and now a leading tourist center of the Black Hills region, stands the old log cabin home of the supposed prototype of that renowned dime novel hero, "Deadwood Dick." In this cabin lived the colorful frontiersman, Richard W. Clarke.

A prospector, Indian scout, frontiersman, and stagecoach driver in his younger days, Richard Clarke, according to local tradition, was the first of several doughty characters on the western border to be known by the alliterative nickname of Deadwood Dick. With only a few facts about Clarke's early exploits and adventures as a driver of the Deadwood stage during the Black Hills gold rush days, the New York dime-novel writers wove such a tissue of romance around his name that the real Clarke was lost — replaced by a fictional hero of almost superhuman stature.

There are few men alive who do not remember reading during their youth one or more of the exciting Deadwood Dick paper-backed novels which were printed in such vast quantities by Erastus Beadle and other New York publishers during the 1870's and 1880's.

In view of Clarke's status as the original Deadwood Dick, his mountainside cabin is an attraction for visitors to Deadwood, along with all the other places associated with glamorous characters of the gold rush period: the site of the old No. 10 Saloon, where Wild Bill Hickok was shot by Jack McCall; the sites of the Gem Theater, the Green Front Saloon, and Chinatown; Mt. Moriah, or "Boot Hill," Cemetery, which contains the graves of Wild Bill Hickok, Calamity Jane, Preacher Smith, and Seth Bullock.

Deadwood Dick's cabin is located on the pine-shaded slope of Sunrise Mountain. Following a footpath to the summit of this mountain, the visitor comes to the grave of Clarke, a grave blasted out of solid rock. From here one can see the town of Deadwood below, crowded into narrow Deadwood Gulch.

When Richard Clarke came to live in his mountainside cabin, he was already widely known as the original of the dime-novel hero.

Log cabin home of the original Deadwood Dick

Perhaps it was because of this that he sought the solitude of a mountain home, not caring for the fame that had come to him. As the *Black Hills Weekly* stated a few years ago, Clark was "pretty much of a lone wolf during his life, refusing to reveal many things about himself."

He was born in England in 1845. After coming to America as a young man, Clarke wandered about for some years and then, with the discovery of gold in the Black Hills, joined a party of prospectors that were going into that region. There he remained for the rest of his long life. He served at various times as an Indian scout, a stagecoach driver, a guard protecting the bullion removed from the Hills, and a deputy United States marshal to suppress lawlessness.

For half his lifetime, however, Deadwood Dick Clarke lived a solitary and circumspect existence in his mountain cabin, and there he died in 1930 in his eighty-fifth year.

From old photographs of Clarke, and from some of his personal belongings, now on display in the Adams Memorial Hall Museum in Deadwood, we learn that the original Deadwood Dick was a frontiersman to the end of his days. He was a tall, well-built man who wore his hair long in the frontier fashion made familiar by Buffalo Bill Cody. Clarke invariably wore the high-top boots, stout leather belt, and fringed buckskin coat of the old-time dweller in the western hills. Among his personal belongings on display in the Deadwood museum are his rifle, compass, animal traps, and placer mining pans.

Index